A Mind of One's Own

This book contains a groundbreaking series of essays which represent Robert Caper's thinking on the nature of psychoanalysis and mental development.

Dr Caper first approaches the problem of rigorously defining psychoanalysis by examining the distinction between psychoanalysis and non-psychoanalytic psychotherapies, then by exploring what emotional problems uniquely characterize a working psychoanalysis, and finally by considering what constitutes psychoanalytic evidence, and how this differs from the type of evidence used in non-psychoanalytic approaches to the mind. He then goes on to consider the constructive and defensive uses of psychoanalytic theory, the relationship between psychoanalysis and artistic and scientific creativity, the relationship between the Oedipus complex and mental independence, and finally offers a critical examination of Klein's concept of the internal object, and Bion's concept of alpha function and his theory of the container.

Written in a clear and forthright style, *A Mind of One's Own* provides an excellent analysis of the nature of psychoanalysis, and a stimulating examination of the clinical effectiveness of this form of treatment.

Dr Robert Caper is a graduate of Reed College and UCLA School of Medicine. He is a training and supervising psychoanalyst at the Psychoanalytic Centre of California, and the author of *Immaterial Facts: Freud's Discovery of Psychic Reality and Klein's Development of His Work*, as well as numerous papers on psychoanalytic theory and technique, many of which appear in this volume.

THE NEW LIBRARY OF PSYCHOANALYSIS

The New Library of Psychoanalysis was launched in 1987 in association with the Institute of Psycho-Analysis, London. Its purpose is to facilitate a greater and more widespread appreciation of what psychoanalysis is really about and to provide a forum for increasing mutual understanding between psychoanalysts and those working in other disciplines such as history, linguistics, literature, medicine, philosophy, psychology and the social sciences. It is intended that the titles selected for publication in the series should deepen and develop psychoanalytic thinking and technique, contribute to psychoanalysis from outside, or contribute to other disciplines from a psychoanalytical perspective.

The Institute, together with the British Psycho-Analytical Society, runs a low-fee psychoanalytic clinic, organizes lectures and scientific events concerned with psychoanalysis, publishes the *International Journal of Psycho-Analysis* (which now incorporates the *International Review of Psycho-Analysis*), and runs the only training course in the UK in psychoanalysis, leading to membership of the International Psychoanalytical Association – the body which preserves internationally agreed standards of training, of professional entry, and of professional ethics and practice for psychoanalysis as initiated and developed by Sigmund Freud. Distinguished members of the Institute have included Michael Balint, Wilfred Bion, Ronald Fairbairn, Anna Freud, Ernest Jones, Melanie Klein, John Rickman and Donald Winnicott.

Volumes 1–11 in the series have been prepared under the general editorship of David Tuckett, with Ronald Britton and Eglé Laufer as associate editors. Subsequent volumes are under the general editorship of Elizabeth Bott Spillus, with, from Volume 17, Donald Campbell, Michael Parsons, Rosine Jozef Perelberg and David Taylor as associate editors.

ALSO IN THIS SERIES

THE NEW LIBRARY OF PSYCHOANALYSIS
32

General Editor: Elizabeth Bott Spillius

A Mind of One's Own

A Kleinian View of Self and Object

Robert Caper

London and New York

To Rochelle, Lisa and Megan,
and to the memory of Annabelle

First published 1999 by Routledge
11 New Fetter Lane, London EC4P 4EE

Sinultaneously published in the USA and Canada
by Routledge
29 West 35th Street, New York, NY 10001

© 1999 Robert Caper

Typeset in Bembo by
Ponting–Green Publishing Services,
Chesham, Buckinghamshire

Printed and bound in Great Britain by
Creative Print and Design (Wales), Ebbw Vale

British Library Cataloguing in Publication Data
A catalogue record for this book is available from the British Library

Library of Congress Cataloguing in Publication Data
Caper, Robert.
A mind of one's own: a Kleinian view of self and object /
Robert Caper.
p.   cm.
Includes bibliographical references and index.
1. Psychoanalysis.   2. Psychoanalytic counseling   I. Title.
BF173.C36   1999
150.19'5–dc21   98–25734
CIP

ISBN 0–415–19911–5 (hbk)
ISBN 0–415–19912–3 (pbk)

Contents

Contents

Acknowledgements

It is a pleasure to be able to acknowledge my debt to Dr Albert Mason for his support, for introducing me to the work of Melanie Klein, Hanna Segal and Wilfred Bion and for his discussions of *folie à deux*; to Drs David Tuckett, Arnold Cooper, Jorge Ahumada and the editorial readers of the *International Journal of Psycho-Analysis* for their generous, thoughtful editorial advice; to Dr Susanna Isaacs Elmhirst for her extremely valuable help with the child and adolescent cases discussed in this book, and to her, Dr Hanna Segal, Miss Betty Joseph and other friends and colleagues who offered me their support, instruction and encouragement; to my patients who have permitted me to use portions of their analyses in the writing of this book; and especially to Mrs Elizabeth Bott Spillius for urging me to write this book, for her advice and persistence as its editor, and for her invaluable discussions of the subjects of identification and internal objects. Finally, I would like to thank my family, without whose patience, support and forbearance I could not have written this book, and especially my wife, whose tireless efforts to get me to write plain and direct English have made the reader's task much easier than it would otherwise have been.

I wish to thank the *International Journal of Psycho-Analysis* and the Institute of Psycho-Analysis, London, for permission to republish Chapter 3, 'Does psychoanalysis heal? A contribution to the theory of psychoanalytic technique,' Chapter 4, 'On the difficulty of making a mutative interpretation, 'Chapter 5, 'What is a clinical fact?', Chapter 7, 'Psychopathology and primitive mental states,' Chapter 8, 'Play, creativity and experimentation,' Chapter 10, 'A mind of one's own' and the excerpt taken from 'A psychoanalytic approach to aesthetics'. I would also like to thank *The Psychoanalytic Quarterly* for permission to republish Chapter 6, 'Psychic reality and the analysis of transference' and Pantheon Books for permission to use the passage from *Genius: The Life and Science of Richard Feynman* by James Gleick.

Preface

Betty Joseph

This lucidly written book consists of a series of apparently disparate papers written over the last few years. But as one reads them one can see emerging the theme that is the title of this book – a mind of one's own – and the book is about how psychoanalysis aims to help the patient achieve a mind of his or her own. To do this it follows a route questioning how psychoanalysis works and the nature of difficulties for both participants, the analyst and the patient; questioning what interpretations as such do; discussing the nature of the relationship between patient and analyst and how an understanding of the complexities of this relationship helps to bring about change. It questions and discusses the nature of change – change from what to what? This opens up the whole area of what we mean by change in psychoanalysis, psychic change. To oversimplify Dr Caper's argument, it concerns the change from narcissistic object relationships and omnipotent, 'delusional' thinking to 'real' object relationships and reality thinking. This discussion, he demonstrates, cannot be taken further without a detailed consideration of what is meant by internal objects and primitive mental states, and he proceeds to do this, now connecting clearly real object relating and having a mind of one's own.

In his previous book *Immaterial Facts*, Dr Caper discussed Freud's ideas on psychic reality and described Melanie Klein's work which he showed was essentially linked with and a continuation of Freud's thinking. In the current book this interest in psychic reality is taken further and is now brought into focus with the achievement of a mind of one's own. The importance of Bion's work to his thinking is clearly elaborated with, for example, a discussion that connects the movement towards mature object relationships with alpha functioning, or to take a further example, the significance of Beta elements to our further understanding of the countertransference.

This is a book which is neither about theory, nor about technique. It examines each step in our thinking about the aims and the difficulties of psychoanalysis and psychoanalysing and thus should – one might assume – help the reader himself to examine these steps and to achieve more of a mind of his own.

Betty Joseph

1

Introduction

This book is based on a series of papers written over the past six years. At the time of writing I did not consciously intend them to have a common theme, but in retrospect it has become clear that there is one, namely the importance for psychological development of distinguishing self from object, and the central role that this difficult psychological disentanglement plays in the therapeutic effect of psychoanalysis. This book is my attempt to provide partial answers to the questions of how psychological development occurs, what psychoanalysis attempts to do to support this, and what sort of theory might help to conceptualize what it tries to do.

These answers have arisen from a number of sources: from theories I have learned, from my attempts to extend and develop them logically, from my own clinical experience, and from my attempts to use this experience to test and elaborate existing theories.

I begin with the difference between psychoanalysis and suggestion, largely because in my own move from psychotherapy to psychoanalysis I slowly realized that what distinguished psychotherapy as practiced by psychiatrists, clinical psychologists, social workers and marriage and family counselors from psychoanalysis is that the former, in my view, is based on suggestion and tactful manipulation of the patient's character, whereas psychoanalysis aimed to achieve something altogether more radical. The aim of psychoanalysis is not to use the patient's existing character structure in an attempt to massage him towards a pre-determined idea of 'better mental health', but to enable him, should he wish and be capable of it – and it has to be said should the analyst also be capable of it – to find out who he is and isn't, and to benefit from the psychological development that ensues from this. When the implications of this are traced out, it turns out to mean that psychoanalysis not only helps the patient distinguish self from object, internal reality from external reality, but also truth from falsehood and impartial investigation from moralism.

This question of the goal of psychoanalysis is the central theme of Chapter

2, 'Psychoanalysis and suggestion: reflections on James Strachey's "The nature of the therapeutic action of psychoanalysis".' In this Chapter I suggest that Strachey's 'mutative interpretation' basically consists of an attempt to help the patient to disentangle internal and external reality, to become more able to distinguish what of the patient himself has been attributed by the patient to the analyst, and what is the analyst as a distinct, separate person.

Chapter 3, 'Does psychoanalysis heal?' and Chapter 4, 'On the difficulty of making a mutative interpretation', develop this thesis further. Following Strachey, I think it useful to regard the patient's view of the analyst, or his view of certain aspects of the analyst, as what Strachey calls an 'external phantasy object.' Unconsciously the patient projects aspects of his 'archaic superego' into the analyst. If these projections are only the patient's phantasy, it is relatively easy for the analyst to distinguish himself from the patient's projection. However, the clinical situation is often complicated by two factors. First, the patient often is able to carry out what Bion calls 'realistic projective identification', that is, the patient is able to evoke in the analyst a state of mind appropriate to the aspects of the patient that the patient unconsciously wants to attribute to the analyst. And second, the analyst, for reasons of his own, may need to play the role of the patient's 'archaic superego.'

If the analyst is drawn into this process, the patient is then unconsciously practicing suggestion on the analyst; patient and analyst have become a two-person version of what Freud (1921b) calls *eine Masse* (a mob) and what Bion (1961) calls a 'basic assumption group.' The patient's realistic projective identification, when its strikes the fertile ground of the analyst's own non-analytic needs, produces in the analyst what Bion calls 'a numbing sense of reality' about the projection, the 'sense of reality' being a feeling that the projection represents an actual reality, and the numbness being an inability to think about or examine the reality of the projection. Much of this interchange happens unconsciously, so that it is often very difficult for the analyst to know what is going on in his own mind, that is, to understand the basis of his own countertransference response to the patient's transference. And this he must do if he is to describe to the patient how the patient unconsciously experiences him and how he has come to do so – that is, if he is to be able to make a mutative interpretation. Very frequently the analyst feels apprehensive about making such an interpretation, afraid of spoiling the 'good' relationship between himself and his patient (the 'good' relationship being based on unconscious collusion between the analyst and patient designed to avoid analysis), afraid that the patient will feel blamed and accused, and that he will be caught up in mutual hatred with the patient. Even-handed description of the processes between analyst and patient becomes difficult and even frightening. Hence the difficulty of making a mutative interpretation. At the same time I stress that patients, however angry they may be at interpretations that unscramble self from other, and morality from realism, may also be grateful for the very process that makes them angry. I describe three clinical examples to illustrate aspects of this process.

It will be obvious by now that the chief influences in my psychoanalytic thinking are, of course, Freud, but also Klein and Bion. The ideas that I have found indispensable for my own thinking include Strachey's (1934 [1969]) notion of the mutative interpretation (which itself drew heavily on the work of Klein), the idea of unconscious phantasy (Isaacs 1952), which Melanie Klein described as 'the most primitive mental activity, [present] in the mind of the infant almost from birth' (Klein 1936b, p. 290), Klein's concepts of the paranoid–schizoid and depressive positions (1935, 1940, 1946), which allow us to understand a fundamental distinction between types of object relationships and mental functioning, Bion's formulations about basic–assumption groups and work groups (Bion 1961), which have helped me greatly in understanding the vicissitudes of the analytic relationship, Klein's ideas of pathological projective identification (Klein 1946) and of the clinical importance of envy (Klein 1957), and Bion's ideas of normal projective identification, alpha and beta elements and the theory of the container (1962a, 1963, 1965). All of these have been crucial to my thinking about the nature of the therapeutic action of psychoanalysis.

In Chapter 5, 'What is a clinical fact?', I propose that what we can interpret about the unconscious is most likely to be true if the interpretation occurs as part of a 'working' analysis, which I define operationally in terms of three recognizable emotional states. The first is what Bion described as a sense of 'isolation within the intimate relationship' of analysis (Bion 1963), a heightened awareness on the part of both participants of what is beyond their control in the analytic relationship. The second is what Donald Meltzer (Meltzer and Williams 1988) calls the 'aesthetic conflict' that one feels in relation to a working analysis, and the third is an awareness of one's own role in producing one's state of mind.

I define a clinical psychoanalytic fact as what becomes clear in an analysis when these emotional states are observed to obtain. Saying that a clinical psychoanalytic fact is what emerges from a working analysis, and that a working analysis may be known by the presence of certain emotional states that themselves may require a great deal of sophistication to detect, leaves us with a feeling of insecurity about whether we can define even our most fundamental notions scientifically. But we cannot avoid this difficulty, unless we are prepared either to abandon the idea that psychoanalysis is a scientific investigation of the mind, or to reduce it to an activity that can be defined by something other than states of mind, i.e., mechanically or behavioristically.

In Chapters 6 ('Psychic reality and the analysis of transference') and 7 ('Psychopathology and primitive mental states') I deal with the problems of how we define transference and how we think about what causes states of mind, particularly with the question of whether the patient's past can be said to cause his present mental state. I suggest, following Klein (1952b), that transference is not a literal repetition of the past but a latter-day version of the same processes of transformation that affected the patient's perception of his objects in the past and that affect his perception of his objects in the present. I then compare this formulation with three competing views of transference which in my view fail to address the critical, and quite common, clinical phenomenon of both analyst and patient feeling unconsciously that the analyst is the patient's archaic superego.

In Chapter 7 I discuss a confusion in psychoanalysis brought about by the use of the term 'primitive mental states' as a euphemism for forces in the mind that are destructive. These forces manifest themselves as a form of narcissistic identification that involves a splitting of self into 'good' and 'bad' parts, and a splitting of the object along similar lines, following which the 'good' aspects of each are recombined to form a 'good' self/object, and the bad aspects recombined to form a 'bad' self/object, and, finally, the 'good' aspects of the self and object are identified with and the bad aspects dis-identified with. Narcissistic identification in the sense I am using the term may proceed via either projection or introjection, usually involving both. It is associated with a state of mind in which the phantasies of splitting and recombination are felt to represent the 'true' reality, while the real state of affairs (i.e. what qualities or characteristics really belong to whom) is correspondingly disregarded. This state of mind is either intensely persecuting or intensely blissful, usually both in alternation. What is destroyed by narcissistic identification is the relationship between the real self and the real object. It is my belief that this form of narcissistic identification co-exists from birth with a more realistic appraisal of what is the self and what is the object. Since both are equally primitive, to describe forces that destroy object relationships merely as 'primitive' is to implicitly deny the constructive forces that exist alongside them (which is unfair to infants). Moreover, by focusing attention on the past, it distracts attention away from the interaction of present-day constructive and destructive forces in the patient's mind (which is unfair to the patient who is trying to recover). In this chapter, I lay particular emphasis on an aspect of narcissistic identification that is not usually emphasized, the recombination of split-up parts of self with split-up parts of the object to produce confusion of self and object.

I describe the idea that adult psychopathology is a revived or persistent normal primitive mental state as a theoretical fallacy that may interfere with analytic work by supporting an evasion of the present-day forces that undermine sane views of what is self and what is object.

In Chapter 8, 'Play, creativity and experimentation,' I suggest that play, which involves normal projective and introjective identification, is a way of exploring the nature of external objects and linking one's knowledge of them with internal reality using normal projective identification, the successful use of which depend on one's ability to recognize the mutual autonomy of the internal and external worlds, or, in other words, to extricate oneself from the confusion between the internal and external worlds that results from narcissistic identifications. (Omnipotence may be regarded simply as this type of confusion.) I also attempt to show the links between children's play, scientific investigation and artistic creativity, all of which, in my view, are the product of a playful use of fantasy and projection to learn about internal and external reality. This is partly an extension of Hanna Segal's work (1952, 1974) on creativity.

In Chapter 9, 'Internal objects', I examine the Kleinian concept of an internal object. In my view an internal object in the paranoid–schizoid position is the product of narcissistic identification and is a concretely experienced phantasy that what is (in reality) an object is not separate from the self, but is instead a part of oneself. An internal object in the paranoid–schizoid position is the product of a type of identification in which both the self and the object are first split into parts, and the parts of the self are then confused with parts of the object. These confused mixtures of self and object are felt to be both possessed and possessing. They are the product of phantasies of omnipotent projection and introjection. One does not really have a relationship with such an object; instead, one feels in the unconscious that one *is* the object, and that the object *is* the self.

An internal object in the depressive position is the product of quite a different process, which results not in a delusional belief that one *is* the object, but rather a feeling that one can only aspire to be *like* the object (if it is loved) or to *not* be like it (if it is hated). This aspiration is uniformly accompanied by the knowledge that one somehow falls short in this regard, that one can only try to be like a loved and admired object, or try not to be like a hated and despised one. In the depressive position, one knows one's reach exceeds one's grasp, and recognizes that heaven is an aspiration, not a realization.

Depressive identification is a function of the part of the ego that is able to recognize and maintain boundaries between self and object. This type of identification is always partial and limited. I suggest that it can begin to emerge only if it is shielded from the power of one's omnipotent identification phantasies by a specific object, the prototype of which is the oedipal father who prohibits entry into (control over) the prototypical object – the oedipal mother. When the oedipal father can be unconsciously acknowledged, what then replaces omnipotent identification with the object is love or hatred for an object felt to be distinct from the self. This love or hatred is what Bion called a link. A link exists between a self that is felt to be different from the object, and an object that is felt to be different from the self. It is fundamentally different from the paranoid–schizoid type of identification, in which self and object are equated.

What Klein called the 'good internalised object' in the depressive position and regarded as 'the core of the ego', is in this view founded on a link – one's love for a good external object, an object recognized to be separate and distinct from oneself. Klein described true self-esteem and inner security as arising from one's relationship with one's good internal objects and from one's capacity to defend them from one's hatred. I would define such security and self-esteem as arising from the capacity to defend one's love for the good external object from one's narcissistic hatred of it. In brief, it is my view that when an object is introjected in the paranoid–schizoid position, it is narcissistically identified with; the self becomes the object and the object becomes the self. In depressive identification, in which the separate identity of the object is recognized, one has only links with good and bad objects.

I explore the impact of the paranoid–schizoid or narcissistic type of identi-fication and the depressive type of identification on the formation of the superego, and I also explore the type of resolution of the Oedipus complex associated with each. I conclude this chapter with a discussion of the implications of this way of looking at internal object relations for our picture of the resolution of the oedipal situation and the institution of a realistic and helpful superego. This discussion of the helpful superego links with my discussion in Chapter 4 of Strachey's 'auxiliary superego.'

In Chapter 10, 'A mind of one's own', I consider, for both analyst and patient, the processes involved in moving from narcissistic to depressive awareness. For the analyst to be able to be receptive to his patient's projections on the one hand, but to be able to think about and interpret them on the other, he needs to have contact both with the patient and with his own internal objects. When engaged in psychoanalysis, the analyst's good internal object is psychoanalysis itself: for the working analyst, it is a good (not idealized) internal object, a situation described by Britton (1989). I conclude, in line with the argument presented in Chapter 9, that analysis is itself an oedipal situation, and that the patient's emer-gence into the depressive position is identical to his working through of this oedipal situation. I describe this connection through a clinical example.

In Chapter 11, 'On alpha function' and Chapter 12, 'A theory of the con-tainer', I attempt to link the ideas discussed in the preceding chapters to Bion's theory of how analysis works. As I remark in Chapter 4, 'On the difficulty of making a mutative interpretation', Bion liked to leave his concepts undefined, 'unsaturated', and hence used such terms as 'beta elements', 'alpha function' and 'alpha elements.' He defines a beta element as a non-mental stimulus that cannot be thought or dreamt about (Bion 1962, p. 6). In my view a beta element may be either a raw sensory stimulus that cannot be thought about because it is not and never has been a thought, or it may be something that once *was* a thought, but has been somehow converted into a non-thought, and is hence unthinkable for that reason.

The job of alpha function, in Bion's view, is to convert beta elements into alpha elements, which can be used for dreaming and thinking. Bion's theory of the container (Bion 1962, 1963) may be viewed as a kind of interpersonal version of alpha function: the patient unconsciously projects beta elements into the analyst using realistic projective identification, following which the analyst uses his alpha function to convert them into alpha elements. The interpretations that the analyst makes allow the patient to become vicariously conscious of what he was previously neither conscious nor unconscious of, since they were at the time still beta elements. The question I address in Chapter 11 is what does alpha function do to beta elements to convert them into alpha elements which can be used for dreaming and thinking. I believe that the exercise of alpha function is precisely the transformation of a delusion into an ordinary idea, and that this transformation requires precisely the kind of differentiation between self and object that is associated with the transition from narcissistic to depressive object relationships.

The exercise of alpha function to recover one's wits in analysis requires work, because the delusion that it must convert to an ordinary thought is part of the world of narcissistic object relationships and the archaic superego and is therefore held with religious conviction. The exercise of alpha function on such a delusion pits the analyst against his own and the patient's archaic superegos, which causes him to feel at the crucial moment that making (or even thinking of) the interpretation is committing a sacrilege. Rationality in the clinical psychoanalytic setting is purchased at the price of defying a type of archaic moral censure from oneself as well as from one's patient.

In Chapter 12 I propose that Bion used the term 'alpha function' to denote two quite different processes, each acting on one of the two types of beta element: one acts on raw sensory data to convert it to a psychologically meaningful entity, and the other acts on an unbearable state of mind to convert it into bearable one. To avoid confusion, I distinguish the former as synthetic alpha function and the latter as analytic alpha function.

Synthetic alpha function converts raw sensory perception into unconscious phantasy by mating it with an instinctual impulse, in the same way that, in Freud's model of dreaming, a day residue is mated with an instinctual impulse to become a dream element or latent dream-thought. In this view, synthetic alpha function requires little psychological work or containment; it is as easy as dreaming normally is. Once produced by synthetic alpha function, unconscious phantasies may then be used as hypotheses for learning from experience through the interplay of non-omnipotent, experimental projection and introjection. As I outlined in Chapter 8, this type of experimentation allows the reality of the external object to modify one's projections, and in this way fosters learning from experience.

The acquisition of a sense of internal and external reality depends on having one's unconscious phantasies proved or, even more important, disproved. This draws a line between internal and external reality, and this line contradicts narcissistic object relationships, the *modus operandi* of which is blurring of the border between internal and external, self and other, truth and falsehood. I call this blurring anti-alpha function.

Anti-alpha function attacks the scientific interplay between unconscious phantasy and perception that I outlined in Chapter 8 by blurring the two with a vengeance – agglomerating them together into monstrosities that are useless for either hypothesis or observation: hallucinations, delusions and bizarre objects. Values based on the recognition of a real and good object and the desire to preserve it are replaced by moralism. Collectively, hallucinations, delusions and the bizarre object with its associated moralism constitute anti–alpha elements.

What makes a state of mind unbearable and therefore in need of either splitting-off or active containment is not only the fact that the contents are painful or distressing, but the predominance in the unbearable state of mind of anti–alpha elements. Anti–alpha elements are not states of mind at all, properly speaking, but concrete experiences that cannot be encompassed or borne because they encompass, invade and deaden the mind.

The metamorphosis of anti–alpha elements requires the calling into play of a form of containment involving the second type of alpha function, analytic alpha function. Analytic alpha function converts anti–alpha elements (hallucinations, delusions and bizarre objects) back into alpha elements (unconscious phantasies, latent dream-thoughts). It restores contact with internal and external reality by de-confusing them, making the individual aware of himself and the other as distinct selves, objects 'proper.'

Analytic alpha function undoes the work of anti–alpha function, which brings it into conflict with the aspect of the personality that is narcissistic and, in the archaic sense, moralistic. Analytic alpha function therefore requires psychological work and containment.

I present clinical examples illustrating Winnicott's concept of 'holding' as an aspect of the subject/object interchange I describe, and distinguish it from the effect of analytic containment through the exercise of analytic alpha function.

It is my view that psychoanalysis developed historically by emerging from suggestion, and each individual analysis develops by emerging from a state of mind in which the forces of suggestion predominate, producing confusion between self and object, into a state of mind in which a distinct self may be in a relationship with a distinct object.

2

Psychoanalysis and suggestion: reflections on James Strachey's 'The nature of the therapeutic action of psychoanalysis'

In 'Group psychology and the analysis of the ego', Freud, following Le Bon, describes the psychology of a certain type of group (*eine Masse*, or mob) as follows:

> [It] is impulsive, changeable and irritable ... nothing about it is premeditated. Though it may desire things passionately, yet this is never so for long, for it is incapable of perseverance. It cannot tolerate any delay between its desire and the fulfilment of what it desires. It has a sense of omnipotence: the notion of impossibility disappears for the individual in a group ... a group knows neither doubt nor uncertainty.
>
> [These] groups have never thirsted after truth. They demand illusions, and cannot do without them. They constantly give what is unreal precedence over what is real; they are almost as strongly influenced by what is untrue as by what is true. They have an evident tendency not to distinguish between the two.
>
> (Freud 1921a, pp. 77–80)

These groups, which were later studied by Bion (1961) under the name of basic-assumption groups, require a leader whose function it is to sustain the group's belief in its omnipotence, and to embody it. If a leader bows to this iron rule, the group will follow him anywhere. As soon as he ceases to do so, he is liquidated as a leader, and replaced with someone more suitable.

The psychology of the individual cannot be extricated from that of the group. Freud conjectured that, 'the psychology of groups is the oldest human psychology; what we have isolated as individual human psychology, by

9

neglecting all traces of the group, has only since come into prominence out of the old group psychology, by a process which may still, perhaps, be described as incomplete' (p. 123).

The aspect of the individual's psychology most firmly embedded in this kind of group mentality is his susceptibility to suggestion. Freud defined suggestion (p. 90) as 'influence without adequate logical foundation'. I would amplify this definition to read: belief in an idea based not on its logic or the evidence for it, but on who has expressed it. The suggestible subject has a relationship to the suggestionist that is like that of a member of a basic-assumption group to its leader. The subject is bound to the suggestionist by ties of love and fear that reflect the subject's relationship to his own omnipotence, of which the suggestionist is simply an embodiment or mirror. As long as the suggestionist embodies the subject's omnipotence, the subject will follow him in the same way and for the same reasons as the basic-assumption group follows its leader. But if the suggestionist ceases to embody the subject's omnipotence, his suggestions will fail. (I wish to emphasize that the type of group functioning that Freud and Le Bon dealt with corresponds most closely to what we would call today mass or mob psychology, and must be carefully distinguished from the type of group activity that is more realistically oriented. Bion (1961) dealt with this latter type of group analytically under the name of 'work group'.)

Since suggestion replaces evidence, logic and truth with the authority of the leader's pronouncements, its effect is to discourage thought and to increase the denial of reality, both internal and external, to cover or evade a problem instead of confronting it.

Psychoanalysis, as we know, claims to exert its therapeutic effect by means that are precisely the opposite of suggestion – by 'lifting' repressions and denial rather than by increasing them. This is a bold claim that has been disputed by many critics, who say that psychoanalysis is itself no more than an elaborate form of suggestion and that it, like all other forms of suggestion, must conceal its true nature or face the risk of losing its effectiveness. Could they not be correct? Could not psychoanalysis be merely an elaborate form of suggestion, the psychoanalyst and patient forming a basic-assumption group of two, and could our belief that real integration occurs in analysis not be based on a very sophisticated suggestion made by our own analysts and the authority of the psychoanalytic establishment to dispel the justifiable suspicion that psychoanalysis is indeed an elaborate type of suggestion?

We have to begin by admitting that the idea that psychoanalysis is a form of suggestion has enough historical truth in it to make it hard to dismiss outright. Suggestion, witting and unwitting, has played an important role in the history of psychoanalytic therapy. But can psychoanalysis be anything *other* than suggestion? This is the problem that James Strachey took up in his classic paper, 'On the nature of the therapeutic action of psychoanalysis' (1934 [1969]).

Strachey begins his paper with a review of the various theories that analysts have had about how psychoanalysis is supposed to work. He points out that, in its earliest stage, psychoanalytic therapy consisted of dream- and symptom-explication. (I omit the period prior to 1897, during which there was no discipline that could really be called psychoanalysis in the modern sense.) Symptoms were viewed as expressions of repressed impulses and ideas. If repression could be got around and the repressed ideas made conscious, then the symptoms would vanish. The therapeutic process was considered to be a quasi-educational one, and the psychoanalyst's task an intellectual one of guessing or deducing from the patient's material what the repressed idea was. But analysts found that such interpretations had little real therapeutic effect. The patient acknowledged only 'intellectually' the unconscious idea that the analyst had deduced and explained to him. 'Real' consciousness of the idea – emotional awareness of it – was still somehow resisted. The therapeutic effect of psychoanalysis at this point was like that of a not very skilled suggestionist.

Analysts then realized that if they could somehow succeed in bringing about in the patient a strong, positive emotional tie to themselves (or, rather, learn to recognize and use the strong positive emotional tie that develops spontaneously), their interpretations would hit home with greater effect – more like that of a *skilled* suggestionist.

In the group situation that Freud considered, suggestion works either because the subject has an unconscious belief in the goodness or authority of the suggestionist, or because he believes in the power and malevolence of the suggestionist. He follows the leader in the former case out of love and in the latter out of fear and terror. In both cases, the patient is in the grip of an idealizing transference – the analyst is either ideally good or ideally bad, but in either case he is omnipotent. The ideas the patient accepts are based not on his own experience but on this compelling quality of his relationship to the leader/suggestionist. He clings to these ideas with a belief strong enough to override his own judgment, which is suppressed in favor of that of the suggestionist. We may note here that the suggestionist's suggestions act in precisely the same way as the subject's own unconscious omnipotent phantasies – they are immune from critical thought and therefore have a kind of absolute power. This is not surprising in light of the fact that idealizing transferences are based on a projection of the patient's own omnipotence into the analyst. It is as though the patient had said to himself, 'OK, my omnipotence isn't working, so I'll get some help from an expert.' The 'expert' in this case is the analyst viewed as expertly omnipotent, someone who does not have to contend with a mind, and in particular does not have to contend with an unruly unconscious. Freud justified this use of positive transference as a means of overcoming the patient's resistances on the grounds that it was a 'benign' type of suggestion that expanded the domain of the patient's ego in the long run.

But analysts soon found that cultivation of an idealizing transference while trying to analyze the unconscious was a risky and uncertain business. Even

11

when the analyst had tried his best to elicit only his patient's positive transference, negative transferences and eroticized positive transferences appeared unbidden. Both of these are, of course, grist for the analytic mill, as we now recognize (thanks in part to Strachey), but if the idea was to win the patient's affections so he would yield to our suggestion that he accept the content of his unconscious, they are a hindrance and an obstacle.

The analyst's dilemma was this: if the effect of analysis as anything more than an intellectual exercise depended on the evocation in the patient of a positive emotional tie to the analyst, then such a tie must be maintained for the analysis to proceed. But if the analyst tries to control the patient by cultivating a positive transference, he will find himself controlled by the patient: we recall that the leader of a basic-assumption group has authority only insofar as he embodies the group's delusions about its own omnipotence. The group member (patient) allows the leader (analyst) to lead (suggest) only insofar as he embodies the group's (patient's) idealized self-image or omnipotence. A leader (analyst) of such a group cannot bring reality to bear in this area, since he is simply ignored or replaced if he tries.

This technical impasse compelled a closer examination of what means may realistically be employed to bring about psychological integration. Many analysts began to give up the idea of doing analysis by accumulating emotional capital in the form of positive transferences, and expending it to 'instill insight' into the patient. They began to pay greater attention to the nature of the transference itself, especially its unconscious roots, which could themselves be uncovered by analysis.

This was a crucial advance, and analysts gradually adopted the analysis of transference itself as a regular goal of psychoanalysis. We can be fairly sure that analysis of the transference itself is not based on suggestion, since the analysis of transference, as long as it is impartial and non-tendentious, attacks the *roots* of suggestion. This marked a definitive break between analysis and suggestion. This radical departure from the previous approach – from trying to get the patient to accept the analyst's deductions about his unconscious by cultivating the patient's belief in the analyst as a friendly authority – opened the way to analysis proper.

It was accompanied by a second major shift in technique. The repressions that analysts had been trying to persuade the patient to overcome referred to memories of events in the past – 'repressed memories'. Interpretations about past events – what Strachey called conflicts over 'dead circumstances' and 'mummified personalities' – that characterize the old non-transference analysis were replaced by the analysis of a live conflict, taking place in the actual, immediate, present psychoanalytic situation, within the patient and about the analyst.

The realization that the transference itself was the proper focus of analysis was no panacea, however. Knowing that one should be analyzing the transference and actually doing so in practice with a specific patient are two different

12

things. But at least this discovery gave a definite direction to psychoanalytic therapy that clearly distinguished it in principle (if not always in practice) from suggestion.

Systematic analytic scrutiny of the transference showed that it was a type of neurosis. Analysts now begin to call the collection of transference manifestations, both positive and negative, that tend to appear when any reasonably free analysis occurs, the 'transference neurosis'. New knowledge about the transference could now be turned to an understanding of suggestion. Suggestion depends on the skillful manipulation of the patient's transference neurosis in order to bring about a result that in the suggestionist's view is 'therapeutic'. The patient being treated with suggestion, for his part, exploited the therapist's need for a positive transference as a lever to nullify any real threat from the therapy to his deeper resistances, by indicating that any attempt to touch them would destroy the positive transference. (Recall that the omnipotent leader of a basic-assumption group retains his position by virtue of a Faustian pact with the members' omnipotence.)

The value of the transference neurosis to psychoanalysis lies in the fact that it is a detailed, current manifestation of the unconscious processes that gave rise to the patient's spontaneous neurosis. The two are different instances of the same underlying psychological structures and processes. If the transference is treated as a neurosis, that is, if it is analyzed to its unconscious roots, then the underlying factors that generated its twin, the spontaneous neurosis for which the patient sought treatment, will also be brought to light. Analytic resolution of the transference neurosis implied a simultaneous solution of the illness. Moreover, any treatment which did *not* analyze the transference to its roots could not claim to have analyzed the spontaneous neurosis either, since the roots of one are the roots of the other. Psychoanalysis proper then consists of the analysis of the transference.

But how, precisely, could the transference neurosis be resolved? It clearly could not be cured by suggestion, since that would amount to using its leverage to destroy itself. The answer to this question had to await three further developments. The first was Freud's discovery of the superego, the second, the discovery that the superego was the major source of resistance in analysis (see Freud 1926, pp. 149–50), and the third was Melanie Klein's work on projection and introjection in the transference.

Strachey relies on Melanie Klein's detailed study of the dynamic formation and maintenance of the superego, which revealed that the superego was the product not only of one's past, but of a number of *currently* active forces. In the unconscious, Klein held, the individual is perpetually projecting his impulses into his external objects, then introjecting these objects, which are now felt to contain these impulses. The character of the introjected objects depends on the character of the impulses directed toward the external objects. Thus, for instance, during the stage of the child's libidinal development in which it is dominated

13

by feelings of oral aggression, its feeling toward its external object will be orally aggressive; it will then introject the object, and the introjected object will now act (in the manner of a superego) in an orally aggressive way toward the child's ego. The next event will be the projection of this orally aggressive introjected object back onto the external object, which will now in its turn appear to be orally aggressive. The fact of the external object being thus felt as dangerous and destructive once more causes the ego to adopt an even more aggressive and destructive attitude toward the object in self-defense. A vicious cycle is thus established. In the course of the development of the normal individual, positive impulses begin to predominate. His attitude toward his external objects will thus become more friendly, and accordingly his introjected object (or superego) will become less severe and his ego's contact with reality will be less distorted. In the case of the neurotic, however, for various reasons – whether on account of frustration or of an incapacity of the ego to tolerate id-impulses, or of an inherent excess of destructive components – this development does not occur, and the individual remains fixated at the pre-genital level. (Strachey viewed this crucial step as the attainment of the genital stage of psychosexual development. Klein later described it as the attainment of the depressive position. For purposes of the present discussion, the two are more or less equivalent.) His ego is thus left exposed to the pressure of a savage id on the one hand and a correspondingly savage superego on the other, and the vicious cycle Strachey outlined is perpetuated. This vicious cycle is the pathological obstacle to the neurotic individual's further growth.

If psychoanalysis works to treat neurosis in any fundamental way, Strachey reasoned, it must make a breach in this neurotic vicious cycle by altering the character of the superego.

The analyst does this by becoming what he calls an 'auxiliary superego'. This occurs as follows: the patient, as part of the process of transference, projects his internal objects (including his superego) into the analyst, making him a 'phantasy object in the external world'. Since *ex hypothesi* the patient is neurotic, bad internal objects predominate, and will tend to be projected more than good ones. And even the 'good' ones that are projected are highly idealized, the products of a defense against the bad ones, and are therefore quite out of touch with reality.

Thus far, it is business as usual, and the result in the analytic relationship is the neurotic vicious cycle (i.e. the transference neurosis). But 'owing to the peculiarity of the analytic circumstances, and the analyst's behaviour,' says Strachey, the introjected analyst tends to be separated off from the rest of the patient's superego. It is experienced as qualitatively distinct – an '*auxiliary* superego' (see Chapter 4 for further discussion of this point).

Strachey explains this by dividing the analytically effective interpretation (or the 'mutative interpretation' as he calls it) into two phases. In the first, the analyst tacitly 'gives permission' for 'a small quantity of the patient's id-impulses to be directed at himself.' In more modern terminology, he tentatively agrees to become the target of the patient's projections, which converts him into what Strachey calls an 'external phantasy object'. He thus becomes a transference object. Without this phase, the analysis would lack the immediacy of the psychologically live relationship mentioned above. However, the success of the first phase poses the immediate danger that the analytic relationship will degenerate into what is sometimes referred to as a 'real' relationship. What this actually means is that the patient's projections are always threatening to turn the real analyst into an external phantasy object.

If the analyst succeeds in not behaving like an archaic good object or like an archaic bad one – in other words, in not playing the role assigned to him either by the positive transference or by the negative transference – the second phase of the mutative interpretation will ensue. Refraining from playing the role assigned to him by the positive or negative transference means precisely resisting the temptation to practice suggestion. This is a difficult state of affairs to maintain. So great is the pressure within the patient to see his external objects as versions of his own unconscious archaic objects that relatively slight behaviors on the analyst's part will feed into this bias and cause the patient to leap to the conclusion that the analyst does in fact correspond to his phantasy object. Much of the so-called 'artificiality' of the analyst's behavior is really more artful than artificial. It is based on a keen appreciation of the power of the unconscious pressure within the patient to experience the analyst as an external phantasy object, and of the resulting delicacy of the position of the analyst who is trying not to feed into the patient's projections.

It is the analyst's task to play no role at all. This is what distinguishes him from the suggestionist: he doesn't play a transference role, but merely makes an observation about the role into which he seems to have been cast by the patient's unconscious. It is the discrepancy between the real analyst and the patient's phantasy analyst that gives the analyst his special status in the patient's mind – special because real objects are not the rule in the mind of the neurotic.

The analyst's failure to behave like a transference object, coupled with his observation about the kind of object the patient feels him to be, converts him, from the patient's point of view, into a more real object. This kind of mental processing, performed on the patient's unconscious projections, is what is meant by containment and analytic receptivity. Containment doesn't mean simply tolerating the patient's projections. It means showing the patient you understand them by interpreting the transference. By virtue of interpreting (rather than playing into) the transference, the analyst becomes a safe and logical receptacle for further projections. In consequence, the process of projection reaches a depth and richness that it could never reach with a non-analytic object (i.e. one unable to disentangle itself convincingly enough from the patient's phantasies). Interpretation fosters and promotes projection, and projection in turn allows interpretation to have a more–than–academic interest.

This attitude of realism on the part of the analyst is not at all the same as emotional detachment; on the contrary, the analyst cannot afford emotional detachment (despite Freud's comparison of the analyst to a surgeon). Since the phenomena on which his interpretations are based are emotional, detachment in the analyst is like blindness in a painter. But the neurotic may mistake the analyst's bearing for an unemotional one because the analytic response to the emotional states generated by the analytic experience is thought not action.

After clarifying what, in his view, distinguishes psychoanalysis from suggestion *in principle*, Strachey goes on to acknowledge a number of difficulties connected to doing analysis *in practice*. Some of these difficulties reveal themselves in symptomatic behavior on the part of the analyst: even when he knows what he should interpret, he may fail to do so, and instead may be undecided whether the proper moment has come; ask questions; give reassurances, advice, or discourse upon theory; give interpretations that are extra-transferential, non-immediate, or inexact; give two or more interpretations simultaneously; and give interpretations while at the same time showing his skepticism about them.

This behavior is a sign that a specific, mutative interpretation is a crucial act *for the analyst*, one that is always difficult for him to perform. Both the analyst and the patient are confronted with danger from their omnipotence when analysis (i.e. reality) is introduced. This danger that both the patient and the analyst sense is connected to the aspect of their personalities (analyst's and patient's) that is devoted to the group/leader relationship. In the case of the analyst, what is endangered is the patient's idealization of him, which he knows is a part of the transference that a mutative interpretation will dissolve. The danger is that he will lose his position as the 'leader' of the basic-assumption group. A mutative interpretation is a crucial act for the analyst because it tests his relationship to his own omnipotence – can he live without it, or, more to the point, can he defy it? (See Mason [1994] and Chapter 4 for further discussion of this point.)

But the cure for this sense of danger in response to reality is (paradoxically) more reality. The analyst's holding fast to reality in the face of this danger is an important element in the analytic setting. It gives the patient a chance to see how the analyst fares when he is himself the direct target of the wrath of his own archaic superego, which is his intrapsychic representative of the basic-assumption group mentality. This provides the patient with a real and realistic hope of coming to terms himself with *his* own archaic superego.

The analyst's ability to hold fast to the realities of the analytic situation – to neither retreat nor counterattack in the face of his and the patient's archaic superegos is, as Strachey emphasized, a crucial test of his relations with his own unconscious impulses.

Adding to the complexity of doing analysis is the fact that, even when the analyst is interpreting the transference with reasonable accuracy, there is a danger that the patient is unconsciously taking the interpretation as a suggestion, a veiled message about what the patient *should* be like. This turns the interpretation back into a suggestion. In addition, the patient may fasten on the inevitable inexactitude of the interpretation so he may use it as a rationalization (Glover 1931). These are among the reasons that interpreting the transference is no panacea. The *fate* of the interpretation must also be traced, and the often subtle reinterpretations and transformations that the interpretation undergoes inside the patient must also be pulled out of the analytic material. This itself is an important part of analysis. (See Chapter 6 for further discussion of this point.)

We must conclude that there is an area of psychoanalysis – what might be called a working analysis – that is quite distinct from suggestion. The area involved would have to be that in which the analyst is constantly trying to undermine the basis of his potential as a suggestionist by interpreting the transferences – the roles assigned to him by the patient of good or bad archaic superego.

This means that, in the end, one either analyzes the transference or practices suggestion willy-nilly. 'Willy-nilly' because if the transference is not analyzed, the patient will retain his unconscious belief in the archaic group/leader situation, and whatever the analyst says will be taken as a leaderly pronouncement, however it was intended. This means that, while the scope of psychoanalysis itself may in principle be unlimited, the scope of any particular, that is, real, analysis is limited by the capacity of the patient and analyst to address the live transference in a realistic way.

Psychoanalysis came into being historically when it differentiated itself from its progenitor, suggestion. It emerges in a logical sense in a similar way; we may differentiate psychoanalysis as a therapy from non-analytic psychotherapies by noting how it differs from suggestion.

It may, perhaps, be important to emphasize that in practice, every psychoanalytic treatment is a mixture of psychoanalysis proper and suggestion. *Suggestion occurs inevitably in every analysis* and much of the analysis consists of understanding the suggestions that have been unwittingly given and taken in it. The distinction between psychoanalysis and treatment that is based on suggestion is that in psychoanalysis the ultimate or proper therapeutic effect of the treatment rests on the exploration of the psychological forces that support suggestion, while success in treatments based on suggestion rests on the exploitation of those forces. Since their effectiveness depends on their remaining unconscious, psychoanalysis undoes the power of suggestion.

Treatments based on suggestion obviously have a place in the practical scheme of things. In times past, when psychoanalysis was still welcomed as part of psychiatry, we used to say that we analyzed what we could understand and medicated what we couldn't. A variation of this is true for suggestion: it is useful when psychoanalysis is unavailable for practical reasons, such as the lack of social or financial support or of psychoanalytic practitioners whose skill and understanding match the severity of the patient's illness. Suggestion also plays a crucial role in some forms of treatment that are not even considered to have a

17

psychotherapeutic component: how much of the healing that takes place in a medical practice is due to the skillful exploitation of the transference role into which the patient has placed the physician? And how much of the effectiveness of psychopharmacologic agents may be attributed to the placebo effect, which is a type of suggestion?

But while suggestion has a place, it also has a price, and this price is exacted on both therapist and patient. The practitioner of suggestion must maintain himself as an idealized good object. This means he must maintain a split in the patient's mind between himself as a good object and himself as a bad object. Maintaining this split means behaving in a way that is consistent with the role of good object into which he hopes to be cast. It also means avoiding behavior that would qualify him as a bad object. This commits the therapist to a pretense which is not provisional, not a tactic that is part of an overall strategy of establishing the truth eventually, but is an essential part of the treatment. The strain of maintaining such a treatment may not be too great with a few patients or with patients who are not very disturbed. But it can be very great with large number of patients or with seriously disturbed ones, and its price is measured in terms of a certain amount of violence the therapist must do to his own sense of truth and of doing something real. The burden of this should not be underestimated. Unless the therapist retreats into cynicism, he risks being crushed by it into the state of agitated depression known as 'burnout'.

The price of suggestion for the patient is even more severe. The therapist maintains the fiction of himself as only a good object by encouraging the patient to displace the role of bad object onto someone else in the patient's life, to the detriment of the patient's relationships with his external objects. Even more serious is the effect of suggestion on the patient's ego and *internal* object world. The split in the therapeutic relationship corresponds to, or, rather, is a manifestation of, a split in the patient's mind between his good and bad internal objects. Fostering the therapeutic split means fostering the corresponding internal split in the patient. The patient is left not only with the already-existing splits within himself unintegrated, but is also (as he needs to be for suggestion to be effective) confused and identified with a 'good' therapist, who in this case is someone who is actively working to seduce the patient away from facing the truth of his internal and external reality. This actually militates *against* the integration of the patient's good and bad internal objects, as well as of the pieces of his ego that have been split apart from one another as part of splitting the object. Part of the price that the patient pays for suggestion is therefore an exacerbation of his transference neurosis, and of its twin, the spontaneous neurosis that the healthy part of the patient hoped to find help with when he entered treatment.

3

Does psychoanalysis heal? A contribution to the theory of psychoanalytic technique★

3.1 Introduction

In his 'Recommendations to physicians practising psycho-analysis' Freud (1912) admonished psychoanalysts to 'model themselves during psychoanalytic treat-ment on … a surgeon of earlier times [who] took as his motto the words: "Je le pansai, Dieu le guérit" '(p. 115). (Ambroise Paré, the seventeenth-century French military surgeon, when praised for his skill in preventing soldiers' wounds from becoming gangrenous, is supposed to have replied: 'I dress the wound, God heals it'.)

If he fails to adopt this attitude, Freud warned, the analyst 'will not only put [himself] in a state of mind which is unfavourable for his work, but will make [himself] helpless against certain resistances of the patient, whose recovery, as we know, primarily depends on the interplay of forces in him.' Freud was cautioning his colleagues against a belief that psychoanalysis can, or should, heal the patient. The fate of the analysis is determined ultimately not by the analyst's interventions *per se*, but by the dynamics of the patient's unconscious. The analyst can only probe the unconscious like a surgeon, while recognizing that the factors governing the patient's ultimate recovery are beyond his control (*Dieu le guérit*).

Far from being the call for indifference to the patient's pain that it has often been misunderstood to be, Freud's analogy between the psychoanalyst and the surgeon is a piece of technical advice based on a realistic modesty, aimed at putting the analyst into a state of mind that is very important, if not essential, for the practice of psychoanalysis. As I will try to show, this modest state of mind

★ This is a slightly revised version of a paper that appeared in the *International Journal of Psycho-Analysis* 73, 283–92 (1994).

also seems to distinguish the practice of psychoanalysis from that of most psychological therapies other than psychoanalysis. (The distinction I am discussing of course does not depend on frequency or length of sessions, use of the couch, or particular arrangements for payment. These are merely practical arrangements whose purpose is only to facilitate what is essential to the practice of analysis, namely the analyst's adoption of a specific state of mind, one characteristic of which this chapter describes.)

Since Freud made this recommendation, certain developments in the theory of psychoanalytic technique have allowed us to see more clearly its basis in the to and fro of the analytic session. I would like to review some of these, beginning with James Strachey's classic paper on 'The nature of the therapeutic action of psychoanalysis' (1934 [1969]).

According to Strachey, the patient in analysis perceives the analyst as what he calls an 'external phantasy object' – a phrase that beautifully conveys the fact that what the patient unconsciously sees in the analyst is a mixture of external reality and projected pieces of the patient's internal reality, the two not being clearly distinguished in the patient's mind. One fairly common example of this occurs when the patient projects his own omnipotence into the analyst, so that the latter becomes in the patient's eyes a magical healer.

The patient's tendency to form external phantasy objects is not confined to the analytic setting, but occurs in all of his object relationships. The neurotic's world is full of such external phantasy objects, and, to the extent that the analyst becomes one in the patient's mind, his utility as an analyst – that is, someone on whom the patient can rely for an experience of external and internal reality in which the two are not confused – may be considerably diminished.

Despite this hazard, the analyst must become an external phantasy object for the analysis to proceed. An external phantasy object is simply a transference figure, and when the patient makes the analyst into one by projecting his omnipotence into him, the analyst has merely assumed a transference value. *What is crucial is that the analyst not join in the patient's phantasies about his omnipotence.* Freud's recommendation seems to me to be directed precisely at this point, the necessity for the analyst to be realistic about his healing powers, if he is to maintain the proper analytic state of mind.

3.2 Projective identification in the analytic process

Since the publication of Strachey's paper, work by Klein (1946) and a number of her followers, including Bion (1967a), Rosenfeld (1971a), Meltzer (1966) and Joseph (1989) on the theory of projective identification has allowed us to understand Strachey's observations about the analyst as an external phantasy object in the transference. We now recognize that in forming the transference, the patient projects a part of himself (in phantasy) into the analyst and subsequently feels that the analyst has become identified with this part. That is, he believes that the projected part is no longer an attribute of himself, but of the analyst instead. When the patient elevates the analyst to the status of a healer, he does so by projecting his omnipotence into the analyst, leading himself to believe that the analyst possesses magical curative powers, and that the analytic process is somehow a longed-for realization of his belief in the particular external phantasy object called a personal god.

We also know that projective identification in the transference is more than a mere phantasy of the patient. The patient actually provokes (through verbal and non-verbal communication) a state of mind in the analyst that corresponds to what the patient is projecting into him in phantasy (Heimann 1950). This state of mind is a type of countertransference that Grinberg (1962) has called projective counteridentification. (This is perhaps an oversimplified statement of a complex issue. The fact that the patient's phantasy – for example, that the analyst is a magical healer – may find a corresponding phantasy in the analyst's mind does not mean that the patient's phantasy has become more than a phantasy. It remains a phantasy, but has now been joined by another one – the analyst's. A *folie à deux* is no less a *folie* than a *folie à un*, and even mass delusions, for all their impact on reality, are still delusions. How it is that the patient's projective identification can have a real impact on the analyst is an important and complex matter, which I discuss further in Chapters 4, 6, 7, 11 and 12.)

Under the impact of the patient's projected omnipotence (and for reasons of his own as well), the analyst may unconsciously agree with the patient that analysis, interpretations or insight are magical – that is, *that they can act as a substitute for the patient's actually solving his problems himself*. If the analyst fails to gain insight into this countertransference, he is in danger of losing sight of his real function, which is only to bring the patient into fresh contact with himself, or, to follow Freud's analogy a bit further, to debride and approximate psychic tissue that has been unnaturally sundered by splitting.

I should make explicit at this point what my assumptions are about the real function of psychoanalysis. It is to assist the patient to integrate repressed or split-off parts of his personality. This idea has a long lineage, going back to Freud's *'wo Es war, werde Ich sein'* and beyond, but, while Freud was probably thinking about something like integrating split-off impulses or affects, I take the role of the psychoanalyst to be helping the patient integrate split-off parts of the personality. By this I mean that the interpretation must ultimately concern the patient's unconscious phantasies of himself in relation to some object, including who the object is, what he is doing to the object, and why he is doing it (Heimann 1950). This internal object relationship is 'doubled' in the transference, and may be approached by the analysis of what Klein (1952b) and Joseph (1985) have called the 'total situation' in the transference.

To the extent that the analyst unconsciously agrees that interpretation or insight can act as a substitute for the patient's actually solving his problems himself, he will abandon his function of helping the patient to integrate split-off parts of his personality and become a magical healer instead. The point to be borne in mind here is that this 'healing' takes place by a process that is precisely the opposite of psychoanalysis that is, by the analyst endorsing the phantasy, consciously or unconsciously, that analysis, interpretation, insight, catharsis or getting in touch with one's feelings can in itself resolve intrapsychic conflicts and thereby act as a substitute for the patient's actually struggling with these conflicts himself. This helps the patient to split off his problems, rather than helping him to come into fresh contact with them within himself. (The analyst and the patient who are thus in collusion each have their own reasons for believing that the analyst can be ultimately responsible for the patient's mind: the analyst because it supports the phantasy that he can heal the patient, and the patient because it supports the phantasy that he need never himself assume responsibility or feel the need for reparation and preservation of a good internal object.)

I would like to illustrate this tendency of analysts to become healers through splitting, and its *sequelae*, with a case history published by Kohut (1979), 'The two analyses of Mr Z'. (In writing this paper, Kohut concealed the fact that 'Mr Z' was Kohut himself, and that Mr Z's first analysis was Kohut's analysis with his training analyst, while his second analysis was a subsequent self-analysis by Kohut.) In Mr Z's first analysis, the analyst, as Kohut later recognized, was dominated by a 'healthy and maturity morality' that led him into 'taking a stand against' the patient's demands on him. This countertransference activity was an attempt to cure the patient of his demandingness. It appeared at the time to work, probably because it forced the analyst to become demanding himself, and this provided the patient (Kohut) with a receptacle into which he could split off and project his own demandingness.

Kohut's second analysis (his self-analysis) differed from his first in important ways. He was able (as the analyst) to demur from the coercive tactics that had formed such an important part of the first analysis. This was clearly a substantial technical improvement, and one that brought obvious and justified relief to both patient and analyst. But now Kohut, having abandoned a technique that unintentionally encouraged the patient to split off something bad into his analyst, began to encourage the patient to do the same thing with his mother. He took at face value the patient's assertions that his psychopathology must have stemmed entirely from his mother's destructive frustration of his healthy attempts to develop. This technical stance was another way of encouraging splitting in the patient. It prevented both analyst and patient from exploring the patient's own contributions to his difficulties, either with his mother or in his first analysis. Kohut the analyst's approach interfered with Kohut the patient's being able to integrate the destructive aspects of his own personality.

Both the 'therapeutic morality' of Kohut's first analysis and the 'empathic' approach of his second were attempts at healing. Neither addressed or respected the hard reality of the conflict between the patient's constructive and destructive impulses; both attempted to deal with this conflict by splitting off or suppressing the patient's destructiveness. In these analyses, the analysts seem to have crossed over the line of wound-dresser, and to have become something like the god that heals. On the one hand, this reinforced the patient's resistance-phantasy of an omnipotent object that will, by 'healing' him, relieve him of the responsibility of finally coming to terms with himself. And on the other, it reinforced his fear that his destructiveness was too powerful even to contemplate, and deprived him of the freedom to communicate about it that he would have had if it had been interpreted. (Kohut indicated that Mr Z's object relationships remained on a rather narcissistic level at the conclusion of his second analysis. This is what one would expect if his destructive impulses were still being projected into his objects, rendering them too dangerous to depend on.)

3.3 Origins of the analyst's need to cure

The transference, expressed in the patient's projective identification into the analyst, exerts a pressure on the analyst to be an omnipotent healer. But what makes the analyst go along with this process, to act in the phantasy with the patient? Freud considered the analyst's need to cure, which forces him to abandon his realistic analytic modesty, to be a defense against his own sadistic impulses: 'I have never been a doctor in the proper sense', he wrote in his Postscript to 'The question of lay analysis' (1927), 'I have no knowledge of having had any craving in my early childhood to have helped suffering humanity. My innate sadistic disposition was not a very strong one, so that I had no need to develop this one of its derivatives … in my youth I felt an overpowering need to understand something of the mysteries of the world and perhaps even to contribute something to their solution.'

The state of mind that Freud had recommended in his paper on technique can be achieved only if the analyst has come to terms with his own sadism and destructive impulses. The reason for this is that the analyst who refrains from suppressing or splitting off the patient's destructiveness, but instead restricts himself merely to bringing the two sides of the conflict between constructive and destructive impulses closer together in the patient's mind, leaves the outcome of the analysis hostage to the patient's ability to resolve this conflict, a resolution that is, of course, by no means guaranteed. If the analyst has himself not succeeded in coming to terms with his own omnipotently destructive impulses, he will have little belief in the adequacy with which such conflicts may be addressed and encompassed. He will then be loath to risk letting the outcome of all his work rest on someone else's ability to do so.

But if the analyst can recognize the sources of his need to relieve the patient's suffering in his own unconscious conflict between loving and destructive impulses, and in his doubts about the adequacy of the former in the face of the latter, he will (at least temporarily) be free of his need to heal the patient. This will allow him to make an interpretation that simply brings together the disparate parts of the patient – that only describes the immediate emotional situation in the analysis as it is, including the patient's unconscious role in it, without needing to prod the patient into health. This is one of the meanings of psychoanalytic containment: the analyst must contain his need to cure the patient.

If the function of the analyst is to help the patient integrate split-off parts of his personality, then a psychoanalytic interpretation would not be an attempt to cure the patient of anything (except perhaps unconscious self-deception), but only a communication about the patient's state of mind. In this view, the analyst would make an interpretation because he believes he sees something of the patient's unconscious clearly enough to communicate about, not because he can judge or direct the interpretation's curative impact on the patient. No one can really predict beforehand what it will mean to the patient if one succeeds in one's interpretive attempts to help him integrate split-off parts of his personality. This makes a true analytic interpretation unsuitable as a therapeutic tool in the conventional sense as a means of bringing about psychic change in any specific therapeutic direction.

3.4 The emotional difficulties of psychoanalysis for the analyst

This constraint on the analyst's therapeutic potency (in the conventional sense of the term) brings to mind Melanie Klein's observation about a painful reality that parents must accept about their relationship to their children:

> the child's development depends on, and to a large extent is formed by, his capacity to find the way to bear inevitable and necessary frustrations [of life] and conflicts of love and hate which are in part caused by them: that is, to find a way between his hate, which is increased by frustrations, and his love and wish for reparation, which brings in their train the sufferings of remorse. The way the child adapts himself to these problems in his mind forms the foundation for all his later social relationships, his adult capacity for love and cultural development. *He can be immensely helped in childhood by the love and understanding of those around him, but these deep problems can neither be solved for him nor abolished.*

(1937, p. 316n, emphasis added)

In the same way, we can say that integration of split-off parts of the patient's personality helps the patient to deal with his difficulties by letting him know what they are, but it doesn't solve or abolish them for him.

This brings us to the difference between working through in analysis and being cured. If the aim of psychoanalysis is to help the patient integrate split-off parts of his personality, then working through would have to mean something like the patient's accepting his unconscious as a part of himself, mourning the attendant loss of self-idealization, and facing the depressive anxieties that follow from this. This contrasts with 'curing' oneself of the newly discovered piece of the unconscious by getting rid of it. Working something through means first facing the fact that one cannot get rid of it.

A dream will illustrate this point. The patient, a woman who had developed an eroticized transference primarily as a defense against awareness of her dependency on her analyst, and who had done a considerable amount of painful and productive work to understand it, had a dream in which she approached the analyst 'like a little girl', sat on his lap, put her head on his shoulder, and began to kiss him tenderly on the neck. He then kissed her on the mouth, which left her feeling confused. In her associations, she made no mention of the erotic element in the dream, focusing instead only on the tender one, and on her confusion about the analyst's reaction, which persisted even after she awoke.

When the analyst asked her if she would be confused in waking reality by a man reacting in that way if she sat on his lap and began to kiss his neck, she realized immediately that her confusion stemmed from a denial of her continued erotization of the analysis. This insight made her quite sad, because, as she said, she thought she had 'gotten rid of that' in the previous work.

This turned out to be precisely the problem. By assuming that this powerful aspect of her personality could be gotten rid of by being interpreted and discussed, she had failed to realize that it was an important reality, not to be dissolved merely by being named. Having now realized this, she was better able to take her unconscious seriously as a real part of her personality, to come to terms with its reality instead of imagining she could get rid of it, which turned out to be an important development in her analysis. This limitation of psychoanalysis as a tool for ridding oneself of unwanted parts of the personality is humbling for both patient and for the analyst, and this disappointment of one's therapeutic ambitions is one of the emotional difficulties of psychoanalysis.

A second emotional difficulty with recognizing that an interpretation of the unconscious does not rid the patient of it is that it offers no safeguard against the eruption of destructive impulses, guilt and feelings of persecution into the analysis. (The more cure-oriented approaches to the patient prevent the emergence of primitive, psychotic transferences. But in this case they are merely split off into the patient's parents, children, spouse, friends and colleagues, who are left to cope with them.) There is then the constant risk that painful and frightening transferences and countertransferences may arise, without any certainty that they can be contained. This is terribly anxiety-provoking. It is difficult to realize that one has such limited powers in the face of such frightening things.

These difficulties, the sense of therapeutic limitation, and the danger of destructive impulses erupting into the analysis at any moment, are consequences of the analyst's decision to analyze rather than heal and, in psychotherapies other than analysis, tend to be circumvented rather than confronted. In my experience, these painful emotions are reliable clinical indicators that the work of analysis is progressing. If these indicators are consistently absent from what is supposed to be an analysis, the analyst should consider the possibility that a pseudo-analysis has taken over.

A third emotional difficulty for the analyst stems from the fact that psychoanalysis is a very peculiar activity, and even, in a certain way, an unnatural one: one is unable to do the natural thing, which is to to offer immediate solace, support or reassurance in the presence of obvious suffering. One can offer only support for the patient's attempts to integrate his mind, and the solace that comes from that. And, while this solace is quite profound, it is often quite slow in arriving, and to refrain from offering the more immediate (if less profound) forms of relief is one of the most difficult injunctions of the rule of abstinence. However, if the analyst is to do his job, he must accept the fact that, by withholding immediate solace, he is in a way 'causing' real suffering in the short run for the sake of the greater long-term relief that comes from psychological integration.

Viewed in this light, the analytic rule of abstinence – that the relationship between patient and analyst cannot really be that of friends (or even family, despite our frequent use of the parent–child analogy to describe the transference) – is not simply a procedural rule and in fact is not a procedural rule at all, but a consequence of the fact that analysis as an activity must necessarily exclude too many of the elements that are vital to any ordinary, natural human relationship. Its power stems from its intense, exclusive and dispassionate focus on the passions of the unconscious. This exclusive intensity produces what Bion (1963, p. 15) called the 'sense of isolation within an intimate relationship' that prevails when each party is aware of his own responsibilities and limits.

3.5 The psychoanalyst as a real object

While it may seem that the analyst's lack of responsibility for whether or not his interpretations heal the patient is a rather cold and inhuman attitude, and perhaps even an irresponsible one, I would argue that precisely the opposite is true – that only by resisting the urge to achieve a cure with an interpretation can the analyst discharge his primary responsibility to the patient, which is not to heal him, but to help him recover himself.

In the long term, this approach brings great relief to patients, even, or rather especially, to more disturbed ones. I believe that this sense of relief arises from the patient's gradual recognition of the analyst's single-minded, even-handed focus on the business at hand, which is to see what is active in the patient's unconscious at the moment, and why. The effect of this is to relieve the patient of a profound anxiety that his inner world cannot be explored realistically, in a balanced way, without evasion, splitting, or the need to fix it immediately.

However, while the healthy part of even disturbed patients feels relief and gratitude at the analyst's ability to bear the patient's projections (as manifested by his ability to do no more than calmly interpret all aspects of the patient's unconscious), a disturbed part of even healthy patients feels that the analyst's exclusive commitment to even-handed interpretation is nothing more than a pointless, artificial device. This part of the patient seems to regard transference figures that act out their roles as external phantasy objects as absolutely real, and the real figure of the analyst as artificial. Such patients will often refer to their relationships with external phantasy objects as 'real relationships', in contrast to the supposed 'artificiality' of the relationship with a real analyst.

What leads the patient to feel the analytic relationship is artificial is, paradoxically, the analyst's very insistence on being real – his careful avoidance of the manifold collusions with the patient's unconscious phantasies that the patient expects of him in his role as an external phantasy object. The patient may perversely idealize these collusions as ordinary sociability or friendliness, common human decency, or warmth and empathy. This leads him to feel that when the analyst is actually analyzing (rather than colluding with) the patient's unconscious phantasies, he is not a real person, not friendly, warm or empathic. It is therefore quite important to keep in mind, when the patient feels that one is being 'real' and empathic, that one may be unwittingly colluding with the patient's perverse attack on the analyst's, and his own, reality sense.

While the analyst's real function is to help the patient to integrate split-off parts of his personality, we must also of course recognize that both the patient and the analyst may have unconscious phantasies of a relationship different from this – for example, that when the analyst is doing analysis, he is a lover, child, adversary, spouse, parent or persecutor. But these are still just phantasies. Of course, these phantasies are real phantasies, and they have real effects on the quality of the relationship between analyst and patient (which is saying no more than that transference and countertransference have a real and undoubted impact), but the real job of the real analyst is to identify and understand the meaning of both the transference and countertransference phantasies in terms of split-off parts of the patient's personality, and to communicate this understanding to the patient. In this view, providing the patient with anything else, such as love, advice, guidance, or support for his self-esteem is the analyst's acting – in his countertransference, and represents his resistance to analysis.

This is not, of course, to suggest that the analyst should be free of countertransference, which would be like saying that the patient should be free of resistance. Even if this were possible, it would be antithetical to the interests of the analysis. Resistance is a valuable indicator that we are nearing an important unconscious phantasy, and we would be lost without it. The same is true of countertransference, as manifested by the analyst's urge to do something other than give a non-partisan interpretation. (Another rather striking connection between resistance and countertransference is the fact that, when we become aware of a countertransference reaction while doing analysis, our initial reaction is often to feel guilty – or rather persecuted – just as we feel when we become aware of our resistance when having analysis. The forces behind these feelings of persecution, which arise in response to our awareness of what is after all only human in ourselves, are an important obstacle to psychological integration, and need to be understood in detail in each analysis.)

Partly in response to our patients' transferences, and partly for reasons of our own, we always unconsciously wish to influence our patients rather than analyze them, and quite regularly we put this wish into effect. But one of the things that distinguishes psychoanalysts from psychotherapists is that when we do use suggestion or influence it is unintentional, whereas such deliberate attempts to alter the patient's state of mind is the major therapeutic currency of non-analytic psychotherapy. And, although we constantly fall short of our goal of simply analyzing our patients, we treat these shortcomings not as something we must simply resign ourselves to as inevitable manifestations of our human fallibility (though they certainly are that), but as opportunities – fuel for further analysis. In this view, the analyst is not someone who maintains a 'neutral' stance above the fray, but someone who is always being drawn into the fray, could not do analysis if he were not in the fray, and who does analysis largely by figuring out what kind of fray he is in.

Klein (1952b) and Joseph (1985) have referred to this as the analysis of 'total situations' in the transference, which Joseph described in the following terms:

> Much of our understanding of the transference comes through our understanding of how our patients act on us to feel things for many varied reasons; how they try to draw us into their defensive systems; how they unconsciously act out with us in the transference, trying to get us to act out with them; how they convey aspects of their inner world built up from infancy – elaborated in childhood and adulthood, experiences often beyond the use of words, which we can often only capture through feelings aroused in us, through our countertransference, used in the broad sense of the word.
>
> (Joseph 1985, p. 157)

Heimann (1950), Money-Kyrle (1956), Segal (1977) and Pick (1985) have also helped to form this view of the interplay of transference and countertransference as a vital element in the psychoanalytic process.

3.6 Technical considerations

One implication of the view I am proposing, namely that the purpose of psychoanalysis is only to help the patient integrate split-off parts of his personality, is that it is not the business of analysis to deliberately bring about the predominance of one or another part of the patient that the analyst regards as healthy.

28

Success in analysis is measured by the degree of integration, not by the degree to which the patient approximates a standard of normality.

To extend Freud's surgical analogy even further, the task of the psychoanalyst might be thought of as freshening the patient's experience of the unconscious by removing the defensive structures that prevent integration of the unconscious, just as the surgeon would freshen the margins of a traumatic wound by removing the dead tissue that prevents healing. This debridement is obviously to be done with a delicate hand; the dead, defensive tissue must be carefully dissected from the patient's living unconscious experiences, both 'good' ones and 'bad' ones, which are themselves to remain as unaltered as possible.

The analyst can only help the patient to think about and experience himself impartially. We may hope that when this integration occurs, good internal objects will in the end predominate over bad ones. We may reassure ourselves by recalling past experiences in which this has indeed happened. But we have no way of guaranteeing it. An analyst, as Meltzer has observed, is like a gardener, weeding and watering the garden so each plant might develop to its full potential. But he does not convert a plane tree into a fir tree or vice versa.

This sobering view of analysis highlights its limits as a therapeutic modality. I believe that these limits are real, and that we should keep them constantly in the backs of our minds. Analysis, like all real objects, is less than we would like it to be.

In a way, this view greatly simplifies the technical demands that the analyst places on himself. He need not worry about the likely therapeutic impact of an interpretation, but only concern himself with giving an accurate, intelligible description of what the patient is doing in the transference and in his internal world, to whom he is doing it, and why. Although I have called this a technique, it would be better to call it an absence of tactics.

In *Envy and Gratitude* Melanie Klein returned to the technical issue that Freud had addressed in 1912. She wrote:

> It makes great demands on the analyst and on the patient to analyse splitting processes and the underlying hate and envy in both the positive and negative transference. One consequence of this difficulty is the tendency of some analysts to reinforce the positive and avoid the negative transference, and to attempt to strengthen feelings of love by taking the role of the good object which the patient has not been able to establish securely in the past. This procedure differs essentially from the technique which, by helping the patient to achieve a better integration of his self, aims at a mitigation of hatred by love.
>
> (1957, pp. 225–6)

This observation touches on the heart of the matter. Omnipotently healing a patient means reinforcing his attempts to split off his destructive impulses, to reassure him that he is after all a good person, and that the therapist, as the

source of this reassurance, is also a good person, without ever seriously exploring the possibility that either one may not be. This is a common feature of
many psychotherapies. Analysis contrasts strongly with these therapies in that it
takes all sides of the patient seriously, so that he may own them rather than
merely be reassured about them.

Klein continues,

> There is indeed an ingrained need for reassurance in everybody, which goes
> back to the earliest relation to the mother. The infant expects her to attend
> not only to all his needs, but also craves for signs of her love whenever he
> experiences anxiety. This longing for reassurance is a vital factor in the ana-
> lytic situation and we must not underrate its importance in our patients,
> adults and children alike. We find that though their conscious, and often
> unconscious, purpose is to be analysed, the patient's strong desire to receive
> evidence of love and appreciation from the analyst, and thus to be reassured,
> is never completely given up ... the analyst who is aware of this will analyse
> the infantile roots of such wishes; otherwise, in identification with the pa-
> tient, the early need for reassurance may strongly influence his counter-
> transference and therefore his technique. This identification may also easily
> tempt the analyst to take the mother's place and give in to the urge imme-
> diately to alleviate the child's (the patient's) anxieties.
>
> (1957, pp. 225–6)

3.7 Conclusion

I have concluded with some remarks on the analyst's technical stance, but the
line of thought I have been following leads to the conclusion that the stance I
am recommending is not a stance at all, in the sense of being a technique that
one can simply adopt. It is a consequence of the analyst having attained a state
of mind that results from having worked through certain emotional difficulties
of being an analyst.

If, as I have assumed, the analyst's role is simply to help the patient experience
neglected aspects of himself and his objects as fully and accurately as possible,
then the analyst must face the fact that this in itself does not provide the patient
with a corrective emotional experience, mitigate the severity of his superego, or
guide him along the correct developmental path. The analyst's acknowledgment
of this limitation – which is equivalent to acknowledging that he can help the
patient to grow, but he cannot 'grow' him – places a psychological burden on
the analyst that is painful and frightening, but that he must take up over and over
again at each step in the analysis, since it is part of a state of mind that the analyst
must have to do analysis. It requires him to recognize that his ever-resurgent
belief in his healing powers is a countertransference reaction that defends him

against his fear that destructiveness – either his own or the patient's – will predominate over loving impulses if the two are brought together and simply left to their own devices. The analyst's belief in these healing powers, in conjunction with the patient's transference phantasies of an object that will cure him omnipotently, forms a *folie à deux* between patient and analyst, a joint delusion that is a vehicle of 'cure' in many types of psychotherapy, but is antithetical to the integrative goal of psychoanalysis.

Finally, to return to Freud's warning that the analyst's failure to adopt the attitude toward the patient that he recommended will put him 'in a state of mind which is unfavourable for his work' and will 'make him helpless against certain resistances of the patient, whose recovery, as we know, depends on the interplay of forces in him'; we can see that the analyst who needs (rather than hopes) to cure the patient is searching for reassurance that his own creativity has not fallen victim to his own destructiveness. The 'resistances of the patient' that this makes him helpless against is the patient's corresponding need for reassurance about his destructiveness. But the patient's recovery, Freud reminds us, depends on the interplay of forces in the patient's unconscious, which are, ultimately and in the final analysis, beyond the reach of the analyst.

The limits that 'dressing the wound' rather than healing it places on the analyst gives an additional meaning to the term psychoanalytic containment: to contain the patient analytically, the analyst must first contain his anxieties about his own destructive impulses, and his omnipotent beliefs about analysis that serve as a defense against them. Only then can he be free of the particular derivative of his omnipotence that makes its appearance as an urge to heal, and only then can he be free to do psychoanalysis.

4

On the difficulty of making a mutative interpretation*

4.1 Introduction

In his classic paper on 'The nature of the therapeutic action of psychoanalysis' (1934), James Strachey suggested that the essence of psychoanalytic therapy lay in a process that he called 'mutative interpretation'. Mutative interpretation consists of two components or phases. In the first, the patient projects one of his internal objects into the analyst, which causes him to feel, consciously or unconsciously, that the analyst possesses certain characteristics that he does not in fact possess. This is familiar to us as what Meltzer (1967) called the 'gathering of the transference'. In the second phase, the patient becomes aware, through the interpretation of the transference, that these characteristics belong in reality not to the analyst, but to himself, or rather, his own internal world. (Compare this with Meltzer's observation that transference is an emanation of psychic reality in the first instance whose internal origin in the reality of internal objects is reluctantly discovered'.)

A mutative interpretation helps the patient to see the analyst as a real external object, and at the same time allows him to recognize a previously unrecognized aspect of his internal object world. These two developments are really just two aspects of the same thing: an undoing of the patient's confusion between his inner and outer worlds, which permits a clearer view of both.

Strachey suggested that the internal object that the patient projects into the analyst in the transference is usually his archaic superego. As a result of this projection, the patient expects to find in the analyst something like an external version of his archaic superego, which is, in its negative aspect, harsh and punitive and in

---

* This is a slightly revised version of a paper that appeared in the *International Journal of Psycho-Analysis* 76, 91–101 (1995).

its positive aspect, warm and seductive. As a result of the mutative interpretation, however, he finds someone not harsh, punitive, warm or seductive, but reasonable and realistic instead. According to Strachey, what serves to distinguish psychoanalysis from all other forms of psychological therapy is that, in other therapies, the therapist acts out the role of archaic superego, consciously or unconsciously, but in psychoanalysis he departs from it in a clear and convincing way.

One of the most striking facts about a mutative interpretation is that making one is very often quite a difficult emotional experience for the analyst. Strachey described this phenomenon in terms that every practicing psychoanalyst will recognize from his own experience:

> Mrs Klein has suggested to me that there must be some quite special internal difficulty to be overcome by the analyst in giving interpretations. And this, I am sure, applies particularly to the giving of mutative interpretations … for there seems to be a constant temptation for the analyst to do something else instead. He may ask questions, or he may give reassurances or advice or discourses upon theory, or he may give interpretations – but interpretations that are not mutative, extra-transference interpretations, interpretations that are non-immediate, or ambiguous, or inexact – or he may give two or more alternative interpretations simultaneously, or he may give interpretations and at the same time show his own scepticism about them. All of this strongly suggests that the giving of a mutative interpretation is a crucial act for the analyst as well as for the patient, and that he is exposing himself to some great danger in doing so.
>
> (Strachey 1934 [1969], pp. 290–1)

The danger Strachey describes here is not, of course, simply due to the fact that the patient may resist the interpretation. This is a sign that the interpretation feels dangerous to the patient, whereas the problem here is that the analyst also feels endangered by it.

A second impressive fact about a mutative interpretation is that, once we have overcome whatever this internal difficulty is and given the interpretation, its content seems very often in retrospect to have been obvious – at times embarrassingly so – and we are left with the feeling that we have just recovered from a temporary deterioration of our intellect.

We recognize, of course, that the splits and repressions within the analyst's personality contribute to his inability to think of the most appropriate interpretation in a timely fashion. But the problem that I have in mind tends to arise with the greatest intensity in the heat of the analytic situation; it is easier to think of the correct interpretation after the session than during it (*l'esprit d'escalier*). This suggests that some specific factor is at work in the interaction between analyst and patient that actually produces a temporary intellectual deterioration in the analyst – a restriction or inhibition of his ego. This phenomenon, that the ego psychologists call the analyst's regression in analysis, is well recognized.

33

In this chapter, I wish to consider two questions: what is the origin of the sense of danger connected to *giving* a mutative interpretation, and what is the source of the intellectual deterioration that prevents the analyst from even *thinking* of one?

4.2 The interplay of transference and countertransference

The most important tool that the analyst has for learning about the patient's unconscious inner world is, of course, the transference, which is, as we know, not just a collection of impulses that the patient feels toward the analyst, or a passing phantasy he has about him, but a complex relationship in which the patient unconsciously regards the analyst as one or another of his internal objects. As Strachey aptly put it, the analyst in the transference becomes an 'external phantasy object' for the patient.

But the patient does more than just phantasize that the analyst is someone he isn't – he 'recruits' the analyst in reality into the role of whatever he represents in the patient's unconscious phantasies. This recruitment consists of the patient using his (largely unconscious but often highly intelligent) ability to perceive, assess and play on the nuances of the analyst's personality to stimulate in him a state of mind that corresponds to the role he is meant to play in the transference. He does this using both verbal and non-verbal means, the way a director might prepare an actor for a part in a play (if he could do so without the actor knowing that he was doing it). This activity is part of what we mean by the term projective identification, and the state of mind stimulated in the analyst is one form of countertransference.

When under the influence of the patient's projective identifications, the analyst actually feels as though he had been pressed into a role in somebody else's phantasy, no matter how difficult it may be for him to describe the specifics of it. At the same time, through lack of insight, he experiences the powerful emotions connected to this role as belonging entirely to himself, and having nothing to do with the patient's psychological impact on him.

By working to extricate himself from the feeling that his emotions are justified entirely by objective realities – what Bion (1961) called the 'numbing feeling of reality' that is produced by projective identification – the analyst is gradually able to recognize the patient's contribution to his countertransference. This places him in a position to treat the patient's projective identifications as a communication – an unconscious effort by the patient to help the analyst learn and think about the patient's inner world, so that he can make an interpretation. This analysis of the patient's projective identifications satisfies one of the patient's unconscious motives for using projective identification in the analysis.

This is, of course, the familiar process by which the patient, using projective identification, puts into the analyst a state of mind that is unbearable for the patient (but, one hopes, bearable for the analyst), following which the analyst, through self-analysis, is able to articulate what the patient could not bear, and make an interpretation of what it is, which presumably then allows the patient to bear it – the Bionian model of containment.

But it is just when the analyst is on the verge of making a mutative interpretation that he is beset by the feeling that he is about to do something harmful, something that will jeopardize his 'good' relationship to the patient. This crisis is not accounted for in the model of Bionian containment as it is usually formulated: projective identification by the patient, followed by containment by the analyst, followed by interpretation of the projection. In that model, the analyst would be glad to have the appropriate interpretation, and, far from experiencing it as a danger, he would welcome the opportunity to give it. Something other than what is accounted for in the conventional model of containment must be at work to produce the analyst's anxiety about his interpretation.

4.3 Clinical examples

A patient entered a Monday analytic session and told his analyst that he had just attended a pop psychology event known as a 'Bradshaw Weekend', from which he had gained many valuable insights about his behavior that he had not gotten 'in four and a half years' with the analyst. He proceeded to list a number of what seemed to be valid insights, all of which, however, the analyst had communicated to him many times in the past. The patient did not acknowledge this, but spoke as though it had all come from his 'Bradshaw Weekend'.

Although feeling quite irritated and threatened, the analyst succeeded with considerable effort in restraining himself and appearing reasonable and accepting of the patient's having benefited from the weekend. The patient went on to speak of his desire to leave analysis soon, hoping, he said, that this would not hurt the analyst who had been 'like a mother and father to me' over the years. He then spoke of his mother's reaction when he announced his desire to leave home: 'there's a cliff, if you want to go jump off of it, go ahead.' The patient went on to say that he felt like he had just gotten his MD degree (the analyst is not a physician) and hoped the analyst would be like a proud father, congratulate him and wish him well.

The patient had left the analyst with the feeling that his work was rather pathetic and slow compared to that of the Bradshaw organization, the success and effectiveness of which he found himself envying. He had briefly considered using this countertransference as the basis of an interpretation about the patient's sense of inadequacy *vis-à-vis* himself, and his envy of the analyst's abilities, but he rejected this idea because he felt that it would have meant that he was being a spoil-sport, enviously denying the patient's good weekend experience, and this made him feel too guilty to make the interpretation. In other words, the projection ruled the day, and the analyst felt that to interpret it would have only been to reveal his own envy of the patient.

A second clinical vignette: after considerable work and progress in her treatment, a thrice-per-week psychotherapy patient requested a fourth session. Analysis of this request revealed that it represented her emergence from a state of despair about anything or anyone ever being able to help her, which the patient was able to acknowledge consciously. Soon after this, she was forced to miss a week of sessions. The analyst agreed to 'make up' the loss by adding a fourth session to each of the three weeks preceding the break. Toward the end of the third week, the patient indicated, without realizing it, that the four-session schedule made it much easier for her to work in the analysis. When the analyst interpreted this, she became tearful and enraged. She accused him of teasing her and of greedily manipulating her into having four sessions, a move that would mean she 'wouldn't be able to buy anything for herself' for many years.

The analyst began to feel depressed and guilty, as though, he later said, he agreed with the patient that he had seduced the patient into a dangerous and destructive addiction, out of his own greed. He forgot completely that all he had done was point out to her that she felt that the fourth session was valuable. The idea that she must keep it arose from the patient's hatred of valuing something she couldn't have.

So powerful was the impact of the patient's projection into the analyst that, even when he realized this, he remained partly in the grip of the feeling that making such an interpretation would only have been a clever attempt to greedily manipulate her into retaining a worthless fourth session, and would certainly have jeopardized his good relationship with the patient.

In both of these examples, the analyst's ability to observe and comment on the here and now of the analytic relationship was interfered with by guilt. What was in reality a scientific endeavor – exploring the patient's unconscious relationship to the analyst – was derailed when the analyst was overcome by the feeling that it was bad in a moral sense, and would, if he did not restrain himself, almost certainly ruin his good relationship with the patient. This suggests that the difficulty that the analyst has in giving a mutative interpretation is connected to the fact that interpretation itself has gotten transformed in his mind from a scientific activity into a moral one.

4.4 Discussion

4.4.1 Strachey's 'auxiliary superego'

Strachey believed that the mutative interpretation exerted its therapeutic effect because it made the analyst into what he called an "auxiliary superego' for the patient. He felt that, in making a mutative interpretation, the analyst draws the patient's attention to the fact that he (the patient) regards him as similar in some way to the patient's archaic superego. But he does so in a way that at the same time demonstrates that he is not the patient's archaic superego. Strachey makes it clear that the analyst does not do this by being kind, tolerant or loving as a way of contrasting himself to the patient's harsh, intolerant superego. This would amount to no more than being an archaic superego in its positive (i.e. seductive) variation – one that controls the patient's mind by 'parental' love and approval rather than 'parental' hatred and disapproval.

Instead, the analyst becomes the one thing that an archaic superego is incapable of being: realistic. Strachey wrote that 'the most important characteristic of the auxiliary superego is that *its advice to the ego is consistently based upon real and contemporary considerations and this in itself serves to differentiate it from the greater part of the original superego*' (1934 [1969], pp. 281–2 [emphasis mine]). But of course advice (or anything else) that is 'based upon real and contemporary considerations' is a function of the ego.

I believe that when Strachey referred to the analyst's function as an 'auxiliary superego', he was really talking about the analyst using his ego. In giving a mutative interpretation, the analyst places his ego where the patient expected to find his own archaic superego. The patient's finding an ego where he expected a superego is the contradiction of expectations that Strachey felt constituted the essential therapeutic effect of psychoanalysis.

To repeat: the archaic superego is capable of either approval or disapproval, but not of assessing what is true. I believe that the reason that the mutative interpretation has its specific effect on the patient is not that the analyst turns out to be a 'good' superego, but that he turns out to be no kind of superego at all. The analyst places himself in a universe different from that of the superego, one of impartial assessment of reality, without any of the disapproval or approval that is the essence of the universe of the archaic superego.

To return to the first question I raised – what is the origin of the sense of danger that the analyst feels in connection with making a mutative interpretation? – what inhibits the analyst from making a mutative interpretation is that in the formation of the transference, something occurs in the analyst's unconscious that is precisely the opposite of what occurs in the patient when the analyst finally makes the interpretation. When Strachey wrote of the patient projecting his archaic superego into the analyst in the first phase of the process, he probably had in mind a phantasy of the patient. This it is, but there is also a reality to it. When we speak of the patient projecting his archaic superego into the analyst, we mean that he causes the analyst somehow in reality to become infected, so to speak, with his archaic superego. The analyst's susceptibility to infection is a function of the strength of his own archaic superego: the patient's projected superego merges with the analyst's, and their combined force pushes the analyst into a state of mind where he experiences the analysis from the point of view of an archaic superego: not as an impartial

scientific exploration of the patient's unconscious (K activity, in Bion's terminology), but something else – a moral, or rather immoral, enterprise. In this
phase of the process, rather than the analyst replacing a part of the patient's
archaic superego with his ego, the patient has replaced (or displaced) the
analyst's ego with his own archaic superego. Put more simply, rather than the
analyst curing the patient, the patient has made the analyst ill. (This is not to
discount the well-recognized problems of giving interpretations, such as the
obscurity of the material, the need to accurately gauge the patient's anxieties
and defenses, and the need for tact. But these problems are all external to the
analyst, whereas the merger of the analyst's and patient's archaic superegos
produces a problem for the analyst that is internal.)

The anxiety that the analysts felt in the examples I have mentioned illustrates
the sense of danger that Strachey connected to making a mutative interpretation. One could argue that in both of these examples, this anxiety stemmed
from the analyst's own ambivalence about psychoanalysis, which made him
unsure whether it wasn't really just a way of enviously stifling the patient's
development, Laius-like, or greedily manipulating money out of the patient.
And I would agree: that sort of perverse view of analysis, being universal in the
unconscious of even experienced analysts, no doubt played a role.

The aspect of the problem that I wish to focus on, however, has to do with
how the unconscious relationship between the analyst and the patient *reinforced*
the analyst's perverse view of analysis – with the fact that some interaction in
the analytic setting had made it much more difficult for him to think *during* the
session about the possibility that his state of mind might be a function of the
patient's projections, than it was *afterward*. The analyst's sense that the mutative
interpretation he is about to give is dangerous arises from his archaic superego.
It has a characteristic quality. The analyst's archaic superego tends to make him
feel that the appropriate interpretation would spoil his good relationship with
the patient – that if he attempts to simply analyze the situation without fear or
favor, he is being cold and unempathic, and if he makes a simple, realistic interpretation in an objective manner, he is being tactless.

But in reality, of course, these anxieties have nothing to do with real empathy
and tact. They stem from the analyst's fear of the patient's archaic superego,
which encroaches on the analyst's ego. True empathy in the analytic sense is
simply a sensitivity to the patient's real and contemporary state of mind, not
reverence for his archaic superego, and real tact consists not of evading pain, but
of finding the least painful way of making an interpretation that inevitably
involves narcissistic injury.

The crisis for the analyst who is on the verge of a mutative interpretation is
that his own ego function – his own grip on reality – comes under attack from
the combined forces of his and the patient's archaic superegos, which are united
in their common belief that a mutative interpretation will ruin the 'good' relationship between patient and analyst. But this so-called 'good' relationship cannot,

of course, be the real working relationship in analysis, which cannot be harmed by interpretation, since it exists primarily to facilitate interpretation. It is a sort of narcissistic fusion between analyst and patient that is in many ways the opposite of a working relationship.

4.4.2 The group superego

If this picture that I am painting – a merger of superegos producing a state of mind in which 'moral' considerations squeeze out scientific exploration, an interest in knowledge and the capacity to work – is beginning to look familiar, it may be because of its resemblance to what Bion described in 1961 as a 'basic-assumption mentality', a psychological state that descends upon one when one becomes a member of a group. The similarities between basic-assumption mentality and that associated with the merger of superegos in an analysis are quite striking: in both a superego-dominated analysis and in the basic-assumption group, there is a deterioration of the capacity for critical thought; in both, there is a superficial and rather manic sense of warm, groupish good feeling, the maintenance of which depends on the absence of critical thought; in both, anyone who directs attention to the actual problems at hand is somehow regarded as an enemy of the group, anti-social, standoffish, hostile and superior; and in both, there is the timeless, mind-numbing feeling that somehow the "group' or the "relationship' is an important good in and of itself, and will heal whatever problems face the group (or the patient and analyst) without the need for specific work on the part of the group members.

One often sees this type of mentality particularly clearly in the early stages of the formation of a group or organization, such as a psychoanalytic society, where the group is idealized while the real problems facing it are denied. Later, when the initial euphoria passes and real problems persist, splitting and scapegoating ensue, with those who are directing attention to the problems being the scapegoats. A similar phenomenon is seen in the initial stages of an analysis.

Could it be that the basic assumption mentality observed by Bion is produced by the confluence of the archaic superegos of the group members? This would be in line with Freud's postulate (1921) that the very feeling of belonging to a 'group' arises through a psychic fusion of the superegos of the members of the group. In that case, the basic-assumption group would be a multiple version of the 'good' analytic relationship.

Bion's 'basic-assumption' group contrasts with what he called a work group, which consists above all of a number of *distinct* individuals cooperating to solve a specific, well-defined problem. The theory of the container, as usually stated, assumes a work-group relationship between patient and analyst. The reason that it does not account for the sense of danger connected with making a mutative interpretation is because that sense arises from the basic-assumption group.

39

4.4.3 *The superego and containment*

I will now turn to the second question that I posed, the intellectual deterioration that seems to affect the analyst who is caught up in the superego-dominated, or basic-assumption type of relationship with the patient. According to Bion, before one can think, one must convert beta elements into alpha elements. Bion tells us that an alpha element is something 'suitable for use as a latent dream thought'. Its importance to Bion's view of the mind can be appreciated when one remembers that in Bion's view unconscious thinking of the sort that occurs in the creation of a dream is the source and origin of our entire mental life.

But what is a beta element? Is it simply a raw material out of which unconscious thoughts must be forged, like Susan Isaacs's (1952) idea of a somatic tension or need, not yet mental, not yet having crossed the border between soma and psyche, that must be transported across this border to become an unconscious phantasy? Perhaps. Is it something that awaits symbolizing, so it may be grappled into its place in the mental fabric? Perhaps. Or is it something too intense to be processed by the unprepared mind, like Freud's idea of infantile sexual overstimulation in his old theory of hysteria? Unbearable because overwhelming? Again, perhaps.

As a rule, Bion liked to leave his concepts undefined, or unsaturated, like an algebraic variable, so they can be evaluated by later experience. But in *Transformations* (1965), Bion himself does some filling in of the concept of beta element. He suggests that one of the things that make beta elements unsuitable for thinking is that they are persecutingly, monotonously moralistic:

> Invariant to beta elements … is the moral component [which] is inseparable from feelings of guilt and responsibility and from a sense that the link between one … object and another, and between these objects and the personality, is moral causation.
>
> (1965, p. 64)

That is, everything that happens is felt to be somehow deliberate, and therefore someone deserves the blame (or credit) for it. As Bion put it, this

> theory of causation, in a scientific sense as far as it has one, is … an instance of carrying over from a moral domain an idea (for want of a better word) into a domain in which its original penumbra of moral associations is inappropriate.
>
> (1965, p. 64)

He called this phenomenon 'usurpation of ego function by superego function'. The ego, in Bion's view, is scientific. It is concerned with seeing things as they are, and not with whose fault anything is. The point that Bion seems to be making is that a state of mind dominated by the archaic superego, in which fault and moral causation are what are important, is actually antithetical to thinking in a realistic way:

> definition and search for meaning ... can be destroyed by the strength of a sense of causation and its moral implications ... causation, responsibility and therefore a controlling force (as opposed to helplessness) provide a framework within which omnipotence reigns.
>
> (1965, p. 64)

In a footnote connecting this deterioration of reality-testing with group phenomena, he adds:

> The group is dominated by morality – I include of course the negative sense that shows as rebellion against morality – and this contributed to the atmosphere of hostility to individual thought on which Freud remarked.
>
> (1965, p. 64)

In another passage from *Transformations*, he makes the same point in a different way:

> Psycho-analysts may find what I have said about theories of causation ... as it exists in knowing about and becoming O, more familiar if they remember how big a part is played in analysis by the need to blame other people and the difficulties of maturation because maturation involves being responsible.
>
> (1965, p. 155)

In short, beta elements are objects that cannot relate to the personality other than by blaming it for something. They are, in other words, pieces of archaic superego. One could simply say here 'superego' rather than 'archaic superego' because, when one considers it carefully, the mature superego – which is the same as Strachey's 'auxiliary superego', characterized by consideration only of 'real and contemporary considerations' – is really ego. The distinction between archaic and mature superego thus becomes superfluous: what we have traditionally called mature superego we may simply call ego, and the term superego now denotes only the archaic variety of superego. In this view, anxiety and guilt about real damage that one has done to one's good external or internal objects, for example, would not arise from the superego at all, but from the ego (since it would be realistic and reasonable, not phantastic and exaggerated).

This brings us to the second question I raised earlier, the source of the intellectual deterioration that prevents the analyst from even thinking of the mutative interpretation. Under the impact of the archaic superego, thought and understanding become painfully difficult if not impossible; one cannot experience the truth about oneself or others as simple facts, but only as occasions for blame. This climate reduces thinking to a mere exercise in blaming, and when one is in this climate, one can avoid attacking oneself or the patient with blame only by putting an end to thinking. This is an important root of the intellectual

41

deterioration (or inhibition of ego function) that prevents the analyst from even thinking of the appropriate interpretation.

Bion's theory of alpha function also suggests how the analyst overcomes this intellectual inhibition so that he can think of the correct interpretation. If alpha function is the conversion of beta elements into something suitable for reality-testing (or scientific thought, as Bion puts it), then one aspect of alpha function must be precisely what the analyst does when he is gearing up to make a mutative interpretation: he disentangles himself from the combined force of his and his patient's archaic superegos, forgetting the supposed 'moral' implications of his interpretations and simply describing to the patient what he experiences about him as realistically as possible.

Alpha function in this view means shifting from being dominated by one's archaic superego to being dominated by one's ego, and in this sense, analysis is a rather purified form of ego functioning. I suggest that an essential part of what we call analytic containment consists of detaching oneself from moralistic considerations, and simply describing what one sees, without fear or favor.

This view is consistent with our knowledge that analytic containment is not an effort to make the patient feel relieved, or good about himself, but only to help him think and feel what is true. Analysis has no more to do with promoting the patient's 'good' superego than it does with promoting his 'bad' one. Both are equally archaic. The concern of analysis is to promote the growth of the patient's ego at the expense of any kind of superego. This means that the analyst should no more endeavor to be a 'good' parent than a 'bad' one. He should endeavor to be only an analyst. (The fact that analysis often comes as a great relief to the patient does not contradict this. The relief comes from the fact that the truth is always less persecuting than the phantasy that had displaced it in the patient's mind. Because of this, the analyst need not concern himself with producing relief in the patient, but only with finding the truth. When the full truth emerges, relief follows as a matter of course.)

Bion saw the value of analysis in the fact that it tried to reach the truth about things, because he felt that truth, or reality-testing, is what brings about development of the patient's ego (a view that Freud would certainly have endorsed). But what does Bion mean by truth? In *Transformations* he formulated a partial criterion for truth that is of interest to us because it is specifically psychoanalytic, and bears on our discussion of ego and superego:

> The painter who works on his public's emotions with an end in view is a propagandist with the outlook of the poster artist. He does not intend his public to be free in its choice of the use to which it puts the communication he makes. The analyst's position is akin to that of the painter who by his art adds to his public's experience. Since psycho-analysts do not aim to run the patient's life but to enable him to run it according to his lights and therefore to know what his lights are, [the analyst's] interpretation ... should [be a]

verbal representation of [his] emotional experience. ... [The interpretation should express] truth without any implication other than the implication that it is true *in the analyst's opinion* ... how is truth to be a criterion for [the analyst's interpretation]? To what has it to be true and how shall we decide whether it is or not? Almost any answer appears to make truth contingent on some circumstance or idea that is itself contingent.

(1965, p. 37, emphasis mine)

In other words, what is truth? Here, in the best Freudian tradition, Bion brings in a piece of clinical experience to shed light on what was threatening to degenerate into a philosophical discussion of the nature of truth:

In practice the problem arises with schizoid personalities in whom the super-ego appears to be developmentally prior to the ego and to deny development and existence itself to the ego. The usurpation by the super-ego of the position that should be occupied by the ego involves imperfect development of the reality principle, exaltation of a 'moral' outlook and lack of respect for the truth. The result is starvation of the psyche and stunted growth. I shall regard this statement as an axiom that resolves more difficulties than it creates.

(1965, pp. 37–8)

Bion's criterion for truth in psychoanalysis is a negative one. A true interpretation, whatever other characteristics it might have, must lack the kind of moralistic outlook that emphasizes what is good or bad. Of course, such an interpretation might still be false (which is why it is important for the analyst to realize that it is only his opinion of the truth), but any interpretation that contains a moralistic implication *must* be false in the analytic sense.

Bion seems to be relating truth in the analytic sense to alpha elements: mental elements that nourish the ego by providing it with *facts* about internal and external reality that it can use in a scientific (i.e. realistic) way. He contrasts these with beta elements, which are not realistic, factual or truthful, but propagandistic.

While the patient's ego needs facts as nourishment, at the same time it must prepare them out of the raw material of beta elements. Analysis provides the patient not with an auxiliary superego, which would simply be another source of beta elements, but with an auxiliary ego, to assist his own ego in maintaining its contact with reality, despite the beta element activity of his archaic superego. (This is in line with the view of the analyst's function that Paula Heimann expressed in her 1956 paper on the 'Dynamics of transference interpretation.')

As part of the very process of doing analysis, of being the patient's auxiliary ego, the analyst is caught up in the conflict between the patient's ego and archaic superego. This conflict, and its attendant anxieties, become the analyst's. To make the appropriate interpretation, he must brave these anxieties within himself by working through the conflict between his own ego and superego. This provides the patient with the best possible opportunity to work through the similar conflict in himself. One of the consequences of this, and one of the peculiarities of analysis is that, if the analyst does it well, then even if the patient does not get better, the analyst will.

4.5 Conclusion

To summarize the main points of this chapter: the sense of danger that the analyst experiences when on the verge of making a mutative interpretation arises from the threat that this poses to the basic-assumption 'group of two' that he forms with the patient; what Strachey called the 'auxiliary superego' in analysis is actually the analyst's ego, and the making of a mutative interpretation requires, among other things, that the analyst's ego struggle with the guilt and anxiety produced by his archaic superego, which is opposed to the mutative interpretation and which is, as an aspect of the basic-assumption group, augmented in its guilt-producing activities by the patient's archaic superego; a successful mutative interpretation is therefore a victory of ego over superego; this process corresponds to part of that denoted by Bion as $\beta \rightarrow \alpha$, and releases the analyst from the intellectual deterioration that the fusion of superegos had produced; this accomplishes one of the purposes of analysis, to help the patient think and feel what is true; Bion regarded truth as necessary for mental survival; and he suggests, as a modest criterion for our concept of analytic truth, that it not be a product of an archaic superego.

5

What is a clinical fact?★

5.1 Introduction

The question, 'what is a clinical fact' is fundamental to our work, and we all proceed as though we know the answer intuitively, which I think we probably do. But defining something explicitly is different from knowing it implicitly.

In a way, definition is a dangerous activity, since there is always the risk that in trying to clarify an issue, we end up instead by embalming it as an 'official' version. But it seems to me that if we approach the matter in a minimalist way, being careful to include in our definition no more than the bare necessities (like Hume's definition of cause and effect as no more than a 'constant conjunction' of certain sense impressions), and leave the rest to be filled in by experience, we minimize the risk of throttling our subject with our attempts to define it.

In this chapter, I will suggest that, while a clinical psychoanalytic fact may itself be simple, detecting one is a very complex matter. And arriving at an agreement about what constitutes a clinical fact – that is, agreeing on how we detect one – may be even more complex and controversial. But it is certainly worth the effort, since some agreement on what constitutes our basic facts seems to be an important precondition for any scientific exchange or, indeed, for the very existence of a scientific community. (Psychoanalytic controversies that arise between people who agree on what the facts are, and how we arrive at them, but disagree on the significance of those facts are resolvable by empirical study. Controversies between people who have different views about what constitutes a psychoanalytic fact may not be resolvable; they may be a sign that the field has divided into multiple disciplines.)

I will approach the question of what a clinical fact is indirectly, by first addressing one that is less controversial: what is a *scientific* fact? (I've said that this

★ This is a slightly revised version of a paper that appeared in the *International Journal of Psycho-Analysis* 75 (5/6), 903–13 (1994).

is a less controversial subject than that of what a psychoanalytic fact is. If one reads philosophy of science, of course, the question of even what constitutes a scientific fact is anything but uncontroversial. But scientists in any given field seem to have a working agreement, even if not explicitly stated, about what qualifies as a fact in their field.)

To make my task as easy as possible, I will start with a simple scientific fact, from the science that deals with the simplest things in the simplest possible way, namely physics. Of course, once we have examined the simplest case, we shouldn't fall prey to the error of thinking that the real world is that simple. But examining a simple case may help us get started on the more complex ones.

The simple case I will start with consists of an experiment we did in the college physics laboratory, an attempt to measure the acceleration on a body due to the earth's gravity ('g'). The apparatus we used was a complicated system in which a weight was attached to the end of a paper tape which was run over a pulley and through an electrode which was set up to produce sparks at regular intervals (I think it was once every tenth of a second). When we let the weight fall and turned on the power to the electrode, the sparks burned holes in the paper tape, and by measuring the distance between the holes, we could see how far the weight had dropped in each succeeding tenth of a second. We could then make a table or graph of this information, and using the techniques of analytic geometry could arrive at a number telling us how fast the weight was accelerating under the force of gravity. This was g.

As I recall, the value we obtained for g was something like 960 cm/sec^2, which is less than the accepted value by about 2 per cent. This wasn't bad at all, considering the crudeness of our apparatus. But the point I want to make is that the validity of our measurement of g depended on a number of factors: the tape mustn't stretch under the pull of the weight; the pulley mustn't slow the tape down through friction; the weight must fall straight down without swinging like a pendulum; the spark timer must fire precisely every tenth of a second as advertised; and so on.

In practice, no real physicists measured g that way, even then. They timed the swing of pendulums, relying on a theory of physics that related the swing of the pendulum to the force of gravity. But we weren't assigned to do it that way, partly because that would have required timers more accurate than those we had available, but mainly because we would have had to use the theory of the pendulum to calculate g, and this was supposed to be a 'direct' measurement. But even the most 'direct' measurement of g depended on a complicated apparatus, all parts of which must work reasonably well for anything of value to emerge. And this is just the simplest case: in practice today, physicists measure these fundamental constants using techniques whose validity depends heavily on the truth of a number of physical theories far more complex than that of the pendulum.

There are many ways we could have run that college experiment, or other measurements of the same thing, that would have been simpler. But without their complexity – the careful establishment of an observational setting, and the reliance on a number of theories about what the observations mean – the results would have had no scientific value. They wouldn't have been more direct or experience-near than the results we got, they simply wouldn't have been phys-ics – they would have just been bad scientific technique. From a naïve point of view, the apparatus was quite complex and operating it required us to be rather fussy. But from the physicist's point of view, it was absolutely minimal.

As this prologue suggests, my answer to the question, What is a clinical fact?, will suggest that even a simple clinical psychoanalytic fact is a creature of a complex apparatus and a lot of theory. This is quite different from the view that 'real' facts are simple observations of the type that are publicly available, no matter how untutored the public, and which may be assembled (or perhaps assemble themselves) to form theories. I am sure that without a rather complex theoretical apparatus, we cannot make even the simplest scientific observations, but only something like random impressions whose barest significance would become a matter of endless speculation. Naïve impressions may be the only type of observation that is possible at first (Freud fondly remembered Charcot ad-monishing him to simply stare at the facts until they began to speak), but perhaps psychoanalysis has reached a point where we may begin to be more comfortable with the fact that even our simplest observation – a 'clinical fact' – is the product of a very complex and delicate observational apparatus.

My approach to the problem of what is a clinical fact will be to try to define an 'apparatus' – the psychoanalytic setting – in which psychoanalytic facts may be observed, without any *a priori* reference to what types of observations might qualify as facts. I assume then that if the psychoanalytic apparatus, like my college gravitometer, is working properly, then whatever emerges will be a legitimate psychoanalytic fact. In the remainder of this chapter, I will address two questions: first, what kind of 'apparatus' seems to be necessary for detecting clinical facts, and how do we know when we've got one? And second, what kinds of observation are found to emerge from this apparatus? In other words, how do we know when we have an observational set-up that detects clinical psychoanalytic facts and not spurious artifacts, and what kinds of facts emerge when it is running properly?

5.2 Evidence of psychoanalysis

The apparatus that produces clinical facts is, of course, psychoanalysis itself; so we could say that clinical psychoanalytic facts are what we observe during those moments when psychoanalysis is going on. But how do we know when psychoanalysis is going on? I cannot, of course, give a description of psy-choanalysis in the same way I can describe the pulleys, tapes and spark timers of my '*g*' measurements, but I can try to give a description of what seem to me to be two or three pieces of evidence that psychoanalysis is occurring. I have arrived at these evidences empirically: when I have observed one or more of them in a session, I have found that I could subsequently place confidence in the clinical 'facts' that the patient and I were then observing.

5.2.1 Isolation within an intimate relationship

I will now illustrate the first of these pieces of evidence with a clinical example. On the night before her initial consultation with me, a patient had the following dream: *She arrived at my office for her consultation, only to find the waiting room full of people. I was nowhere in sight. She went into the consulting room, and discovered me showing another crowd of admiring people some fabrics or tapestries I had designed. She felt obliged to admire them as well, but at the same time felt cheated out of her consultation. I was evidently so much in need of her praise for my work, however, that she couldn't complain without feeling terribly guilty.*

Among her associations were the feelings that she had always had to serve other people, which she resented, but did not feel she could complain about; that she was never doing enough for them; and that she somehow was always inadvertently failing to discharge her obligations. I said that the dream suggested that, although she hoped to get some help from me, she feared she would end up instead having to help me in some way. She agreed, adding that she had dreamt of me as one more in the endless line of people who demanded her help when she needed help from them. She was surprised and embarrassed at her portrayal of me, and said by way of explanation that her mother had been a depressed, fragile and easily overwhelmed woman whom she had apparently 'transferred' onto me.

This dream was her initial communication about a relationship with me that persisted almost unchanged for two and a half years. The first sign of a real shift came during a session several weeks before the long summer break, in which the patient seemed to be worried that I had become overwhelmed by my work with her, and that my summer break represented just that. When I pointed this out, she agreed, and explained it in the same way as she had explained the dream, as well as a number of similar episodes that had occurred since then, as 'transference' from past experience with her mother.

Although I had never really felt satisfied with these explanations, I also had not been able to see why, and had more or less fallen into the habit of giving them silent assent. But this time I was struck by the lifeless manner with which she spoke, and by the fact that she afterward lapsed into silence. When she did speak again, I noticed that it was in a cautious and tentative way, being careful (I felt) not to say anything that might cause me any distress or make me feel there was any work I had to do for her. It occurred to me that, although she had meant by her interpretation that she realized that her state of mind reflected a past reality now dead and inappropriate to the present, she was acting as though I were indeed quite fragile in present reality. Her analysis of her state of mind did not seem to meet her actual experience of it; it seemed, rather, to be a half-hearted attempt to talk herself out of her present experience of me by labeling it transference.

I then began to feel an unexpected sense of irritation at the patient's concern about me. If my job was indeed to help her understand what she was experiencing, then her attempt at making my work easier was having the opposite effect: working with such a reticent patient was much harder than with a candid one, no matter how troublesome the latter might be. (This is not an uncommon experience. Everyone has found themselves in the position of being helped by someone they wished would not be so helpful.)

I told her, with some trepidation, that, while she was aware of feeling that I was overwhelmed, and wanted to help me, I thought she was unaware that her reticence was helping to make me helpless. As I feared, she at once felt angry and hurt.

Her reaction confirmed a suspicion that was just beginning to dawn on me: despite her interpretation about her experience of me being a carry-over from the past, she still took it as an unquestionable *present* fact that I was exhausted. In this light, her attempts to lighten my burden were then the only possible way that she could hope to help me. My comment could therefore only represent to her my ingratitude for her efforts. Hence her feeling wounded.

The unconscious beliefs about my exhaustion on which her reaction rested suggested that she was not just confusing me with a past figure, or having a phantasy (in the ordinary sense of the word) about me in the present, but actually experiencing me in the present as exhausted and overwhelmed by her. I now realized that what had been irritating me was that this experience carried with it a sense of conviction so strong that it seemed to admit literally no doubt, rendering the interpretations I made about it completely impotent: insofar as they did not support this picture of me, she simply ignored them.

(Strictly speaking, they were consciously acknowledged, but ignored by her unconscious. 'Ignored by her unconscious' merely means that she was ignoring them without knowing that she was ignoring them. But *I* knew it, or rather something in *my* unconscious knew it; hence my irritation, inexplicable until I interpreted it to myself.) Despite her evident desire to think about what made her see me as so incapable, she seemed unable to overcome an emotional certainty about my exhausted state that was so fundamental and undoubted that it made serious consideration of any alternative impossible. When I told her this, she again fell silent. But this silence, unlike her previous reticence, had a thoughtful quality to it. When she broke it, she said very soberly that she now realized her analysis *had* been governed by a profound belief – an unwavering certainty not affected by the experience of the analysis – that I was indeed too fragile to bear the burden of her as a patient. She felt both sad and astonished to find how it had persisted despite the many times she had tried to convince herself it was merely a carry-over from the past. But she now saw, as if for the first time, that it had

49

been both present since the first day and the first dream, and, up until now, untouched by interpretation.

She had established contact not just with the 'fragile mother' that material reality had imposed on her, but with something she was also making fragile in her mind. The 'making fragile' was her *relationship* to her internal object, her role in the formation of her psychic reality or internal object world. Her sadness and aston-ishment were a response to her sudden awareness that she played an *active role* in forming the internal 'mother' that she had projected into me in the transference.

For some time following this session, the analytic work took on a sense of solidity and conviction that I hadn't seen in it before. It was as though the analysis itself had suddenly emerged through a film into the real world: the patient was in contact with how she made her internal objects different from her external ones, and this enabled her to see the difference between them and therefore to be in contact with her real, external analyst.

If I had to describe the emotional tenor of the analysis during this period, I would say that it was dominated by an unusual sense of clarity, tinged with sadness and anxiety. The clarity arose, I believe, from a de-confusion of the former state of affairs, in which the patient was unable to see me as I was, distinct from her internal objects, and I was unable to disentangle myself from the transference role into which she had cast me. The anxious sadness was partly the patient's and partly mine – hers over the recognition of how powerless she had been against her unconscious need to have me helpless, and mine over a similar recognition: it had taken me two and a half years to give an effective interpretation of her first dream. This was a blow to my therapeutic omnipo-tence that left me feeling quite powerless as well. This recognition showed both of us how little influence I had over her unconscious, and how 'being in analysis' was not in itself any guarantee of progress or development; neither of us could make me able to 'fix' her unconscious. The sadness and anxiety we felt as a result of this was the complement of the sense of clarity and sanity – both were due to a new appreciation of our separateness from each other.

Earlier I raised the question of the requisite apparatus for detecting clinical facts – how do we know when we are getting *psychoanalytic* facts and not some-thing else? I would like to propose this emotional constellation – a certain combination of clarity about who's who and who is doing what in the session, and sadness – as a criterion for the occurrence of psychoanalysis, and therefore that what is emerging is a psychoanalytic fact.

In *Elements of Psychoanalysis*, Wilfred Bion also described this problem and this emotional constellation in the following terms:

> considering any psycho-analytical session as an emotional experience, what elements in it must be selected to make it clear that the experience had been a psycho-analysis and could have been nothing else ... The dictum that an analysis must be conducted in an atmosphere of deprivation is usually under-

stood to mean that the analyst must resist any impulse in himself to gratify the desires of his analysands or to crave gratification for his own. To narrow the expression of this statement without contracting the area covered by it; at no time must either analyst or analysand lose the *sense of isolation within the intimate relationship of analysis* ... the analyst should not lose, or deprive his patient of, the sense of isolation that belongs to the knowledge that the circumstances that have led to analysis and the consequences that may in future arise from it are a responsibility that can be shared with nobody.

(Bion 1963, pp. 14–16, emphasis mine)

Although patient and analyst are working together on the analysis, they are both in it alone. Bion goes on,

[Psychoanalytic] detachment can only be achieved at the cost of painful feelings of loneliness and abandonment experienced (1) by the primitive animal mental inheritance from which detachment is effected [which he defines as 'the primitive mind and the primitive social capacity of the individual as a political or group animal'] and (2) by the aspects of the personality that succeed in detaching themselves ...

(1963, p. 16)

The desire, shared by patient and analyst alike, not to be so alone is what the rule of analytic abstinence really frustrates.

My patient's sad astonishment arose from her recognition of her role in maintaining me as a fragile object. Her sudden awareness of her responsibility for maintaining me in this state despite all the interpretations we had both made produced the senses of sadness and anxiety. But at the same time we both experienced a sense of clarity – it had become clear who was who in the analysis. I believe this is an example of what Bion meant by a sense of 'isolation within an intimate relationship': isolation in the sense that one is aware of one's individual role in the relationship, and intimacy that can come only from contact between two *separate* individuals.

The analysis that I have just made of my clinical experience could no doubt be formulated in other psychoanalytic 'languages', or theoretical frameworks. If my description of the clinical material has been adequate, those who speak other languages should be able to recognize it and translate it into their own terms. The same is true of the following example.

5.2.2. The aesthetic conflict

The second piece of evidence of psychoanalysis that I wish to propose is related to a type of response that certain patients have to interpretations that they find helpful and profoundly moving. I would like to illustrate this response

51

with another clinical vignette, from the analysis of a woman who related a dream in which she was *jogging around a pool 'for her health', and then looking at some silk blouses on a rack (she said that this was a type of blouse that was worn under the jacket of the type of suit she had worn the day before). These suddenly changed into some cheaper silk blouses, whose texture was not as fine and whose colors were not as subtle. She didn't really like them, but told herself they were really OK, that they were just worn under jackets and mostly didn't show anyway, and that, as her sister had always told her, she was always too picky, and anyway, the good ones were very expensive – they cost almost as much as the suit itself.* After relating this dream, she commented that, while these arguments against the blouse sounded convincing, they were fallacious, since a good silk blouse really makes the whole outfit.

She connected jogging for her health to the analysis, and the silk blouses to the previous day's session. On that day, she had worn a suit she had been given by her mother, and felt vaguely dissatisfied with it, but was frustrated because she could not put her finger on exactly what displeased her. I asked her what she would prefer, and she said she would like the skirt to be either tighter or shorter. I said that she seemed to feel that it was too dowdy for her – that she would prefer something sexier. This remark surprised her greatly; it seemed exactly right to her, but she had no idea that that had been the problem. Her surprise surprised me, since it seemed quite clear that that is what she had been complaining about. (This brought to mind Bion's remark that an interpretation should be about something obvious but unobserved. This is an ideal, but one can actually achieve it from time to time.)

Furthermore, she felt profoundly moved and relieved by my comment. In the year since that session, the patient reports that it produced a deep and enduring change in her ability to wear the kind of clothes she likes. It was, she later said, as though my saying what I did had really allowed her to feel that she could wear the kind of clothes she wanted to, and did not have to accept what her mother wore, or what others might prefer her to wear. (This also led eventually to productive work on her capacity to 'wear' and display her own opinions, and not those of her objects.) My seemingly innocuous and rather banal observation clearly had deep ramifications for her: it turned out that I had been a representative in the transference of some internal figure – probably an archaic superego – that was trying to desexualize her. My comment presented her with what was apparently a surprising piece of evidence that I was *not* interested in desexualizing her.

My comment had caused her to experience something of which she had been quite unaware about her immediate relationship to me. After a few minutes she connected it to an episode in her childhood. I felt that this was a dead association (that is, it felt dead), one designed to get her away from an important immediate experience with me, and its implications, but I did not say so.

To return now to the dream: the fine silk blouse represented the interpretation that she had found so important the previous day, and the transition from the fine blouse to the cheaper imitation represented the transition from the live, immediate situation to the dead associative cliché about the past – a recoiling from the impact of the immediate experience of the analytic session to an 'explanation' that was a dead imitation of analysis. In her dream, she recognized this explanation of her state of mind as not the real thing, but was trying to convince herself with a series of rationalizations that appeared to support the idea that the sterile explanation of the live experience was more or less as good as the live thing, and that, in any event, it didn't make any real difference anyway because the subject of the interpretation, like the blouse, didn't 'really' show, since it was an inner state. Besides, she was being too picky to want a real analysis when her sister wasn't having one, and wasn't analysis very expensive? But she also knew unconsciously that the inner state does show through (if only partially), and, as the inner blouse 'makes' the whole outfit, the part of her inner world that shows somehow makes her the person she is.

The conflict represented in the dream is over whether she can allow herself to experience the impact of what she felt was a beautiful and important interpretation, or whether her desire for this will succumb to the propagandistic internal accusations of being too picky and self-important, and of spending an extravagant amount of money (and emotion) contacting a live internal state that 'didn't really show' and was in any event 'not really that much better' than the less expensive, dead one. These accusations have the effect of devaluing an important experience – one that has since proved quite valuable for the patient's emotional development – and of making her feel somehow guilty for valuing and wanting it. They represent an envious internal attack on the good object (the fine silk blouse), as well as on the part of herself that cares about it (here called picky and selfish). Note that this is not an example of a negative reaction to what the *analyst* thinks has been a good interpretation; it is a negative reaction to an interpretation that the patient herself found profoundly moving and helpful.

This kind of envious internal attack is the second type of evidence for a psychoanalytic process that I wish to propose. In this case, the reaction was relatively mild; my patient had a dream in which she felt guilty about the fine blouse she had been given the opportunity to buy. I would not consider this a negative therapeutic reaction, but it is easy to see how, if it had been much more severe, the guilt and self-hatred over having the interpretation could have produced what we would recognize as a classic negative therapeutic reaction.

In the example I described, my patient's sense of the beauty of the interpretation, and hence her ability to cling to the live experience of the analysis, was undermined by an envious internal attack. Her struggle was like that of Aeneas's faithful helmsman, who steered the ship through the night, resisting the temptations of sleep, until the enraged god Somnus finally tore him from his station and threw him into the sea. But Aeneas, emerging the next morning, saw not only that the helmsman was gone, but that a part of the ship's tiller had been ripped away as well. So he knew from the evidence of the struggle (my patient's dream) that the helmsman had remained true.

I do not think that it is difficult to understand why this sort of reaction – mild or severe – should qualify as a criterion of psychoanalysis. An analytic interpretation – even a painful one, as in my first example – produces a sense of sanity in the patient, and a greater capacity to think and feel. These capacities are the life of the mind, and the Kleinian habit of comparing interpretations with food is no mere metaphor or genetic reconstruction. The mind needs reliable information about itself – truth, if you will – just as much as the body needs food. Whoever has the ability to provide this is in an enviable position indeed. And, unless the patient is completely free of envy (and if there are such creatures, I would like to see one), he will envy something as enviable as a working psychoanalyst.

This conflict is similar phenomenologically to what Donald Meltzer has called the 'aesthetic conflict' (Meltzer 1988), a conflict that arises within the patient when he experiences the truth of an interpretation as beautiful, in fact, as *unbearably* beautiful. Meltzer's clinical observations about a type of conflict arising in response to analytic progress are lucid and important, and he has done us a service by pointing out that it is what the patient experiences as *beautiful* that triggers this conflict. I disagree, however, with his formulation of its causes: I believe that he neglects the role of envy in producing the clinical picture he so eloquently describes.

5.3 Psychic reality

Having tried to give some account of how we might be able to tell if our apparatus for detecting clinical facts is working properly, I would like to go on to suggest that if our apparatus is working properly, the facts it yields will turn out to be elements of one's inner world or psychic reality. Before continuing, I should explain more precisely what I mean by psychic reality.

Freud developed the concept of psychic reality after he was forced to abandon his seduction theory of hysteria, which, as we know, was based on the idea that certain external events (such as sexual molestation during childhood) would of themselves produce a neurosis in later life. (This theory seems to be enjoying a resurgence.) In its place, he realized that the external event, which may in itself be quite minor, must combine itself with a certain type of unconscious phantasy – one, for example, that was an expression of the sexual drives – to produce a *subjective* experience which would then, perhaps, lead to a neurosis. This subjective event is a piece of *psychic* reality; it is to be distinguished from the associated external event itself, a piece of *material* reality. Freud recognized that both components – the unconscious wishful phantasy and the material event – were required for an event to have an impact on the unconscious. The event and the unconscious wish must be congruent in the sense that the external event must be usable by an unconscious wishful phantasy as a vehicle for its expression. The model for this is dreaming, where the external event (day residue) serves, in Freud's analogy, as the entrepreneur while the unconscious wish acts as capitalist (Freud 1915–17). In this sense, our unconscious is always dreaming.

What was crucial for a neurotic symptom to develop in Freud's view was not that one simply have a phantasy or suffer an external event, but that the two should combine to produce a piece of psychic reality. He concluded that 'neurotic symptoms were not related directly to actual events, but to wishful phantasies, and that as far as the neurosis was concerned, psychical reality was of more importance than material reality' (Freud 1925).

Contact with one's psychic reality therefore puts one in contact with one's *relationship* to the external world – how one reacts (in phantasy) to the events that present themselves to one's experience. This is in certain ways the opposite of the idea that analysis enables one to become aware of the repressed *external* events that have had an impact on one's mind, which is really a modern version of Freud's pre-psychoanalytic seduction or trauma theory.

The next major advance in our appreciation of psychic reality came with Melanie Klein's discovery of the internal object. Freud's concept of psychic reality was of a vague combination of instinct-driven phantasy and external events. Klein's discovery of the internal object put flesh on Freud's skeleton. She described how children's unconscious phantasies of swallowing their objects produce a phantastic inner world that they feel to be concretely real. It is a version of the outer one, but a version that has been altered in important ways:

> The baby, having incorporated his parents, feels them to be live people inside his body in the concrete way in which deep unconscious phantasies are experienced – they are, in his mind, 'internal' or 'inner' objects, as I have termed them. Thus an inner world is being built up in the child's unconscious mind, corresponding to his actual experiences and the impression he gains from people and the external world, and yet altered by his own phantasies and impulses ... [I]n the baby's mind, the 'internal' mother is bound up with the 'external' one, of whom she is a 'double', though one which at once undergoes alterations in his mind through the very process of internalization; that is to say, his image is influenced by his phantasies, and by internal stimuli and internal experiences of all kinds. When external situations which he lives through become internalized – and I hold that they do, from the earliest days onwards – they follow the same pattern: they also become 'doubles' of real situations, and are again altered for the same reasons.
>
> (Klein 1940, pp. 345–6)

In this view, an internal object is clearly not simply our perception of an external one, or our mental representation of it. It is far more than that: Mrs Klein used the term 'internal object' as a shorthand way of describing her observation that children have phantasies that they swallow their objects, which then survive inside them like Jonah in the whale. Children feel these internal objects to be friendly or hostile, healthy or ill, localized or invasive, good or bad, and so on.

Internal objects in this sense are creatures of our psychic reality: they represent our external objects existing inside us *in whatever condition we feel they are as a result of our relationship to them – that is, our (phantasied) treatment of them inside ourselves.*

What we as conscious adults would recognize as something existing in our minds, our unconscious experiences predominantly as something bodily. (This unconscious experience is represented by conscious phrases for our states of mind, such as 'a gut feeling'.) Our internal objects are a manifestation of both how our objects feel or act toward us and how we feel about our objects. The two combine to produce an object that we unconsciously experience as being inside us in a very specific state; we are in a very specific relationship to them, and they are in a very specific relationship to us. That is, we are doing something to them and they are doing something in kind to us.

I suggest that 'internal objects' are how we experience on a primitive level what we would speak of on a more mature level as 'states of mind'. We may wish to use the term 'internal object' in other senses, of course, but this is one aspect of what an internal object is. I do not believe it is really correct to say that our 'unconscious internal objects' *produce* our states of mind: our internal objects *are* our states of mind. For example, 'containing a good internal object' is a vivid way of expressing what we would otherwise call 'feeling love'. We do not feel love *for* our good internal object, or because we *contain* a good internal object; the feeling of 'having a good internal object' *is* our feeling of love. Similarly, we do not feel guilty *because* we have a damaged internal object; what we call guilt is the same as the feeling of something that we care about existing in a damaged state inside us. And we do not feel depressed *because* we have a beaten-down internal object; our depression is the same as the feeling of having something flattened inside us, and so on.

I believe that Klein's discovery of the internal object world – the universe of all of our internal objects – was a great advance in our understanding of states of mind because, while what we call a state of mind may be the same as an internal object, our internal objects – detailed unconscious phantasies of what we contain – are far more vivid, detailed and varied than our ordinary vocabulary for states of mind – such as depression, guilt, love, security, elation, and so on – can convey. A large amount of the time consumed by a psychoanalysis is devoted to capturing the very details, nuances and ramifications of the states of mind so crudely represented by these terms.

In both of the clinical examples I have cited, the patients became aware not only of their states of mind, but of *their roles* in producing their states of mind. It seems to me that this type of insight is a unique product of psychoanalysis, and that it may therefore serve as a more general indicator that our analytic apparatus is working properly.

5.4 Discussion

It might be objected that this rather elaborate way of looking at a clinical fact is too restrictive. Wouldn't it be better to allow anything that occurs in a session – any feeling, for example – to count as a fact, and to build up our theories on them later on? I think that this is an appealing argument, but I think it is ill-advised. My formulation of what a clinical fact is – a state of mind, whether we picture it as an internal object or in some other way – is complex. And so is my formulation of the emotional 'apparatus' that we use to detect it: psychoanalysis itself, signified (in part) by the emergence of certain emotional states. But they seem to me, despite their complexity, to be no more than bare, minimal necessities.

In any event, it is certainly important to come to some working agreement about what a basic fact is if we are to communicate with each other, even if we can't make it explicit. The 'criteria' I have proposed for knowing when psychoanalysis is occurring are not meant to be exhaustive, exclusive, or definitive. Other criteria can be suggested, and the ones I have suggested may be found to be inadequate. They are merely the ones that seem important to me as I examine my own clinical experience. But whether or not we agree with any given formulation about *what* criteria signify that analysis and nothing else is occurring, it seems probable that the hallmark of a psychoanalysis in progress will turn out to be an emotional climate of the sort I have illustrated here.

What I am suggesting here is that there are certain emotional states that we can observe in the course of an analysis, and that these observable states are signs of a working analysis. I am claiming that what we and the patient can see in the presence of these emotional states is empirically reliable in the same way that a working physical instrument gives reliable information about the physical world. The difference is that a working psychoanalytic apparatus gives us reliable information about the psychical world. This information does not consist of 'facts' that are not subject to interpretation; on the contrary, what I am identifying is precisely what qualifies as the subject of interpretation.

I recognize that gauging an emotional climate is not the same as seeing that pulleys run smoothly, tape doesn't stretch and timers are accurate. But I believe that it is a task that is imposed on us by the nature of our work, and cannot be abandoned for something more mechanical. The stuff we are trying to measure consists of states of mind, and our instrument for measuring it – as work since Racker (1968) on transference and countertransference has made clear – is also an emotional state.

Saying merely that a clinical psychoanalytic fact is what emerges from an analysis, and that an analysis may be known by the presence of certain emotional states (which themselves may require a great deal of sophistication to detect) leaves us with a sense of insecurity about whether or not we can even define in words some of our most fundamental scientific notions, let alone communicate them to a broader public, or even among ourselves. I don't believe that the solution to this sense of insecurity lies in trying to make psychoanalysis more expressible in the scientific language we have. I think we would do better to try to change the language of science into something more psychoanalytic.

At present only poets and artists are able to capture these kinds of experiences so that they retain their meaning outside the context of the events immediately surrounding them. But if we respect how terribly difficult this is, and how much hard work lies behind the artist's easy grace, we may be able to arrive at a precise, *scientific* account of clinical facts that will have real meaning outside the context of the analysis itself.

If this sounds too daunting, or like something that will take us too far from our scientific base, we can recall – returning to the physics lab I began with – that even Newton had to invent a whole new mathematical language – the differential calculus – before he could capture physical motion. The calculus proved extremely controversial, since, unlike conventional forms of mathematics, it dealt not with exact quantities, but only with approximations of them (or as Bishop Berkeley, one of the critics of the calculus put it, 'the ghosts of departed quantities'). The controversy over whether or not Newtonian mechanics was proper science raged for a hundred years. So perhaps we can take heart from that, and not abandon our *métier* for the sake of an illusory scientific propriety.

6

Psychic reality and the analysis of transference

6.1 Psychic reality

In his first theory of hysteria, Freud held that the patient's neurosis was the product of an actual external event – a sexual molestation occurring in childhood, the memory of which had been repressed. After formulating this theory, he set about trying to prove it by attempting to recover the repressed memory in a series of analyses carried out in the mid-1890s. He was unable to do so, however, even in a single case, and the difficulties he encountered in the attempt led him by 1897 to conclude that the pathogenesis of a neurosis was more complex than he had supposed: he now recognized that the source of neurosis was not simply a repressed memory of a past external event, but an unconscious phantasy that had been reinforced by a congruent external event. This discovery was the first step of a path that, by 1925, led him to turn his original theory of the pathogenesis of neurosis on its head. External events now played a secondary role, and, while they might reinforce or strengthen an unconscious phantasy, they were no longer even required for the development of a neurosis. On the other hand, if the required unconscious phantasy was present, it would produce a neurosis even without much assistance from external reality (Freud 1925). In a neurosis, he concluded, unconscious phantasies have the same impact in the mind as actual events. He formulated this by writing that 'as far as the neurosis is concerned, psychical reality is of more importance than material reality' (1925, p. 34).

The problem that faced Freud now was how to account for the fact that certain unconscious phantasies could have this kind impact on the mind, as well as for the fact that they could maintain this impact in the face of all the evidence

* This is a slightly revised version of a paper that appeared in *The Psycholanalytical Quarterly* 66 (1), 18–33 (1997).

that contemporary external reality – the here and now – presented against them. Although he did not state the problem in this form, what he had to account for was the presence of unconscious delusions in neurotic patients.

Freud believed that only certain phantasies had the power to make one delusional in this way, namely phantasies that were the expression of repressed sexual impulses – repressed libido. The idea was that instincts cause phantasies (or, as Susan Isaacs put it [Isaacs 1952], unconscious phantasy is the mental representation of somatic instinctual processes), and that if these phantasies are repressed, they may become confused with the subject's perceptions and memories, without the subject being aware of the confusion. But this still left the problem unresolved, since everyone has repressed sexual phantasies, but not everyone becomes unconsciously delusional (i.e., neurotic), or at least, not everyone becomes so to the same degree.

In 1946, Melanie Klein described a certain type of unconscious phantasy that made one feel that the attributes of one's own personality could be removed from oneself and placed into an object. She called this unconscious phantasy projective identification, and suggested that it had the power to override reality-testing and confuse the perception of inner and outer reality. Aspects of oneself – such as one's impulses, wishes and phantasies – are then experienced as being in the external world (Klein 1946). (This corresponds to what Britton [1989] called 'attributive projective identifications.')

In logical terms, projective identification might be called a meta-phantasy. It is not an ordinary phantasy about ourselves or our objects. It is a phantasy about our phantasies. It makes us feel that our phantasies are a part of objective reality. Projective identification produces unconscious delusions about what belongs to the world and what to ourselves.

Klein's work implied that it was not a quality of the libido (such as its sexual nature) or the fact that it was repressed that enabled it to cause confusions between phantasy and reality. It was rather that one had a certain type of phantasy about one's mind: one felt that bits of it (including one's phantasies) could be projected into the external world. This gives them (from the subject's point of view) the status of concrete realities. That is, they are 'real' in the patient's psychic reality, in his subjective, unconscious experience of the world.

6.2 Transference

Melanie Klein's theory of projective identification indicates that it causes a type of confusion between one's self and one's object in which the subject attributes aspects of himself to his object (instead of to himself). Unconscious phantasies therefore have the power to affect one's perception of reality *to the extent that they are deployed via projective identification.* The theory of projective identification provides an answer to the question of how unconscious phantasies become unconscious delusions in the neurotic patient. They do so to the degree that the patient's use of projective identification makes them seem part of the objective world.

This theory also has obvious implications for our understanding of the transference. I will try to outline these implications and to explore their usefulness in the practical analysis of transference, especially of transferences in patients who are often considered too fragile or too structurally defective for psychoanalysis.

In this chapter, I will use the term 'transference' to refer specifically to the type of confusion in the patient's mind between himself and the analyst that is brought about by projective identification (see 3.2). I am therefore ascribing the transference to the same processes that cause neurosis. This is what we would expect from the facts that (a) a transference neurosis spontaneously arises to replace the patient's pre-existing neurosis in analysis, and (b) resolution of the transference neurosis through analysis resolves the pre-existing neurosis. This is obviously not the only way in which one can view transference, but since the purpose of this chapter is to explore where such a view might lead us, it is the one I shall focus on. After presenting this view of the transference, I shall compare it to certain others.

To summarize: as I am viewing it, transference is the result of a process by means of which the patient projects aspects of his current inner world into the outer world (i.e., into the analyst) in a delusional manner. This way of looking at the transference is related to Money-Kyrle's idea (1968) that all patients, not just psychotic ones, suffer from unconscious delusions.

It is often said that the transference is a repetition of the patient's relationship with objects from his past, experienced with the analyst in the present, instead of being remembered from the past. I think that this is true, but I am struck by the fact that this statement is just as true if one puts it the other way around: that the relationships that the patient seems to have had with his objects in the past are a 'repetition' of the patient's present relationship with the analyst. To put it in a more balanced way, the patient's version of the past, conscious and unconscious, is subject to a number of distortions – that is, confusions between external reality and phantasy – and the transference relationship that he has with the analyst is subject to precisely the same distortions. This is because the 'past', as the patient experiences it in the present (so to speak), and the transference are influenced by the same active, present-day dynamic processes. These processes – the patient's characteristic way of confusing himself with his objects – constitute one aspect of his experience of the present and past alike (see also 7.1).

Until the patient has reached the point through analysis where he is able to resolve the transference – that is, undo his confusion between internal and external reality, his conscious and unconscious recollections of his past must be taken with reservations. (Of course, the resolution of the transference is never an absolute *fait accompli*. The transformations I am describing are relative.) One of the consequences of this is that only at the end of an analysis can we obtain a reasonably reliable history of the patient's past.

This corresponds to the observation that the patient's past, especially the character of his parents, tends to change during the course of an analysis. And it does so in a way that is precisely parallel with the patient's changing perception of the analyst. The analytic transference may or may not be a repetition of the patient's past relationships with real objects. It is highly likely to be a repetition of the patient's past relationships with transference objects, and this is a crucial difference.

We may understand the patient's experience of the analysis itself – the analysis as it exists in his psychic reality – by separating the two sources of this experience. The first is what the analyst actually said or did, the manner, when, in what context, and so on; in other words, all of the different ways by means of which the analyst tries to communicate. The second is how the patient transforms the analyst's words and behavior – how he interprets them. The product of these two is the patient's subjective experience of the interpretation.

If we have a fairly clear idea of what the analyst said and how he said it, and if we can also get an estimate of how the patient experienced it, then we can deduce something about how the former was transformed into the latter. We can say, 'the patient responded *as though* we had said or done such-and-such.' This transformation is the patient's unconscious contribution to the transference. I believe that this is one of the things that Bion was getting at with his idea of 'transformations' (1965): given 'a' being transformed to 'b', what are the rules that govern the transformation? Patients cannot take an interpretation simply as an interpretation until they are well into the resolution of the transference (or, what is equivalent, when the use of projective identification diminishes significantly). But the ways in which they mistake the interpretation are highly interesting, and form the material of a close analysis. (This is in agreement with the point raised in Faimberg's [1996] paper, 'Listening to listening'.)

While we may understand the patient's experience of the analysis itself by separating the two sources of this experience, it is also true that these two phenomena obviously affect each other in complex ways. Given this fact, is it really possible to perform such a separation of the components of the patient's experience of the analyst? Many observers have pointed out that the analyst's behavior and state of mind may be perceived accurately by the patient and will in this case contribute to his transference. This is certainly true, but it does not justify the conclusion that one may not separate out the analyst's and patient's respective contributions. Furthermore, it is likely that the analyst's behavior acts only to reinforce the patient's unconscious projective-identification phantasies, which would be active in any event without this augmentation, and without which the analyst's behavior would have no effect on the transference. This is a complex matter which may perhaps be clarified by the following clinical example.

6.3 Clinical example

Following a period of analysis in which some light had been shed on certain longstanding, unconscious characterologic problems, a patient began a session by telling me of the problem he was having getting a reliable estimate for repair of earthquake damage to his home. He was not satisfied with the estimates he had gotten, for he felt they were too low, and would cause his insurance company to issue benefits that were also too low. As he went on, it became clear that he hoped to use the proceeds from his insurance claim, not just to repair the damage from the earthquake, but to improve his home. When I asked him how he planned to do this, since the insurance benefits were carefully calculated to cover only damage from the earthquake, and the patient would still be responsible for a substantial co-payment, he said that he believed that the estimators would identify hidden, structural damage that wasn't really there; hence they would pay him for damage that didn't exist, and he would use this money to remodel and thereby increase the value of his home.

I asked him how he knew that the structural damage that the estimators might think was present wasn't really present. Had he opened up his walls to look? He said he hadn't, and had no intention of doing so. When I said he sounded as though he didn't want to know, and that his plan might result in 'improving' a home that had fundamental structural flaws, he simply reiterated his belief that there were none.

This struck me as completely illogical. But instead of accepting the patient's abandonment of logic as a given, I began to try to show him the flaws in his reasoning. In retrospect, it is clear that this was an attempt on my part to force him to 'see reason' by the use of logic, instead of interpreting his resistance to it by the use of analysis. After a while, I realized my mistake, and began to think about the possible reasons for his lack of logic. I recalled that in the past, he had often identified himself with his house, and I then said that he was worried that what the analysis had been uncovering recently represented fundamental flaws in his psychic structure, and that he was trying to find a way of remodeling himself – of looking better or more valuable – without having to see what he feared was internal damage that he couldn't afford to repair. The patient greeted this interpretation with skepticism and a great deal of resistance.

The following day, he reported a dream in which *he was lying on a couch, holding his penis in his hand. A man was lying next to him, dilating his own anus with his fingers while groaning from the pain and effort, and instructing the patient on how to insert his penis into the man's rectum. He protested that he couldn't do it, since there was no lubricant, and the man told him to masturbate and squeeze a few drops of semen out of his penis to act as a lubricant. The man then pulled his fingers out of his anus, and the patient saw they were covered with shit. He felt terribly disgusted, and told the man that he would never do as he asked.*

He said that the couch was probably the analytic couch, and the man next to him was probably me, but had no further associations. I said that the dream seemed to represent his subjective experience of the previous session, in which he felt that I was motivated by a desire to cast doubt on what was really a potent and ingenious plan to remodel and improve his house and his personality. My words were not meaningful, but simply sounds indicating that I was dilating my anus in preparation for covering his erect penis – his potent plan – with shit (disguised as interpretations) while triumphing over him in the process; if I couldn't have a penis like his, at least I could sully his. His interpretation (as conveyed by the dream) of my communications was that they were an envious attack on his creativity in having arrived at a good plan. In the previous session, I had evidently given him detailed instructions (my arguing the illogic of his house plans, in contrast to my usual style) which would, had he not seen through them, have resulted in his falling prey to what he regarded unconsciously as my impotent, homosexual, anal obsessions with non-existent structural problems, which would undermine what he considered to be his manly, can-do attitude.

If we assume that the dream represented the patient's unconscious experience of the previous session, given what transpired in the session, and given the dream, we may ask how the patient had transformed the former to produce the latter. The answer to this will shed light on the patient's role in producing this specific transference. If the same type of operation is seen repeatedly – that is, if the patient tends to transform his experiences in the same way in different contexts – we have learned something about the patient's habitual unconscious contributions to his experience of the analysis. We may regard this as an unconscious 'bias' that converts his external reality into his psychic reality in a characteristic (characterological) way. It may be that what we call character or personality is no more than the sum total of such 'biases'. (I realize that the term 'bias' has a negative connotation, but I wish to use it in a neutral way, as in the dictionary definition: 'an inclination of temperament or outlook'.)

The situation is complicated by the fact that in the actual session, I had not simply made an interpretation (about his anxiety that his personality contained hidden damage that the analysis had not overestimated), I had before that debated the logic of his reasoning about his house. The latter was, in fact, a sign of real analytic impotence. By arguing, I was acting out my own phantasy of projective identification with the patient: I was trying to force or inject my understanding of the illogic of his plan into his mind – that is, attempting to control it – rather than simply communicating my observations, allowing the patient to accept or reject them, and trying to understand what he did and why.

This means that, at the very least, the patient's characterization of me in the dream was not *completely* delusional. He had projected into reality, my analytic impotence as manifested by my arguing my point. Given this fact, wouldn't we have to say that the analytic session was indeed hopelessly muddied by my non-analytic activity, and give up any attempt to discern the transference from it? I don't believe so. The dream focused entirely on one aspect of the session (my use of non-interpretation – logical argument), which it portrayed as an attempted homosexual rape, while ignoring the interpretation that followed it. While my attempt at logical persuasion was my contribution to the dream, the exaggeration of it into a violent and humiliating act, and the selection of it as the only thing I did in the session were the patient's contribution to the formation of the dream. They represented his unconscious transformation of the session experience into a transference. It is not correct, in other words, to say that the patient's dream was *simply* a response to the reality of the previous session. My debating my point acted as an actual event that became available to be 'adopted' and transformed by the patient's pre-existing phantasy that I envied his potency. Without this adoption it would have had little impact, and we can, from the details of the transformation, discern the outlines of the transference. This example illustrates how it is possible to separate out the analyst's contribution to the analytic experience from the patient's, to isolate, so to speak, the patient's transformation of the analyst's interpretation, imperfect though that might be, and from that transformation to begin to draw certain conclusions about the transference.

The approach to evaluating the transference that I am describing leaves out the question of *why* I engaged in non-analytic activity, i.e., it leaves out the question of my countertransference. This neglect does not, of course, mean that I believe that understanding the countertransference is not an important source of information about the transference. I have not taken up the countertransference aspects of the session because, indispensable as they are for the conduct of an analysis, what I am trying to explore is not why I did what I did, but why the patient *thought* I did what I did. This type of information does not replace or conflict with what the countertransference may tell us about the transference, it is merely independent of it. It may therefore be used to confirm or amplify the impressions that one gets from countertransference analysis, and as a check against the inherent unreliability of countertransference analysis.

Countertransference analysis is often helpful in deciphering the role in which the analyst has been cast in the patient's transference. A study of the transformations that the analyst undergoes while being internalized by the patient provides different information about the same thing. This is not surprising if both are simply different manifestations of an active confusion between external and internal reality brought about through projective identification.

Contrast the situation in the session I have described with an ideal one in which both patient and analyst are able to take an interpretation as an interpretation – as a mere observation, free of value judgment, which may be right or wrong, about the patient's state of mind, and which the patient is able to accept or reject. One measure of analytic development is the amount of movement that one has been able to make toward this type of relationship to the interpretation. This is as true of the analyst's analytic development as it is of the patient's. The extent to which the patient and analyst deviate from this ideal is a measure of the unresolved transference and countertransference respectively.

Even approximating this ideal relationship to the interpretation is a considerable achievement. I have described previously the state of mind that the analyst must struggle to have, and some of the forces within himself that he must struggle with, if he is to achieve this sort of relationship to his interpretations (Chapters 3 and 4). The patient's relationship to the interpretation involves a similar struggle.

6.4 Transference analysis

If we work in the transference by studying the patient's relationship to the interpretation, and in particular what I have been calling the patient's transformation of the interpretation, our further interpretations (and our psychoanalytic theories) will arise from direct experience of what happens inside the consulting room, in the present, examined as it happens, while it is still alive. Our reconstructions of our patient's past object relationships – and even our interpretations about their present relationships external to the analysis – derive their power and sense of conviction both for patient and analyst only from this type of close analysis of the transference.

Basing the analysis strictly on observations of what Donald Meltzer (1967) has called the 'phenomenology of the consulting room' places it on a firm empirical basis. Once the patient has gained real insight into his habitual unconscious contributions to his experience of the analysis, especially through analysis of the immediate analytic relationship, he can appreciate his role in the formation of his outside relationships, past and present (as distinct from the roles of others), and the roles of others in these relationships (as distinct from his). In this way the analysis becomes integrated into his real life.

I would now like to compare the approach to the transference that I am describing with certain other approaches. These approaches may be grouped into three categories. In the first, the analyst employs the patient's communications about the past to gain insight into the transference. An example of this is the view – reductionist in my opinion – that the transference is a consequence, a faithful copy, of a past external reality. It seems to me that this view commits the same error that Freud did when he regarded neurosis as caused by a repressed memory of actual past events, with no active contribution from the patient. It takes the patient and analyst away from what may be learned empirically from the present relationship about the patient's role in his life and his neurosis.

In my approach, communications from the patient about his relationships with past objects are accepted in a highly provisional way. The reason for this is that, while the patient is undoubtedly giving us an account of past events as he experienced them, his past experiences are as subject to the distortions arising from projective identification as the present transference itself. The past therefore cannot be used to gain insight into the origins of the transference, since past relationships and the present transference are merely two different manifestations of the same thing.

This point was made by Melanie Klein in her paper on 'The origins of transference' (1952b, p. 53): 'I hold that transference originates in the same processes which in the earliest stages [of life] determine object relations.' She added (p. 54) that, 'altogether, in the young infant's mind every external experience is interwoven with his phantasies and on the other hand every phantasy contains elements of actual experience, and it is only by analysing the transference situation to its depth that we are able to discover the past both in its realistic and phantastic aspects.'

A second commonly employed approach to the transference simply takes the patient's subjective experience of the analyst as a reliable indicator of how the analyst actually is, with perhaps minor contributions from the patient's unconscious phantasies, which needn't be attended to until much later in the analysis. This also ignores the patient's contribution to his own present experience, which is the essence of Freud's discoveries about psychic reality.

A third approach that many analysts have adopted is connected to the idea of 'intersubjectivity' (Stolorow, Brandchaft and Atwood 1987) or the 'analytic third' (Ogden 1994). Unlike the two just mentioned, this idea acknowledges the fact that there are two sources of the patient's subjective experience, the analyst's words and manner, on one hand, and what I have called the patient's transformations of them, on the other. But it locates the experience of the analysis as it exists in the patient's psychic reality somewhere *between* the patient and analyst, in such a form that the respective contributions of each cannot be resolved. This seems to be a way of denying that the transference can be analyzed: analysis, after all, means resolution into components.

6.5 Analysis of the archaic superego

These three ways of approaching the transference all have the effect of defending the patient from insight into his personal contribution to the present relationship with the analyst, and by implication into his contributions to other object relationships as well. They relieve the patient of a sense of responsibility for himself by attributing his experience of the analytic relationship to the effects of his parents' behavior in the past, or the analyst's behavior in the present, or by locating it in a space between patient and analyst, in which events occur that are not clearly anyone's responsibility.

The approach I describe in this chapter has the opposite effect: it places the patient in contact with his role (or rather the role of his unconscious wishes and phantasies) in forming his experience of the world, past and present, and hence in conditioning his relationships with his objects.

Many patients have an urgent need to deflect responsibility for themselves into the past, or into the analyst, or into the void of intersubjective space, as a defense against the sense of blameworthiness that besets them if they feel responsible. This sense of blame emanates from their archaic superegos. It is most intense in patients who are often considered to be fragile, or to have structural defects that render them unable to withstand ordinary analysis. I believe that what appears to be a fragile or defective structure is often the result of an extremely punitive archaic superego. It seems to me that if we are to assist our patients as much as possible, we must not collude with their need to deflect responsibility for themselves, but rather help them understand what makes the responsibility so unbearable.

My experience discussing these matters with colleagues of various theoretical orientations has led me to suspect that how we conceptualize the transference may depend on what our therapeutic objectives are. We may decide on a therapeutic goal, and then construct or adopt a theory of transference that fits in with that goal. If the goal is to protect the patient from assaults by his archaic superego, then we will adopt theories of transference that allow us to interpret it in such a way that the assaults get diverted toward the patient's objects, rather than toward himself. If, however, we believe that the archaic superego can be analyzed, then we will adopt a theory (as I have done) that allows us to interpret the transference in a way that brings the archaic superego overtly into the analytic relationship.

The difficulty with this approach is that the analyst then becomes the patient's archaic superego in the transference – i.e., a paranoid transference arises. But if it can be analyzed, then the patient will be greatly helped to resolve the most paranoid aspects of his relationships to his objects, and deepen and enrich those relationships as a result. If, however, we do not believe that such a transference can be analyzed, we will fear it and avoid it at all costs (see 3.3).

Protecting the patient from his archaic superego has its uses. It is a legitimate therapeutic approach that is justified by its relieving suffering in cases where a more thoroughgoing analysis is not available. But such an approach carries real risks. From a therapeutic point of view, if we fail to help the patient to be more responsible for the aspects of his personality that he is projecting into his objects, then his objects and his object relationships will pay the price. And from a scientific point of view, if we misrepresent such an approach (to ourselves or others) as a scientific investigation of the mind – i.e., as psychoanalysis – we will end up tailoring our theories of transference so that they justify this approach, and thereby jeopardize the scientific integrity of psychoanalysis. An enlightened use of this approach requires us to be aware of these risks.

The arousal of the archaic superego *in vivo*, though it poses the risk of difficult and painful analytic problems, also provides an unparalleled opportunity for insights into the patient's need to form transferences. For very often the patient's need to rid himself of unwanted aspects of his personality and to adopt those of the object's personality through projective identification is not simply because acknowledgment of who one is is painful, but because it is literally unbearable. What makes it unbearable is the tendency of the archaic superego to attack one for who one is. Analysis of this problem offers the possibility of a fundamental rearrangement of the patient's psychological forces, and permanent relief of neurotic symptomatology.

This means that concentrating on the immediate analytic relationship is not only an optimal approach from an empirical point of view – from the point of view of obtaining reliable information about the patient's unconscious – it also provides the best opportunity for the analysis of the force within the patient – his archaic superego – that compels the use of projective identification, which is what drives and maintains much of the transference. Analysis of the archaic superego in cases such as these therefore offers the best opportunity for a truly analytic resolution of the transference.

Psychopathology and primitive mental states*

7.1 Primitive mental states

The question I wish to address in this chapter is whether psychological illness in the adult can be regarded as a regression or a fixation to a 'primitive mental state'. I take the term 'primitive mental state' to refer to an early stage of normal psychological development.

While the detailed nature of early stages of normal psychological development is still largely unknown, what we already know about psychological development makes certain conclusions about these early stages almost inescapable. In his 'Formulations on the two principles of mental functioning' (1911), Freud hypothesized a primitive form of mental life consisting of a state of hallucinatory gratification, an egg-like form of existence in which omnipotent phantasy (i.e., wish-fulfilling hallucinations) substitutes for contact with reality, and reality itself is disregarded. This form of mental life is governed by the pleasure principle. But as Freud himself pointed out, and as is obvious in any event, hallucinating that one's hunger has been satisfied does not really satisfy hunger, and reality (in the form of biological need) eventually supervenes, requiring the infant to make contact with a real source of food and to behave realistically in relation to it. An organism whose mental life was organized *entirely* along the lines of hallucinatory wish fulfillment could not really exist for long, if for no other reason than that such complete ignorance of reality would inevitably lead to a fatal collision with it. We must therefore conclude *on principle* that there is some reality sense in even the most primitive of mental states, and that a stage of development entirely devoid of reality sense cannot exist at any point in life. (In Freudian terms, this means that the second of Freud's two

---

* This is a slightly revised version of a paper that appeared in the *International Journal of Psycho-Analysis* 80, 539–51 (1998).

principles of mental functioning, the reality principle, must exist alongside the pleasure principle even from the very beginning of post-natal life.)

The pioneering papers of Klein (1952a) and Bick (1964), supported by the more recent work of Bower (1977), Stern (1985), Trevarthen and Logotheti (1989) and Trevarthen (1993) have given empirical support to this conclusion by offering observations that suggest that even small infants have impressive capacities for contact with real objects, and for communicating with them in real ways. Emde's notion of affective attunement between infant and mother as an important condition for normal development (1988a, 1988b) implies not only that the mother is capable of assessing the infant's state of mind, but also that the infant is capable of assessing the mother's (otherwise the mother's attunement to the infant would have no effect on the infant).

All of this means that an orientation toward reality, i.e., some awareness of what is internal reality and what isn't, must be part of any normal primitive mental state. This is simply a way of saying that there must exist from birth onwards some contact with an object that is not confused with the self, and with a self not confused with an object. This type of unconfused contact with self and object allows one to experience both, and therefore to learn from one's experiences. In Chapter 8, I argue that, given this bare beginning of a capacity to know self from object, if nothing interferes, infants and young children quickly develop a *substantial* capacity for learning from experience. Children, even young children, are innately skilled experimentalists. This may not always be apparent, but that is only because children and infants are learning things that we adults know so well that we forget that we ever needed to learn them, but which, if we did not know them, we would be hard pressed to learn. (This point will be familiar to anyone who has ever tried to get a computer to work, where the problem is that computers don't know anything at all – they have no common sense – and consequently have to be told everything explicitly. Going through such an exercise makes us aware of how complex even the simplest tasks are, that is, how much we take for granted in what we do, how much we know that we don't know we know, and don't know even has to be known until we have to instruct a mindless machine how to do it.) Children must learn to feel their way through the enormous complexity of even the simple tasks of living step by step. What is crucial here is not how much or how little the infant or child might know, but its *capacity* to learn from experience. The capacity to learn from experience is not measured by where one is on a learning curve, but by the velocity with which one is able to move along it regardless of the starting point. If we consider how much a normal infant learns in, say, the first two years of life, then its contact with reality compares favorably with that of any other stage of life. (The capacity to learn from experience, may, incidentally, be taken to be as true a measure of contact with reality in adults as it is in children.)

We consider a normal infant normal precisely because, however rapid its transitions from bliss to uncontrollable anxiety or fear and back again, and whatever evidence it demonstrates of magical thinking (i.e., what in the adult would be regarded as delusions), we believe that time will modify them. A child in whom these states of mind are not modified with time will slowly but surely come to be regarded as abnormal, as will an adult. Normal children may be subject to transitory delusions and hallucinations, but they are able to work their way out of them without the aid of special psychological treatment. This is not true of ill children or ill adults, and this is one of the major differences between normality and illness.

This means that an ill adult is not simply an older version of a normal child, although he or she may be an older version of an ill child. Freud held in his 'Analysis of a phobia in a five-year-old boy' (1909) and 'From the history of an infantile neurosis' (1918), that adult psychopathology is merely an extension of an infantile neurosis that had, perhaps, in the meantime become temporarily submerged by an appearance of normality. He was not suggesting that adults who are ill have regressed to a *normal* primitive mental state, but that they are older versions of children whose mental states were *abnormal*. Illness in the adult is not a regression or a fixation to a normal primitive mental state, *but a non-progression from an abnormal one.*

7.2 Abnormal mental states and the failure to learn from experience

The persistence of a primitive mental state into adulthood is due to a failure of what Wilfred Bion (1962) called learning from experience – a failure of the capacity to allow experience to modify the infantile delusions (unconscious magical thinking) that are part of early normal mental development. These delusions may be viewed as the product of pre-genital (oral, anal and phallic) psychological forces, which manifest themselves in the mind as omnipotent unconscious phantasies of splitting, projection and introjection (Klein 1932; Isaacs 1952). Such phantasies consist, among other things, of splitting of the self and object into idealized good and bad parts, projection of parts of the self into objects, and introjection of parts of the object into the self. Acting in concert, they produce a subjective experience in which the object and the self are first split into idealized good and bad parts, following which the good parts are recombined into an idealized good self/object, and the bad parts into an ideal-ized bad self/object. The good self/object is identified with, and the bad self/object is dis-identified with, i.e. ejected. Klein called the state of mind in which these phantasies are dominant the paranoid-schizoid position, and the object relationships that result from these phantasies, part-object relationships.

In the paranoid-schizoid position, what to an outside observer would be self and object are both split into parts which are then recombined with one an-other with complete disregard for which parts belong to whom. 'Good' parts of self and object are regarded as belonging to the self, while 'bad' parts of self and object are regarded as belonging to the object. It is true that we speak of the 'good object' in the paranoid–schizoid position, but careful examination shows that such an object is strongly felt to be a possession of the self, really as much a part of the self as the hand or foot. The psychological operations that bring about this state of mind (omnipotent projection and introjection) may collectively be called narcissistic identification.

States of narcissistic identification do not include the capacity to perceive the self as it is (i.e., as a whole self), or the object as it is (i.e., as a whole object), or the capacity to 'place oneself in someone else's shoes'. This means that the ability to have contact with the mind of another, or even to be aware that someone else has what we would call a mind of their own, is severely restricted in these states. The omnipotent phantasies that produce narcissistic identification are indistinguishable from a delusion that one has, or is, the needed object, and that one doesn't have unsatisfied needs or mental pain. Their role in the mind is therefore precisely that of the wish-fulfilling hallucinations that Freud posited in his 'Formulations on the two principles of mental functioning'.

Roger Money-Kyrle (1968) has provided a valuable insight into the *clinical* usefulness of Freud's 'Two principles' with his suggestion that psychopathology is due to the presence of unconscious delusions – ideas that are fixed and not subject to modification by ordinary experience, but on which reality might nonetheless be brought to bear through the extraordinary experience of psychoanalysis. One of the main therapeutic effects of psychoanalysis, in my view, is precisely this bringing of reality to bear on the unconscious delusions that underlie narcissistic identifications, thereby helping the patient to be able to distinguish self and object, phantasy from external reality. This allows him to have clear contact with internal reality (the self) and external reality (the object), that is, experiences in which the two are not confused, and from which he may learn about both. Prior to this de-confusion, he could have contact neither with his phantasies nor with his perceptions of external reality *per se*, but only with the confused mixture of the two that constitutes delusions.

7.3 Unconscious delusions and unconscious phantasies

At this point, it may be useful to emphasize that omnipotent unconscious phantasies – unconscious delusions – and ordinary unconscious phantasies not only differ from each other, but play roles in the mind that are diametrically opposed. While unconscious delusions undermine one's capacity to learn from experience, unconscious phantasy is an essential component of learning from experience, since one of the major ways in which we learn about reality is by posing hypotheses about it in the form of phantasies, then testing them against perception (Chapter 8). Omnipotent unconscious phantasies (unconscious delusions) differ from ordinary phantasies precisely on this point: they cannot be tested against or disproven by perception. Psychopathology is associated with the predominance in the mind of unconscious delusions that cannot be used as hypotheses that may be brought into relation with perception. Unlike phantasies or thoughts, which can be experienced as hypothetical, delusions are felt to be concretely real, more like dogma than ideas.

Money-Kyrle held that once reality is brought to bear on unconscious delusions through analysis, they become ordinary unconscious phantasies. If this occurs, they cease to act as obstructions to learning from experience and may instead be used to foster it. This is the result one hopes for from analysis.

But it is not the only possible outcome of the encounter between analysis and unconscious delusion. When delusions encounter experiences that might undermine them, instead of the delusion being modified by the experience, the experience may instead be folded into the delusional system through such maneuvers as selective attention to the experience, the manipulation of reality so that it corresponds to the delusion (via what Bion called realistic projective identification), or through the patient's unvoiced reinterpretation of the analyst's interpretations, so that his subjective experience of the interpretations seems to support the delusion. This last maneuver falls into the category of what Bion called transformations in hallucinosis (1965, p. 144), and reversal of perspective (1963, pp. 50–63).

7.4 Clinical illustration

I can illustrate some of these mechanisms by expanding on the clinical example that I gave in Chapter 4.

The analyst in this case was an experienced psychotherapist who was treating his first analytic case under supervision. The patient was a businessman in his forties who came to analysis because of chronic depression related to feelings of unbearable inferiority. After a period of analysis, it became apparent that his emotional life was dominated by envy and the defenses against it: he viewed the world as a dog-eat-dog arena, in which he had to maintain a constant vigil against being exploited and triumphed over. He envied other men's sexual prowess, but became terrified if he felt that a woman was interested in him sexually, since he viewed a sexual relationship as a form of predation in which the woman could satisfy herself only by draining him and leaving him behind as an empty shell. These anxieties were related to his unconscious conviction that all relationships would eventually succumb to mutual destructive envy between the people involved.

At the same time, he suffered from terrible guilt in his dealings with others: he constantly worried that he was exploiting his employees (especially the female ones), which caused him to bend over backwards to be fair in his dealings with them, in a futile attempt to avoid the guilt. In his sessions, he tried desperately to be a 'good' patient, but always felt that he was failing. In reality, his associations often did have an artificial, forced quality, as though he was trying hard to comply with an analytic 'requirement' that he associate freely when he was not capable of any real spontaneity. This lack of spontaneity turned out to be connected to his feeling under terrible pressure because he felt that the analyst was enviously judging his associations, and always finding them wanting.

When having intercourse with his wife, he would sometimes feel confused about whether it was his penis going into her, or her penis going into him – he had eliminated the sexual differences that might give rise to envy on the part of either of them. The idea that it was her penis entering him did not seem unpleasurable to him, a fact that alarmed him greatly – was he a homosexual? He had phantasies of sucking the analyst's penis, which seemed to represent both a masochistic placation of the threatening, envious analyst and a way of magically possessing the analyst's potency, in order to diminish his own envy of it.

He was addicted to anal masturbation, often using a carrot. Despite a paucity of conscious associations to these masturbatory activities, it gradually became clear that he felt very guilty and persecuted about it, and a review of the material seemed to indicate that it represented his way of taking in food in general – whether mother's breast as an infant or the analyst's interpretations as an adult. He covered them with shit while at the same time exciting himself through his misuse of them – a triumphant, envious devaluation of the object that he needed.

The session I wish to describe in some detail occurred on a Monday. The patient entered and told his analyst that he had just attended a pop psychology event known as a 'Bradshaw Weekend', from which he had gained many valuable insights about his behavior that he had not gotten 'in four and a half years' with the analyst. He proceeded to list a number of what seemed to be valid insights, all of which, however, the analyst had communicated to him many times in the past. The patient did not acknowledge this, but spoke as though it had all come from his 'Bradshaw Weekend'.

Although feeling quite irritated and threatened, the analyst succeeded with considerable effort in restraining himself and appearing reasonable and accepting of the patient's having benefited from the weekend. The patient went on to speak of his desire to leave analysis soon, hoping, he said, that this would not hurt the analyst who had been 'like a mother and father to me' over the years. He then spoke of his mother's reaction when he announced his desire to leave home: 'there's a cliff, if you want to go jump off of it, go ahead.' The patient went on to say that he felt like he had just gotten his MD degree (the analyst was not a physician) and hoped the analyst would be like a proud father, congratulate him and wish him well.

The patient had left the analyst with the feeling that his work was rather pathetic and slow compared to that of the Bradshaw organization, the success and effectiveness of which he found himself envying. He had briefly considered using this countertransference as the basis of an interpretation about the patient's sense of inadequacy *vis-à-vis* himself, his envy of the analyst's abilities, and his defending himself from them by projecting both into the analyst. But he rejected this idea (despite its consistency with what he knew about the patient's difficulties with envy, his tendency to project it, and the fact that the 'Bradshaw' insights had all appeared in the analysis before) because he felt that it would have made the patient see him as a spoil-sport, enviously denying the patient's good weekend experience. This is an example of reversal of perspective. The patient would interpret the analyst's interpretation as a confirmation that it was the analyst who was filled with envy, not himself. The situation in this case was complicated by the analyst having made a similar reversal about his own work, which left him feeling that the patient's accusation would somehow be correct. At the same time, he had the vague feeling that, by remaining silent on the matter, he was somehow prostituting himself by implicitly assenting to what the patient had said.

In this session, the patient had been enacting his masturbatory phantasies. His account of the 'Bradshaw Weekend' excited him with the feeling that he was now the possessor of all the new insights, as in his masturbation he felt that he now possessed mother's breast and the analyst's penis. At the same time, he covered the actual analyst with shit, rendering him a slow, plodding and envious little boy. This enactment was the vehicle of a realistic projective identification, by means of which the patient projected his feelings of smallness into the analyst, while at the same time identifying himself with the analyst's potency and capacity for insight.

Reversal of perspective, realistic projective identification and transformation in hallucinosis are psychotic rather than neurotic defenses. (Realistic projective identification may also be used in the service of communication, rather than for the consolidation of a delusion. In this case, it is being used by the non-psychotic part of the personality for non-defensive purposes.) When used as a psychotic mechanism, they pose difficult technical problems for the analyst, who may be unaware of them for a long time, and who may, as in the clinical example, find it difficult to describe them to the patient even when he does finally become aware of them. The problem for the analyst is not just an intellectual one, but an emotional one as well. These operations are defenses against the considerable pain, anxiety and feelings of smallness that the patient experiences when his unconscious delusions are brought into proper register with reality through an accurate interpretation. The analyst may himself resist making interpretations that cause such evident pain out of an understandable but short-sighted reluctance to be the bearer of painful news for his patient. This resistance may eventually become institutionalized in the form of fallacious theories that create the appearance of analytic insight while allowing the analyst to evade drawing the patient's attention to the painful awareness that he is deluded and has been incapable, in the area covered by the delusions, of learning from his previous experiences. The idea that psychopathology is due to a regression or a fixation to a normal primitive mental state, rather than a failure to emerge from an abnormal one is a denial of the fact that something *within the patient* has been actively interfering with his contact with himself and his objects, and has therefore damaged his psychological development.

7.5 A theoretical fallacy

The evidence that I have presented above about the relationship – or lack of it – between adult psychopathology and normal primitive mental states suggests that the idea that ill adults are ill because they have regressed to or are fixated at early or primitive states of mind, that they are simply 'stuck' in the psychological situation of a normal infant or child, is based on a confusion between normal primitiveness and childhood pathology. Psychoanalysts have been aware of this confusion for some time. Kohut, for example, wrote that 'reactions of clinging dependence of adults, if they are regressions to childhood situations, refer not to the normal oral phase of development but to childhood psychopathology' (Kohut 1959, p. 475). But, despite the widespread recognition of this fallacy, it persists nonetheless as a respectable (or at least semi-respectable) part of the theoretical structure of psychoanalysis. The persistence of an idea known to be false, or at least the falseness of which is knowable if one examines it closely enough, suggests that it serves a defensive purpose.

The defensive use of theory is obviously not without precedent. We recall that in the first of his *Three Essays on the Theory of Sexuality*, Freud proposed that what we call perversions were actually normal infantile sexual activities that had, for some reason, persisted into adulthood as a fixation or regression. Normally, infantile (by which he meant pre-genital) sexual activity is integrated, or rather subordinated, by genitality into adult sexuality where its vestiges persist as foreplay. Freud said that what we call perversion in the adult is merely an outcropping of normal infantile sexuality – 'primitive' sexuality, if you will – in an unusually intense or dominant form in adult life.

One effect of this view of perversion, and perhaps (for all we know) one of Freud's intentions as well, was defensive – it destigmatized perversions that would otherwise be subjected to social stigma. After all, he argued, if the people responsible for some of our most revered cultural achievements were, for example, homosexual, how degenerate or pathological could homosexuality be? I think that by arguing for this view of perversion, Freud did a lot of well-meaning damage to psychoanalysis, damage that has persisted for many decades. I don't mean to bash Freud for this. This view of perversion followed from the theories of infantile sexuality, repression, and the unconscious sexual roots of neurosis that, prior to the discovery of destructive impulses, were all he had on hand to explain psychopathology.

But as Meltzer (1972), Stoller (1994 [1986]) and others have pointed out, while there are indeed forms of sexuality in the adult that represent persistent, normal 'primitive' infantile sexuality, they should not be called perversions, but rather polymorphisms. Both Meltzer and Stoller go on to say that, in addition to these polymorphisms, there are what we might call *real* perversions. Real perversions are sexual in a way, but, unlike polymorphisms, their essence is not sexual, but destructive. That is, they are activities that hijack sexuality to accomplish ends that are fundamentally destructive. What gets destroyed are relationships with real objects, among them real sexual relationships.

Thanks to this work, we are no longer constrained to define perversion behaviorally or superficially (as Freud did in his *Three Essays*) as sex between members of the same sex, or between adults and children, or humans and animals, or humans and inanimate objects, or as sexuality not leading to genital intercourse. We can define it in a psychoanalytic way, purely in terms of the unconscious forces and phantasies behind it: is the activity sexual or destructive in the unconscious? This work has enabled us to see that sexual perversion is not a matter of behavior, but of a certain kind of unconscious object relationship. Sexual activity between members of the same sex may or may not be perverse (that is, it may be perverse or polymorphous), and the same is true of sexual activity between members of different sexes.

Meltzer showed that Freud's theory of perversion in the *Three Essays* was really a theory of polymorphism that left out the essential feature of true perversion, namely an unconscious destruction of object relationships. The result of this was that Freud could not clearly distinguish perversions (destructive object relationships) from innocuous polymorphisms (primitive object relationships).

I suggest that the idea that psychopathology is a regression or fixation to a normal primitive or early mental state is a product of the same type of well-meaning fallacy that Freud committed with regard to perversions. By holding that ill adults have regressed to the state of mind of a normal infant or small child, we have confused destructive states of mind with normal ones (that is, ones containing a capacity for development), in the same way that Freud had confused perversion with normal polymorphism.

(Interestingly, Freud, as we know, believed from quite early on – probably from the mid-1890s – that 'neurosis was the negative of perversion', meaning that neurotic symptoms simultaneously represented overt defenses against, and covert expressions of, unconscious perversions (which in his view were normal infantile sexual impulses). But when he modified his theory of neurosis to take destructive impulses into account, he failed to see the implications that this would have for his theory of perversion. Meltzer's revision of the theory of perversion, which holds that what makes an impulse perverse is not its infantile sexual nature, but its fundamentally destructive (i.e., anti-sexual) nature, restores the original formulation of the relationship between neurosis and perversion.)

Glover (1931) has given us a brilliant and quite general account of how entities that *seem* quite similar, but are really quite different, may be used as the basis of what he called an 'inexact interpretation', an interpretation that serves the resistance to analysis while appearing to be a part of analysis. Freud's confusion of perversion and polymorphism is an example of Glover's 'inexact interpretation'. He confused the two by failing to take into account that perversions act through the destruction of links with real objects.

The notion that contemporary psychopathology is a regression or fixation to normal 'primitive mental states' is another example of an inexact interpretation. It fastens on the fact that psychopathological states often contain the splitting, idealization, concreteness and phantastic anxieties and grandiosity that are also found in normal infantile mental states to support the idea that pathology is merely a continuation of an infantile state. This explanation exploits these similarities while covering over the fact that pathological states differ from primitive ones in lacking the potential for spontaneous development that turns normal primitive mental states into ordinary adult ones, given only time. The reassuring inexactitude of this view of psychopathology is an expression of our fear of making clear to our patients and ourselves that we are dealing with contemporary destructive forces, not primitive developmental ones. What these forces destroy is the very capacity on which mental health and development depends – the capacity to have proper object relationships, that is, object relationships that permit one to make contact with the self and the object as they are, which in turn allows one to learn about self and object from one's experiences. The destruction of object-links does not, incidentally, necessarily constitute evidence of a destructive instinct (although it clearly does not rule it out either). We may, if we wish, attribute it simply to a bias in favor of omnipotence of thought (Freud's pleasure principle).

7.6 Psychoanalytic reconstruction

Given that we cannot equate present pathological mental states with normal primitive mental states, is it still possible to reconstruct past mental states, and, if so, is this useful analytically? Before considering this, I would like to clarify what I mean by a reconstruction with a hypothetical clinical example: a patient in analysis becomes slowly but very surely convinced that the only real problem in his life is the analyst. It becomes more and more clear, if one listens to the patient, that there is no problem that could not be traced to some sin on the analyst's part. The patient's conviction is so contagious that the analyst begins to believe it himself, and accordingly begins to fear that the patient was dying analytically, and that the analysis was killing him. He of course battles against this idea, but, due to the mixture of guilt, frustration and exasperation that he is feeling by now, he begins to think to himself irritably, 'I don't know *what's* the matter with this patient.' Upon cooler reflection, he feels that the patient was inducing in him this sense of being the patient's only problem by means of massive projective identification. (I have lifted this example bodily from Bion [1967a, p. 104].)

From these observations he may construct the following scenario about the patient's mental state as an infant: the patient's mother had cared for him in infancy in a dutiful way, but had no real rapport with her child. She was unable to decipher the cause or meaning of the child's cries, which was that the child feared that it was dying, and which should have stimulated in *her* the fear that the child was dying. Instead of experiencing this fear, she pushed it away, and adopted the attitude of 'I don't know *what's* the matter with that child.' As a result, the child, denied the use of normal projective identification because he had an unresponsive 'container' (or, alternatively, because of an empathic failure in the mother), grew into an adult who used projective identification in a massive way, as if to compensate for what he had been deprived of early in life, and this is what he is doing in the analysis.

The analyst could attribute the transference he was observing to early infancy because the patient felt that the analyst was his *only* problem. He could reason that if the patient was in a state of mind where all his problems had to do with a *single* object, the primitive state being recreated in the analysis would be that of a young infant with its mother. The idea that the mother was guilty and exasperated at being unable to understand her infant would be based on the analyst's own guilt and exasperation over the fact that all his efforts seemed only to produce a situation in which he is harming instead of helping his patient.

This is a coherent construction of a primitive mental state called 'having an unresponsive or unempathic container' or 'being denied the use of normal projective identification.' An analyst might construct such a scenario, and might make interpretations based on it. But he needn't do so. He could also construct another scenario based on the following assumption: the patient's feeling that the analysis was harming him and was the sum total of all that was wrong with his life was due to the patient's having launched an unconscious envious attack on the analyst's *good* work. The analyst's guilt and exasperation would then be due to his having been overcome by the patient's envious projections, so that he was 'buying' them rather than interpreting them (even to himself). This would lead to a scenario in which the problem would not be that the patient's mother was an inadequate container, but that the patient, as an infant, had more than adequate envy of the mother's adequate ability to contain. This is a second, equally plausible construction of the patient's mental state as an infant, based on the same clinical observations.

This presents us with a dilemma. What should we tell the patient about his infantile relationship to his mother? Which reconstruction should we interpret? The answer I would suggest is neither. From the clinical data available, we cannot decide between the two scenarios about the patient as an infant with his mother. From a scientific point of view, we have to admit that they are both possible, and maintain an open mind on the subject. But more importantly, neither reconstruction would serve any *analytic* purpose. On the contrary, making an interpretation of the form, 'you feel this way about me now because when you were an infant, etc.,' saturates the observable phenomena of the consulting room by explaining them (away) in terms of a past hypothetical reality. This is not just useless analytically, it is worse than useless.

The reason it is worse than useless is that it forecloses the possibility of further understanding the present transference relationship by obstructing it with a putative 'explanation' based on speculations about past experience. In analysis, we do not arrive at our understanding of the transference by gathering knowledge about, or trying to reconstruct, the patient's past; on the contrary, we understand the past in terms of the transference. The analytic 'past' is a reconstruction based on the transference (Chapter 6). There is no special therapeutic virtue in being able to reduce the present transference (of which we have direct knowledge) to a hypothetical past (of which we have no direct knowledge). In fact, such a reduction, if it is taken to mean that the present transference has been *caused* by the past (hypothetical) reconstruction, has an anti-therapeutic effect. It explains away the present, live transference in terms of a dead, speculative past.

This does not, however, mean that reconstructions of the past have no place in analysis. The right time to make a link to a past 'primitive mental state' is when the question of how things got the way they are – the appeal to historical causes for present pathology – has ceased to be a burning question. When the present (meaning the transference) is sufficiently understood, that is, when the patient has been able to integrate through the work of analysis the aspects of his personality that he has been denying or splitting off and projecting into the analyst, then the past necessarily becomes clear, since he has by that time also stopped projecting into *it*. But the burning need to know what happened in the past, i.e., 'how I got this way in the first place', has also greatly diminished by then. The reason for this is that an *anxiety* to know these answers (as distinct from an interest in one's history) is a manifestation of the need to project into the past. A historical reconstruction should sort out who was who in the past, in the same way that an interpretation sorts out who is who in the present. This is its real value. But the former is possible only after the latter has occurred. The anxiety about 'what happened' in the past is often a displacement of the need to know what *is* happening – who is doing what – in the analytic relationship. When the latter is satisfied, the former tends to be as well. What is left when this need has diminished through analysis is a feeling that the past is of historical interest, but that it is not the kind of history on which one's vital interests depend. The patient has been freed of his bondage to the past. The passion to know 'what happened' tends to evaporate once one is able to acknowledge what *is* happening. (A similar point has been made by Gill [1990].)

7.7 Summary and conclusions

To summarize my argument to this point:

1   Normal primitive mental states contain omnipotent phantasies that in an adult would be classified as delusions and hallucinations, but they also contain sufficient reality sense to allow the infant's omnipotent unconscious phantasies (unconscious delusions) to develop spontaneously into ordinary unconscious phantasies through learning from experience.
2   Psychopathology of the type requiring psychoanalytic treatment is connected to unconscious omnipotent phantasies (delusions). It is not due to a regression to a normal primitive mental state, since in a normal primitive mental state, such delusions and their resultant inhibitions, symptoms and anxieties are gradually and spontaneously overcome through learning from experience.
3   The unconscious delusions related to psychopathology are so persistent because they are insulated from the effects of the learning from experience that would ordinarily convert them into unconscious phantasies by the psychotic defenses of transformations in hallucinosis, reversal of perspective and realistic projective identification. Together, these distort experience in such a way that reality appears to confirm, not challenge, the delusions, making learning impossible.
4   The theory that psychopathology is due to a regression or fixation to a normal primitive mental state acts as a defense against the awareness that the mental states associated with psychopathology are not normal primitive ones, and that they differ from normal primitive mental states by containing forces that are sufficiently destructive of learning from experience to have prevented the patient's mental state from evolving in a normal fashion.

If the analyst does not explain away the patient's current unconscious delusions as manifestations of a hypothetical normal primitive mental state, but instead uses interpretations that are sufficiently exact about the patient's use of reversal of perspective, transformations in hallucinosis and realistic projective identification, he puts the patient in the extremely painful position of having to face how much his delusions have and do cost him in terms of failed development. The pain of this recognition may cause the patient to redouble his use of psychotic mechanisms to undermine the analyst's sense of reality – his contact with the patient – as though the psychotic aspect of his personality recognizes that the analyst's dropping the use of inexact and euphemistic interpretations means that the analyst has become sane about its activities, and it now feels it must do something to restore the status quo ante.

This clinical situation puts the analyst's relationship to his own sense of reality to a stringent test, and it presents a serious and very real danger for the patient, because the analyst's reality sense is precisely what he needs to depend on if he is to use the analyst's help to free himself of his unconscious delusions. If the analyst succeeds in maintaining his own sanity in the face of the attempts by the psychotic aspect of the patient to undermine it, he can move the analysis forward.

But he will be greatly hampered in his efforts to help the patient through analysis if he is unable to clearly identify the ways in which the psychotic aspect of the patient's personality evades the pain of facing his delusions and thereby destroys the patient's capacity to use the analysis to learn from experience. It may help the analyst to face these forces in the patient squarely if he can keep in mind that there is also a sane aspect of the patient that is in alliance with the analyst and in conflict with the forces that are attempting to undermine his own, and the analyst's sanity. The psychotic aspect of the personality behaves as though governed by the principle that mental pain must be avoided at any cost – even at the cost of one's sanity (clear contact with self and object). While Freud's pleasure principle may not correspond exactly to the mental state of any actual infant, it is a very close description of the mode of operation of the psychotic part of the personality.

This conflict between the patient's sane and psychotic aspects is a source of great anguish and suffering that deserves our utmost respect and calls for great tact in interpretation. But tact is not avoidance, and if we try to avoid the pain and conflict that effective interpretation evokes by offering plausible-sounding but unsound, 'inexact' interpretations about primitive mental states, we do not spare the patient his suffering, we merely leave him alone with it.

8

Play, creativity and experimentation*

8.1 Introduction

The topic that I wish to explore in this chapter is the connection between the ability to play, create and experiment, on one hand, and the nature of one's object relationships, on the other. There is an extensive psychoanalytic literature on the subject of creativity, beginning with Freud's 'Creative writers and day-dreaming' (1908), and I will not attempt a comprehensive review of this literature here. I will approach my topic by considering a single symptom: the inability to play. This symptom was first described in a psychotic patient sixty-five years ago by Melanie Klein in her paper, 'The importance of symbol formation in the development of the ego' (1930), which was also, I believe, the first case report of the psychoanalytic treatment of a psychotic patient. The patient in this case was a four-year-old boy named Dick, who had the vocabulary and intellectual attainments of a child of about fifteen to eighteen months. From the very beginning of his life he had only rarely displayed anxiety, and was largely devoid of affects. He had almost no interests, no contact with his environment, and he was unable to play. From the clinical description Mrs Klein gave, it seems very likely that Dick would have been diagnosed today as suffering from Kanner's autism (Kanner 1944).

The impression his first visit left on Mrs Klein was that his behavior was quite different from that which she had observed in neurotic children. She described how he moved to and fro in an aimless way, and ran around her just as if she were a piece of furniture. He showed no interest in any of the objects in the room, and the expression of his eyes and face was fixed, far-away and lacking in interest.

* Originally published in the *International Journal of Psycho-Analysis* 77 (5) 859–69 (1996).

Her analysis of Dick indicated that his inability to play was connected to his inability to think in a symbolic way, which in turn seemed to be connected to the type of relationship that he formed with his objects. This is the area that I would like to explore in detail. To anticipate the conclusions I will draw: because Dick formed a certain type of relationship with his objects, he could not think symbolically; because he could not think symbolically, he could not play, and because he could not play, he was unable to learn from his experiences about himself and his world.

An inability to play is a major handicap in people of all ages, since it prevents them from making contact with reality. This statement may seem surprising at first, since play is usually associated with phantasy rather than reality. But phantasy is, of course, an important part of internal reality, and we have known for a long time that playing is a way of establishing contact with and expressing one's internal reality. This is the basis on which we are able to use observations of play as part of child therapy and child analysis. The thesis that I would like to propose is that play is an essential means of establishing contact with *external* reality as well. More precisely, playing is an important means of exploring the relationship between internal reality and external reality.

8.2 Playing and experimentation

Let me explain what I mean by this. The most striking overt feature of people in psychotic states is their disordered relationship to external reality. One important feature of the psychotic's *internal* or psychic reality must therefore be that there is something about it that interferes with his ability to make contact with external reality.

There is also obviously something in the psychic reality of the psychotic that interferes with his ability to make contact with *it* – which is just a way of saying that people in psychotic states are notoriously lacking in insight. I believe these two disabilities are really only two different manifestations of a single underlying process.

My thesis is that *one establishes contact with external reality in part by linking it in a particular way to internal reality, that one establishes contact with internal reality in part by linking it in the same way to external reality, and that this link is basically playful.*

When a child plays, he learns about the external world by deploying his phantasies in an experimental way. In his biography of the theoretical physicist Richard Feynman, James Gleick (1992, p. 19) captured this aspect of playing when he wrote that

> children are innate scientists, probing, puttering, experimenting with the possible and impossible in a confused local universe. Children and scientists share an outlook on life. *If I do this, what will happen?* is both the motto of the

child at play and the ... refrain of the ... scientist. Every child is observer, analyst, and taxonomist ... constructing theories and promptly shedding them when they no longer fit. The unfamiliar and the strange – these are the domain of all children and scientists.

The roots of experimental investigation of the world – both the everyday and more formal scientific varieties – lie in the play of infants and children. (Scientists often refer to their work as 'playing' with ideas or with new tools.)

Melanie Klein (1921) considered the impulse to find out how the world works so fundamental that she gave it the status of an instinct – the 'instinct to know'. In the Kleinian view, instincts always give rise to unconscious phantasies of doing something that would satisfy the instinctual urge. I think that what Klein had in mind at first with her 'instinct to know' was that the infant had a phantasy of getting inside the mother's body to see what was there, but she came later to realize that the infant's phantasy is, to use the current catch-phrase, more interactive than that. Infants do not just observe their objects in a passive Baconian way, sitting back and cataloging their observations until a pattern emerges, they actively probe them to see what will happen – what they will do. (This assertion will, I believe, be supported by anyone who has had prolonged or intimate contact with an infant.) This makes infants unconscious experimentalists. The test probe they use in their explorations of their objects is what Bion (1967a) called 'realistic' projective identification and Spillius (1988, p. 83) called 'evocatory projective identification' – the ability to evoke certain states of mind in the object through verbal and non-verbal behavior.

8.3 Experimental play in psychoanalysis

In this view, normal child's play is a latter-day version of what was originally an exploration of the inside of the primal object – either the mother's body, or her mind, or perhaps both, or perhaps even both experienced as the same thing. Like all psychoanalytic theories of mental life in infancy, this one is a reconstruction based on the analyst's experience in the analytic session. What is this experience? In analysis, the patient plays with the analyst's mind, evoking countertransference responses in it by using 'realistic projective identification'. In this way he can learn a great deal about the analyst: 'If I do this to him, what will happen?' One establishes contact with that part of external reality that we call other minds through the active deployment of projections. What is projected is a state of mind, and what it is projected into is the mind of the object. We evoke these states of mind in our object's minds for many reasons, which may include loving impulses, or sadistic ones, or the fact that the state of mind that we are inducing in the object is unbearable for us, and that we therefore need to evacuate it, and we feel that somehow if we can induce it in our objects we have magically removed it from our own minds. But among the many reasons we project into our objects' minds, one is to *find out* about their minds. It seems to me that this kind of probing is the only way of learning anything about the interior of our objects – what they are like inside – which is what really concerns us about our objects anyway. Someone's mind is a mystery to us until we see how it reacts to something.

This is one aspect of playing. A second aspect is connected to the fact that when children play, they are not just testing the world to see what it is like, they are also externalizing their internal phantasy world. I say 'externalizing' rather than 'representing' because play is more than a representation of unconscious phantasy. It is a way of getting something from inside to outside so we can see what it is, in the spirit of E.M. Forster's question, 'How do I know what I think until I've had a chance to hear what I have to say?'

In the same way, the patient in analysis projects aspects of his internal world into the analyst so that he may explore the nature of whatever aspect of his internal reality he is projecting into the analyst. The question he poses is 'If I do this to him, what will happen?'; but more precisely it is, 'If I make him feel what I feel, what will he do?' Will he explode (i.e., is what I am projecting explosive)? Will he find it pleasurable, annoying, incomprehensible (i.e., is what I am projecting pleasurable, annoying or incomprehensible)? The analyst's response to the patient's projective probe tells the patient about the probe – his own projection, a piece of *his* internal world.

This kind of projective testing allows us to test and thereby learn about our internal and external realities at the same time: we learn about the minds of our objects by projecting into them our inner states (to see how they react), and we learn about our own inner states by using the minds of our objects as instruments for measuring them (by seeing how they reacted). This is obviously not a perfect set-up for controlled experimentation, since we are dealing with two unknowns at the same time, but with enough repetition with enough different objects, we do manage to learn quite a lot about ourselves and our objects in this way. It is obviously important here to have a number of *different* objects, so that we are not forced to rely on the idiosyncrasies of only one object to inform us about ourselves. This may be one motive for the child to expand his object world beyond that of his primal objects.

For any of this to work properly, however, internal and external reality must be kept separate in one's mind. If the two become too confused, one cannot use either to test or play off against the other, and this means that one is hard pressed to establish contact with (learn about) either. This is where the psychotic patient comes to grief. Because of the type of relationship that the psychotic patient forms with his objects, internal and external reality become so confused that neither can be used to learn about the other, and contact is therefore lost with both. Symbolic thinking breaks down and the psychotic patient is unable to play with the world in an experimental way. (The use of the term 'psychotic' here is meant to apply equally to the psychotic part of the non-psychotic patient's personality.) This is because he experiences his projections not as experiments with limited consequences, but as wholesale, catastrophic alterations of his objects. And because of the confusion between self and object in these states, these catastrophic alterations of the object are felt to be indistinguishable from wholesale catastrophic alterations of the self.

I believe that one of the major reasons that trauma is traumatic is that in traumatic situations there is a collapse of the distinction between internal and external reality. Traumas correspond too closely to the unconscious phantasies that one has projected into the traumatizing object. It is as though the projection of our phantasies into external reality has taken over the object, so that the difference between the projection and the object disappears. This produces severe confusions in one's mind between internal and external reality. The projection now seems no longer playful or experimental, but deadly serious. The result is that belief in omnipotence is reinforced and one's grip on reality further weakened. It is not simply the nature of the trauma or the content of the phantasy that is pathogenic, but the closeness of the correspondence between the two. A very close fit reinforces confusion between external and internal reality. This diminishes one's ability to learn from subsequent experience or experiments in the affected area – one is terrified of getting a repetition of what had turned into a runaway experiment – and this is what is truly pathogenic.

I have been writing as though we were dealing with a causal sequence of events, like a row of dominoes: a confusion between self and object leads to a breakdown of symbolic thought, and because of that, one is unable to play, and because of that, one cannot use experimentation to learn about oneself and the world. I have put it this way because it is easier to write about it this way, but in fact, there is not a causal chain: all of these are simply different aspects of the same thing, which may be described as a loss of autonomy of the self from the world, and of the external world from the self.

8.4 Experimental disasters in psychotic states

A person in a psychotic state projects into his objects in such a way that severe confusions between inner and outer reality are constantly arising, and this tends to make all of his experiences traumatic. For such a person, a projection into the object is not a test probe, it is something that he feels turns the object into the projection, that engulfs the object and infiltrates its every pore. There is no possibility for the object to react to the projection, since the projection is felt to so dominate the object that it literally becomes indistinguishable from the projection.

This eliminates the possibility of learning about the object through projective probing. Furthermore, insofar as the object is able to react (that is, insofar as the patient does not feel his projections have been so omnipotent that they have taken the object over completely), the patient feels that the reaction is one that engulfs, infiltrates and destroys *his* mind. This feeling is the basis of the psychotic patient's fear of being taken over or of having his mind controlled by the analyst. Needless to say, a patient who is convinced that the analyst is trying to infiltrate or destroy his mind cannot use the analyst to help him learn about his internal reality.

These catastrophic effects of the attempts of someone in a psychotic state to use projection were illustrated in the analysis of a seven-year-old girl who entered a psychotic state when she saw her divorced father with a woman friend, and became quickly convinced that she knew just what they were up to. By this I mean that she didn't just have what she could recognize as phantasies about what they might be doing together, she had an absolute conviction that left no room for doubt – in other words, a delusion. As time went on, she began to phantasize a sexual relationship between them in precise physical detail. I noticed that there was something about the way she was talking that would have made sense only if she had been present in the room observing the couple actually having sex. Her phantasies had been projected into the couple with such force – she had confused the inner reality of her phantasies so throughly with the external reality of her objects – that the result resembled a hallucination. In fact, I believe that when she was really caught up in this, she *was* hallucinating instead of thinking.

Here her suspicion or belief about her father's sexual activities had engulfed the external reality (which, as far as I could gather, offered only modest confirmatory evidence) so completely that the two had collapsed into one another. There was no longer a state of mind that could be played off against reality, or a reality that could be played into by the use of projection as a probe, but a hallucination in which the two had collapsed into each other. (Ronald Britton [1994] has explored this type of confusion, where what he calls 'belief' in one's unconscious phantasies can eliminate the power of conflicting perceptions.)

During this time, the sight of her father also began to drive her mad. The external reality (his presence) felt to her as though it were engulfing her mind, and stopping her from having an internal world, a mind of her own. She felt that he had become a sort of hallucination in reverse, i.e., that she had become something like a hallucination of his, that he was infiltrating and controlling her mind so thoroughly that its independent existence was threatened.

When I interpreted to her how she was speaking of her father's (supposed) affair as though she were actually seeing it in front of her, she slowly began to realize how close to delusional her thinking had become, and her sense of persecution diminished. Her certainty about the significance of her seeing the two together also diminished and her reaction to its possible meaning became less persecuting. She could once more see herself and her object, her internal and external reality, as separate and distinct.

8.5 Experimentation and sexuality

I believe that the fact that the patient's delusion concerned a sexual couple was no mere accident. Thinking disorders that lead to the type of concreteness found in this clinical illustration are often connected to delusions about sexuality. Reality-testing is connected to the state of one's *internal* sexual parents, and one's relationship to them. The precise state of one's internal sexual parents, i.e., the degree to which one has been able to accept an internal parental couple whose sexuality is pleasurable, creative and non-destructive, plays an important role in one's ability to establish the kind of playful, experimental relationship to reality that I have been describing. (See also McDougall [1995], Chasseguet-Smirgel [1984] and Britton [1989].)

What I mean by this is that an ego that is normally linked to reality, i.e., that is able to *observe* reality, to allow one's wishes to become subject to reality, and to learn from experience, is like a mother linked sexually to a father in a pleasurable and creative way. Such an ego is capable of allowing itself to be penetrated by reality, and to thrive and grow from the penetration, rather than feel humiliated by it.

At the same time, the capacity to experiment with nature – to probe it with questions and projections – requires one to be able to actively penetrate one's objects without feeling that one is committing a destructive invasion. That is, one must be able to have an internal sexual father whose activity is a helpful penetration, not a destructive one.

Both of these capacities – the capacity for receptive observation and the capacity for active inquiry and experimentation – are therefore equivalent to a third, the capacity to conceive of sexual intercourse as an activity between two people that is mutually beneficial. (This point was the subject of an early paper by Klein [1931].) The ability to learn from experience is therefore connected to the state of one's internal combined parents, meaning the unconscious phantasies that one has about their intercourse.

What seems to be crucial in this picture of a mutually beneficial intercourse is the feeling that the parents retain a *mutual autonomy* from one another in the process: one does not feel that either parent is taking over, invading, merging with, swallowing up or otherwise destroying the identity of the other. This is equivalent to a feeling that we may probe our object's minds without destroying them, and that we may be receptive to our object's projections without being destroyed ourselves.

At the same time, the child must recognize the parents' sexual relationship as a fact that is autonomous of its wishes. One of the benefits of resolution of the Oedipus complex is that it establishes in the child's mind the parents' sexuality as an autonomous fact, and this leaves behind a salubrious decrease in the child's omnipotence. One realizes the difference between one's real place in the world and one's wished-for place. If the Oedipus complex is not adequately resolved, belief in omnipotence remains too great and the ego will not be able to experiment with reality, since it will then feel that its phantasies are too powerful to play with safely. This leads to the somewhat surprising conclusion that *if the sexual autonomy of the parents cannot be accepted, what is subverted is ultimately the autonomy of one's own ego in its playful and experimental link to reality.*

Seen in this light, normal play, a normal sexual life, and normal intellectual functioning all require a capacity for a certain type of playful or experimental projective and introjective link with one's objects. We would therefore expect a disturbance of any one to be associated with disturbances in the other two.

8.6 Symbol formation and creativity

Both play and scientific experimentation depend on the capacity to form symbols. To form symbols, one must preserve the distinction between the symbol itself and what is symbolized. One's phantasies must not be felt to take over and dominate the object into which one projects them, and the external world must not dominate or take over the internal phantasy world. Each has its own domain, and the domain of each must be respected if play or scientific experimentation is to be possible. Put another way, the internal and external worlds must be autonomous of one another for playing and scientific experimentation to be psychologically possible.

These considerations apply to the relationship between internal and external reality in artistic creativity as well. Hanna Segal has shown one aspect of this in her paper on 'Delusion and artistic creativity' (Segal 1974), where she uses the material of William Golding's novel *The Spire* to investigate the nature of creativity. This is a fascinating paper that I cannot hope to summarize here, but I would like to mention one part of it that bears directly on the problem of symbolic thought. The novel takes place in the Middle Ages and its protagonist, Jocelin, is the dean of a cathedral who dreams of adding to it a huge spire. He claims that the spire will reflect the glory of God, but it is clear from the story that it is his own glory that he wishes it to reflect (he plans to have his own image on all four sides of the spire, and he compares the completed structure to a man's body, with the gigantic spire arising from the middle).

Jocelin cannot build his spire without the aid of a master builder, Roger Mason, who refuses to cooperate because he does not believe that the structure will stand; the cathedral's foundations are too weak to support it. Excavation proves the builder right, but this only strengthens Jocelin's determination to proceed.

The contrast between Jocelin and Roger Mason is one between grandiose, delusional narcissism and sober realism. But it is also a contrast between sterility and creativity. Jocelin claims that the spire is an expression of love for his object – God – but it is clear that he has identified himself with God and that the spire is really an expression of his love for an idealized image of himself. He is incapable of constructing anything real, however, because he sacrifices his perception of reality for the sake of maintaining his narcissistic delusions. Like the cathedral, his delusional system lacks foundation in reality. Roger Mason's view of what he can do is constrained by reality, and is hence much more modest, but, unlike Jocelin, he is capable of creating something real.

The point that Segal is making here is that the artist must acknowledge and respect the autonomy of his medium, its actual potentialities and limitations, if his work is to be a real creative expression of his inner world. By 'autonomy of his medium', I mean the fact that his materials have qualities of their own to which his phantasies must yield if they are to achieve artistic expression in the real world. If the artist cannot keep in some corner of his mind the difference between what he wishes to do and what his skill and materials allow him to do, his work cannot be realized, because it will lack foundation in reality.

This is one side of the creative process. Segal takes up another side in her paper on 'A psychoanalytic approach to aesthetics' (Segal 1952), in which she describes her analysis of a young girl

> … with a definite gift for painting. An acute rivalry with her mother had made her give up painting in her early teens. After some analysis she started to paint again and was working as a decorative artist. She did decorative handicraft work in preference to what she sometimes called 'real painting,' and this was because she knew that, though correct, neat and pretty, her work failed to be moving and aesthetically significant. In her manic way, she usually denied that this caused her any concern. At the time when I was trying to interpret her unconscious sadistic attacks on her father, the internalization of her mutilated and destroyed father, and the resulting depression, she told me the following dream: She had seen a picture in a shop which represented a wounded man lying alone and desolate in a dark forest. She felt quite overwhelmed with emotion and admiration for this picture; she thought it represented the actual essence of life; if she could only paint like that she would be a really great painter.
>
> It soon appeared that the meaning of the dream was that if she could only acknowledge her depression about the wounding and destruction of her father, she would then be able to express it in her painting and would achieve real art … her dream showed something that had not been in any way indicated or interpreted by me: namely the effect on her painting of her persistent denial of depression.

(1952, p. 191)

If the artist's work is to have real aesthetic value (as opposed to mere 'prettiness'), she must also respect the autonomy of her inner world. What she seeks to express has no importance or value if it is not a part of her actual psychic reality. This means that she must recognize that her unconscious, no less than the external world, is independent of her wishes, an autonomous source of creativity that she is no more able to control than the child is able to control the sexual creativity of the parents. In this case, the patient's creativity had been stifled by her refusal to acknowledge the autonomous reality of her inner world. The creative builder in Golding's novel was constrained by the reality of his materials – the external world – and Segal's patient needed to be constrained by the reality of her inner world – to be true to it – if she would accomplish something substantial – 'be a really great painter.'

Creative expression is the consequence of a simultaneous respect for the autonomy of both external and psychic reality. Each must be recognized as independent of one's omnipotent wishes – one must 'submit' to them – if a creative merger is to occur. The artist must somehow find the intersection between his irreducible psychic reality and the irreducible nature of material reality.

From this point of view, one becomes hard pressed to distinguish purely artistic creations from scientific creativity, or either from free play. Both true artistic creations and creative scientific theories owe their validity to their being faithfully subservient to realities beyond the investigator's control.

8.7 Conclusion

Playing is an experimental probing of external reality – the object's mind – with pieces of internal reality – one's own states of mind. By seeing what happens when we project a state of mind into our object's mind, we learn something about both our object's mind and our own projection.

For this to work as a means of learning about our internal and external worlds, however, the two must be kept separate. There must be a limit to what one feels is the power of one's thoughts over the mind of the object, and there must be a similar limitation on the power of the object's mind over one's own. This is where psychotic patients (including Dick) come to grief; they are unable to play and experiment because they feel that their experiments occur not on an 'experimental' scale – with limited effects on external reality, especially on the minds of their objects – but to be full-scale alterations of the world – 'runaway experiments'.

Not keeping the internal and external worlds separate (that is, not recognizing their mutual autonomy) means that we equate our projections with the external object's state of mind; we feel that they have actually altered our object's mind in an omnipotent way. Similarly, we feel that our external object's state of mind can invade, control and alter ours.

The capacity to project in an experimental way, to have an awareness of how little power we have to control the mind of the object, and to accept this without feeling that the object's mind is therefore dominating ours, is connected in turn to the ability to have a picture of good sexual intercourse. Projecting into external objects without feeling one is risking disaster, or has taken them over, is like being a sexual father who can penetrate mother without harming her. Accepting the verdict of reality without feeling that one's phantasies have been the victim of a disaster is like being a sexual mother who can allow the father to penetrate her without feeling destroyed. Put the other way around, one feels that one's projections are disastrous events and that submitting to reality is the same as accepting a humiliating defeat if one has similar views of the roles of father and mother in the primal scene.

The creative artist as well must be able to recognize the realities of his medium if his phantasy is to be successfully realized in the external world. But he must also be able to recognize the realities of his internal world if his creation is to have any real value. Viewed in this way, artistic creation and scientific investigation become hard to distinguish in their essence. Both depend on the ability to recognize the autonomy of external and internal reality both from each other and from one's wishes about them. Both require a rather 'hard-nosed' attitude about what is real externally and what is real internally (i.e., aesthetically or scientifically meaningful). Awareness of the mutual autonomy of external and internal realities creates a space or gap in which one may 'play' with external reality without feeling that one's phantasies have had too great an effect on it (so that we are not inhibited in our creative or experimental play). At the same time, this gap keeps our phantasies safe from too much of an impact of external reality, so we are still free to imagine. (The creative scientist, like the creative artist, must have free imagination; the physicist Michael Faraday said that 'nothing is too wonderful to be true', and the geneticist J.B.S. Haldane has said that 'the universe is not only stranger than we imagine, it is stranger than we *can* imagine.')

In this chapter, I have described an aspect of reality-testing that rests on playful exploration of the inner and outer worlds. The psychotic's phantasies are not usable for establishing contact with his objects because the peculiarities of his relationship to his objects make it impossible for him to project into them *in the experimental way that we all learn in our play*. A projection that normally acts as an experimental hypothesis becomes instead a delusional conviction, and what should be an opportunity for learning from experience through contact with our objects becomes instead the threat of being driven mad by them.

To return to the subject of Klein's paper, the importance of symbol formation in the development of the ego, one of the reasons that symbol formation is important in the development of the ego is that when people cannot experience their phantasies as mere symbols – that is, when they cannot recognize the mutual autonomy of what is in their minds and what is outside their minds – they cannot project in a normal way, and therefore cannot learn about the inner and outer worlds through playing and experimentation.

9

Internal objects

9.1 Unconscious conceptions

The psychoanalysis of young children, which allows a very precise, clear, specific concrete picture of the unconscious conceptions of the mind, led me to use ... the term 'internal objects' or 'inner objects' and 'good' and 'bad' objects. My reason for preferring this term to the classic definition, that of 'an object installed in the ego' is that the term 'inner object' is more specific since it exactly expresses what the child's unconscious, and for that matter the adult's in deep layers, feels about it. In these layers it is not felt to be part of the mind in the sense, as we have learnt to understand it, of the superego being the parents' voices inside one's mind. This is the concept we find in the higher strata of the unconscious. In the deeper layers, however, it is felt to be a physical being, or rather a multitude of beings, which with all their activities, friendly and hostile, lodge inside one's body, particularly inside the abdomen, a conception to which physiological processes and sensations of all kinds, in the past and in the present, have contributed.

(D16, Melanie Klein Trust Papers, Wellcome Library,
quoted in Hinshelwood [1997], pp. 894–5)

As Klein indicates in this note, she coined the term 'internal object' to denote a psychological entity that is located 'deeper' in the unconscious than the classical superego. The type of internal object that Klein was describing is, to be more precise, a more concrete and psychotic phenomenon than the classical superego: it is not felt to be in the mind, but in the body. In modern jargon, it has not been 'mentalized'. What Klein called the 'deeper layers' of the unconscious are the layers that are most dominated by unconscious phantasy. (I use the term in Isaacs's [1952] sense of the word: something existing in the borderland between psyche and soma – the mental expression of instinct that is most

95

immediately adjacent to somatic process.) In this area of the mind, phantasies are indistinguishable from bodily processes. 'Unmentalized' phenomena are mental events that are not experienced as mental events. From an objective point of view, they are phantasies, and are – like all phantasies – mental. But from the subject's point of view, they are concrete, physical events. The mind's conception of itself at this deep level of the unconscious as a physical entity means that its contents are not felt to be susceptible to critical thought, but are instead experienced as immutable facts. (This level of the unconscious is the locus of Freud's hallucinatory gratification.) In addition, perceptions of the external world received at this level of the unconscious tend to become so saturated with these concrete, instinct-laden phantasies there that they seem indistinguishable from them.

Such perceptions, saturated with phantasy that does not feel like phantasy, are experienced without the slightest inkling that they contain phantasy, or might be erroneous representations of the external world. (There is no negation in Freud's system Ucs. and it is not known for its epistemic humility.) These are the internal objects that Klein discussed in the passage quoted above. These saturated, concretized perceptions, appearing to the subject as indubitable facts, are of great importance in determining how one experiences both one's inner and outer worlds. This corresponds to Freud's observation (1925, p. 34) that psychic reality is of more importance than material reality in the formation of a neurosis.

An internal object (and I am here still using the term as Klein did in the passage quoted above) is the product of an identification with an external object. But this identification is not a simple process. Both the object and the self are split during the process of identification into 'good' and 'bad' parts, following which the 'good' parts of the self and object are recombined with each other and introjected (i.e., experienced as part of the self), while the 'bad' parts of self and object are similarly recombined and projected (i.e. experienced as object). What is 'identified' with in the paranoid-schizoid position is therefore a confused mixture of parts of the self and parts of the object. (See also Chapter 7.)

Identification in the paranoid-schizoid position is (like projection) partly a defense against the many anxieties associated with the fact that one is only oneself and no one else. Just as projection defends one against an unbearable sense of who one is by attributing the unbearable aspects of oneself to an object, identification defends one against an unbearable sense of who one isn't, by attributing indispensable aspects of an object to oneself.

Our concept of identification arose from the ideas of incorporation and introjection. Freud introduced incorporation in his *Three Essays on the Theory of Sexuality* (1905), and Ferenczi introduced introjection in his paper on 'Introjection and transference' (1909). While Freud and Ferenczi stressed the sexual basis of these phantasies, what is important about them for purposes of this discussion is their close relation to instinct – the fact that they operate in the deeper layers of the unconscious, in which, as Freud said, there are 'no indications of reality' (Freud 1985, p. 264). This renders them omnipotent: introjection and incorporation are not felt to be simply phantasies, but are instead felt to portray a concrete reality about who or what one is, who or what one's objects are, what they can do to one and what one can do to them. The phantasies of introjection, splitting, incorporation and projection that make up identification in the paranoid-schizoid position are believed uncritically – believed without any suspicion that they are mere beliefs or phantasies.

The therapeutic effect of psychoanalysis is based partly on the observation that if omnipotent or concrete phantasies can be converted into ordinary (i.e., non-concrete or non-omnipotent) wishes or phantasies, their impact on the mind becomes far less important. This conversion is no easy task; the phantasies in question satisfy some exciting, instinct-laden wish, or relieve some important anxiety, which means that the support that reality fails to provide for them is compensated for by the charge of excitement they engender, or by the relief from anxiety that they provide.

In my view, the internal objects that Klein referred to in the passage quoted above are the concrete products of such omnipotent phantasies. She found that when her child patients identified with an object, they incorporated it in unconscious phantasy into their bodies. What Klein called the 'parents' voices inside one's mind', which she connected to the 'higher strata of the unconscious', are quite different from these concrete internal objects. These voices are not experienced as the parents being concretely inside one, but are instead experienced as phantasies about the parents – beliefs that the parents' voices are inside one, so to speak, but beliefs that are recognized as different from concrete realities.

The feeling in this type of identification is *not* that one's identity has undergone a concrete alteration, but instead that one has a relationship with an object that is felt to be in one's mind. This type of identification is distinguished by being regularly accompanied by the knowledge that one is *not* the object.

These two different types of internal experiences result from two rather different types of identification, operating at two different levels of the unconscious. The state of mind characterized by the unconscious belief that one has the object concretely inside one corresponds to identification in the paranoid-schizoid position. The state of mind associated with a non-concrete relationship to an object, which involves the knowledge that one is physically and mentally distinct from the object, corresponds to identification in the depressive position. In the remainder of this paper, I shall discuss these two different types of identification, and the different types of internal experience that result from them. Despite Klein's caveat, both types of experience have come to be called internal objects. To avoid confusion, I shall refer to them as paranoid-schizoid and depressive internal objects.

These two types of identification and the two types of internal object resulting from them constitute the two ends of a spectrum. Identifications and internal objects that we encounter clinically lie somewhere on this spectrum, and are composed of combinations of the two types in varying proportions. I shall begin with a discussion of the paranoid-schizoid type of internal object, and then take up the question of depressive internal objects.

9.2 Paranoid-schizoid internal objects

Freud's theory of identification as a sexual activity emerges readily from his theory of sexuality. As we know, for each type of sexual impulse he delineated a source, an aim and an object: the source of a sexual impulse is an erogenous zone – a specific part of the body – and its aim is a specific kind of contact, by definition pleasurable, between the erogenous zone and some physical object, the object of the impulse. Incorporation in this scheme is simply the aim of the sexual impulses that arise in the mouth: sucking and swallowing.

Sexual impulses are constantly active in the form of unconscious, if not conscious, phantasies. If a real object with which sexual contact may be made is not available, we will unconsciously phantasize such pleasurable contact in accordance with the pleasure principle (Freud 1911). To the degree that a phantasy is deeply unconscious and split off from conscious awareness, it retains the vividness and subjective reality of a masturbation phantasy or an unconscious delusional belief. The classical Freudian theory of identification as a sexual activity fails to do justice to many of the subtleties that we now recognize as part of the process of identification, and especially to the subtlety of identification in the depressive position, but it seems to be quite a good description of the type of identification found in the paranoid-schizoid position. Freud's sexual theory of identification is a theory of paranoid-schizoid identification.

Klein's theory of internal objects is a logical extension of Freud's sexual theory of identification: if we believe we can swallow our objects, we must then believe they reside inside us. Klein's patients felt that their objects (or parts of them) then resided inside their bodies, as a world of concrete internal objects that paralleled their world of external objects. But this parallel is only very approximate: partly because of the splitting of self and object and the confusion that arises from the recombination of parts of the self with parts of the object that occurs in this kind of identification, the internal object world is quite different from the external object world.

One of the earliest formulations of the discrepancy between the world of external objects and the internal object world appeared in 'The psychological principles of early analysis' (Klein 1926), in which Melanie Klein suggested that the severe, primitive oedipal anxieties from which her small patient, Rita, suffered in her relationship to her parents were connected not to her external parents, but to phantasized introjects: Rita's fears of being attacked in her bed arose, Klein believed, not from the 'real [i.e., external] mother, but from an introjected mother.' Similarly, what hindered Rita's oedipal desire to steal the mother's babies was not her external father, but the 'introjected father'.

Rita's anxieties arose not from her relationship with her external parents, but from her relationship with an internal object – an omnipotent phantasy that led her to feel that she had a version of her parents concretely inside her. By virtue of their being inside her, they were were privy to her every thought and wish, and, by virtue of the same thing, she was utterly defenseless against them. To put it another way, if she could believe that she could swallow her parents, chew them up, or absorb them into her body, she must also have believed that they could swallow, chew or absorb her from their location inside her.

Klein concluded that internal objects such as Rita's archaic superego are formed by a type of identification that is the product of two kinds of omnipotent phantasy: one causing the subject to feel that the external object is different from what it really is (concrete projection into the object), and the other causing the subject to feel that the external object is located inside him, that is, experienced as a part of the self instead of as an object (concrete identification with the object). Concrete projection into an object is also a sexual phantasy, combining oral (spitting), anal and urethral eroticism. It produces experiences and beliefs that are as physical and immune from doubt as phantasies of incorporation.

This way of looking at identification and its sequelae later crystallized into her notion of projective identification (1946), which is one form of the paranoid–schizoid or narcissistic type of identification – identifications in which parts of the self and parts of the object become confused. Her conclusions about the superego were in accord with Freud's mature view of the role of identification in the formation of mental structure. In *Civilization and Its Discontents* (1930, p. 130), and the *New Introductory Lectures on Psychoanalysis* (1933, p. 62), Freud suggested that the superego is formed by a complicated identification with the parents, in which the child does not identify with the actual parents, but rather with his unconscious phantasy about the parents, which is by no means always the same as the actual parents.

The superego formed by projective identification is felt to reside concretely inside one, to be able to read and control one's mind, and to have the capacity to produce intense anxiety. It is not felt to be subject to rational or critical thought (since it is not, on this deeper level, felt to be mental), and, in consequence, one finds oneself resorting to desperate magical defenses to ward it off. These qualities of the archaic superego make it hard (at times, practically impossible) to distinguish having one from a delusion of being possessed. We experience the superego through identification as a part of ourselves, a possession of ours. But we also experience ourselves as a possession of it. The patient Victor Tausk described in his paper on the 'Influencing machine' (Tausk 1919[1933]) exemplifies this latter state of mind. She felt that she was enslaved by a machine constructed to be her mechanical double, and that her movements and sensations were determined by those of the machine. Paula Heimann (1942, p. 9) observed a similar clinical phenomenon in a patient who felt herself to be 'inhabited by devils. These devils ... roamed about inside her caused her physical pain and illnesses, inhibited all her activities, especially in painting, and compelled her to do things she did not want to do.'

The primitive superego may produce an intense feeling of well-being or euphoria as readily as a sense of terror and persecution. The former type of relationship to the primitive superego is found in certain states of mania and in certain types of groups, where the leader of the group is invested by the members with the qualities of a primitive superego. (According to Freud [1921a], the Church is an example of such a group. Bion [1961] has given us a general treatment of such groups.) In the extreme cases, having a 'good' primitive superego produces an experience of being possessed by a holy spirit, a sort of oceanic union with God, while having a bad one produces an experience of being under the control of an extremely destructive and omnipotent force. Outside of psychotic states, the *conscious* experience of an archaic good or bad superego is rarely as extreme as this, but the *unconscious* experience of having one nonetheless does seem to correspond to ideas of possession and of being possessed even in non-psychotic states.

The experience of being possessed, controlled and invaded by an object is a manifestation of an omnipotent phantasy in which the boundaries between the object and the self have become blurred or non-existent, so that one feels that one is simultaneously taking it over and being taken over by it. It is not projective identification *per se* – the unconscious phantasy that one is projecting into the object as well as identifying with it – that creates this weakening of boundaries, since a phantasy of omnipotently *introjecting* an object will have the same result. It is the narcissistic character of the identification (i.e. the omnipotent nature of the phantasy) that is crucial here, and this may occur as part of either projection, introjection, or of a combination of both. Because of the confusion between self and object that occurs in this type of identification, the resulting internal object is not a true object. What I mean by this is that the 'object' in such cases is a confusion of bits of the self and bits of the object, with the distinction between the two having been lost, and with all being regarded equally as attributes of the object. The relationship that one has with such an internal object is not a relationship with an object, but with an internalized chimera of self and object.

Clinically, the degree of control that such an internal object is felt to exert over the ego, and the power of the ego's unconscious phantasies to alter the character of such an object allow us to recognize that we are dealing with a relationship between ego and object in which neither is distinct from the other. I will call this type of relationship a pseudo-object relationship. (Recall that I am trying to characterize two ends of a spectrum, and that the identifications and internal objects we encounter clinically lie somewhere between the two ends as complex mixtures of true and pseudo-objects.)

9.3 Depressive internal objects

The second major type of internal object, the type associated with non-narcissistic (i.e., depressive) identification was delineated by Melanie Klein in a series of papers (1935, 1936a, 1937, 1940), in which she took up a problem that Freud had addressed twenty years earlier in 'Mourning and melancholia' (1917): the relationship between normal mourning and depressive illness. Her detailed examination of mourning and depression forms the basis for her theory of the depressive position. At the heart of this theory was the problem of identification. She observed (in agreement with Freud) that the loss of a loved object precipitates unconscious hatred toward it, which results in an internal struggle between one's love and hatred for the object. The pain of mourning is due to this struggle, and to the guilt and remorse that one feels as a result of hating a person that one also loves. Hatred gains the upper hand at first, with the result that one's love for the lost object – and one's capacity to love in general – are temporarily extinguished. This produces the mourner's loss of interest in the world – he loves nothing in it.

In normal mourning, the strength of the mourner's love is eventually recovered, and interest in the world returns. This means that he has in the end been able to retain his love for the lost object even in the face of the pain and frustration of its loss. This pain is an ongoing phenomenon – it is reawakened, though in a gradually attenuated form, every time one thinks of the lost object, forever. It becomes a fact of life for the mourner. What we refer to as working through a loss is a process that has no clear ending and is sustained only at the cost of a certain amount of mental pain.

The capacity to bear this pain for the sake of retaining the object is itself constantly in danger of getting lost if hatred of the lost object gains the upper hand. It is this second loss, the loss of the capacity to bear the pain of the loss of the object, that poses the threat of depressive illness. Depressive illness arises not from the loss of the object, but from the loss of the capacity to acknowledge that an object that one loves has been lost – that it is *not* a part of the self – while still loving it; in other words, to mourn.

A patient in the grip of depressive illness cannot fully regain his interest in the world, which is a sign that his capacity to love his good object has not overcome his hatred of it. The depressive's loss of self-esteem is partly due to his unconscious awareness of his inability to love his real objects (that is, objects that he does not feel are part of himself) and partly due to the fact that he denies the loss of the object by concretely identifying with the (now predominantly unloved) object.

The fundamental difference between normal mourning and depressive illness is that in the former, one's love for the good object ultimately predominates over one's hatred of it despite the recognition that it is non-self. Klein held that this type of mourning is a part of normal development – or rather, that mourning in adulthood is a recapitulation of a process that is universal in normal

101

development and that originates with weaning. She referred to the mourner's (or child's) love predominating over hatred as 'securing the good, internalized object'. This object is the product of successful mourning.

This type of internalized object is radically different from the paranoid-schizoid internal object that we considered in the previous section. It is not a pseudo-object set up as a defense against loss ('I have not lost the object – in fact, I cannot lose the object, since I *am* the object'), but a true object. It is the result of one's capacity to acknowledge a narcissistic loss (i.e., that 'the object is not a part of me') without having one's love for the lost object destroyed by one's narcissistic hatred of it. The two types of internal object are the products of processes that are not only different from each other, but are the precise opposite of each other in a number of important respects. (It is interesting to note that Freud seemed to return to this problem of narcissism and identification at the very end of his life when he wrote (Freud 1939, p. 299): ' "Having" and "being" in children. Children like expressing an object-relation by an identification: "I am the object". "Having" is the later of the two. After the loss of the object it relapses into being. Example: the breast. "The breast is part of me, I am the breast". Only later: "I have it" – that is, "I am not it"…').

A true object relationship respects the boundaries (psychological and physical) of the object (and of the self). In a true object relationship, one may love or hate an object, but one somehow recognizes that those are merely one's own feelings about it, and that, for better or worse, one's feelings *per se* (as distinct from one's actions) don't invade and alter it. By the same token, one does not feel that the relationship with the object makes one a different person, or allows one to invade or engulf the object, or allows the object to invade or engulf one, but merely that it provides one with an experience which one may then use (or not use) as part of one's development. A feeding from the breast as a true object gives only milk (just as contact with the analyst's mind gives only understanding); the breast (or analyst) remains separate, intact and uninvaded following the experience, as does the self.

Good and bad aspects of the object are experienced as closer together – as belonging more to the same object. Similarly, good and bad aspects of the self are more appreciated as different parts of a single whole. In other words, splitting tends to become less wide in the depressive position. At the same time, there is less confusion between ego and object: what belongs to ego is more and more seen as such, and what belongs to the object is also seen more as such: splitting in the depressive position also becomes more realistic.

In contrast to this, the pseudo-object relationships of the paranoid-schizoid position are associated with severe confusions between self and object, together with derealization and depersonalization, paranoid anxieties of being invaded by the bad object, and a sense of loss of vital aspects of the self. In extreme cases, where the use of omnipotent projection and identification have gone very far, we arrive at the derangement of psychic reality found in psychosis.

But what does it mean to speak of a good internal object in the depressive position – an object that is at the same time a true object and a part of oneself? A fundamental condition for the existence of the good internal object in the depressive position is that one has worked through one's narcissistic hatred of the true object and that one's love for it or its good qualities predominate over one's hatred. By 'working through' one's hatred of the object, I do not mean freeing oneself of it, but, on the contrary, living with it without giving in to it. This emotional tie with the good internal object in the depressive position is not a wish–fulfilling identification that equates the needed object with the ego, but rather a hard-won emotional link between the ego, on one hand, and, on the other, an object that one has had to work very hard to recognize as *not* part of the self.

Depressive identification is a function of a part of the ego that is able to recognize and maintain boundaries between self and object. This type of identification is always partial and limited. I suggest that it can begin to emerge only if it is shielded from the sexual drive to pleasurably incorporate the object concretely into the ego, on one hand, and from the anxious pressures to get away from who one is – from the fact that one is only oneself and no one else, on the other. This shielding is provided by a specific object, the prototype of which is the oedipal father who prohibits entry into (control over) the proto-typical object – the oedipal mother. The state of mind that permits this type of identification to predominate is one in which the oedipal father is tolerated despite the frustrations that are imposed by his prohibitions. This tolerance of the oedipal father allows one to recognize one's position in the oedipal triangle, which permits one to lose and mourn one's omnipotence and sense of possessing the object. This loss is painful, but to the degree that it can be accepted (meaning successfully mourned), the sense of having one's mind controlled *by* the object is relieved.

The tolerated oedipal father enforces a sense of who's who, which is an important component of sanity. One's tolerance of this father can be lost at any time, and is in fact in constant danger of being lost through the activity of narcissistic forces: as soon as the needed object is acknowledged to be external (that is, as soon as it is experienced as an object under the aegis of the oedipal father, who enforces boundaries between self and object), the narcissistic aspect of the personality will hate and attack it (if for no other reason than its being both good and *not* part of the self, it produces a narcissistic wound). This inevitable conflict over the capacity to have a true object relationship accounts for the sorrow, guilt and grief that is an inescapable part of realistic object relationships. The preservation of one's love for the good object in the face of one's hatred of it depends on the capacity to bear these painful feelings.

If these feelings can be borne, the result is the development of true self-esteem and inner security. True self-esteem (as opposed to mania) seems to be the product of a successful struggle to preserve one's love for the good object in the face of one's narcissistic hatred and destructive envy of it. One is then able to feel *worthy* of the good or loved object. Inner security therefore does not come simply from being loved. The presence of a good external object – for example, a mother who loves an infant and is therefore worthy of its love – is clearly necessary if one is to love her, and therefore to have any love to preserve. But it is not sufficient. One must then undergo an internal struggle with one's destructive narcissism, which attacks the good object precisely because it is a true object, instead of a good part of the self, and also attacks the part of the self that loves the true good object, which it regards as a traitor to its cause.

9.4 Clinical example

The way in which both object and self come under attack during this depressive struggle is illustrated by a vignette from the analysis of a patient who suffered from clinical depression. She began a Monday session feeling persecuted because she was unable to meet a request to help organize a complex fund-raiser at her daughter's school, a task she would have had to add to her many other school activities. This request faced her with her limitations, always a difficult problem for her, because it produced a conflict with a deep need to be competent, self-sufficient and independent. She simultaneously began to feel despair about her prospects in the analysis, which seemed, as it had many times in the past, to be connected to her unconscious hatred of the idea that it might help her where she had been unable to help herself, an idea that came into conflict with the same need for self-sufficiency. This in turn led to unconscious attacks on the analysis, along the lines of 'if I can't help myself, then you can't help me either'. The session helped her see this, and to feel that her situation in the analysis was not as hopeless as she thought, which gave her palpable, conscious relief.

She began the next day's session with a dream: *She was in a fortress of some kind that belonged to space aliens. She was their captive. She was in a maze with grey-black metal or plastic 'high-tech type' walls. She was trying to escape, and managed to grab weapons from two of the aliens, with which she killed them. She then escapes, starts to run and is soon pleased and relieved to find herself flying. She decides she doesn't need one of the weapons, and drops it. She sees a tremendous fireball where it hits the ground, and feels sorry for the people who had died in it.* (As she related the dream, this sorrow did not sound sincere.)

Her associations to this dream were characteristically very sparse. In response to a question if she had 'any thoughts' about the dream, she said 'No', and followed it with a terse and rather annoyed 'I don't know what it means'. After a long silence, she said she was 'pounding on the piano yesterday' while her children were playing. When she had finished, they asked her to continue, since they were playing pirates and were using the music as background.

104

I said that the dream represented her unconscious experience of the Monday session, which was quite different from the conscious relief she had felt, and was an unconscious reaction to that relief. The aliens represented the analyst on whom she depends and which a part of her loves. The relief she experienced in the previous day's session made her aware that I could see things in a way that was different – alien – from hers. While she consciously experienced this as as a good thing (and myself as a good and needed object), unconsciously she felt that this was a terrible threat. Her *dependence* on an analysis that goes beyond her own capacities (represented by the advanced technology of the high-tech grey-black metal or plastic walls) is experienced by a part of her as being a *captive* of this alien force. (This seems to be what happens when she experiences her objects as not her, while she is still under the dominance of the narcissistic aspect of her personality: if the object is not part of her, she must be part of it.) If, however, she can place me in the background, that is, if she can feel that I am just 'pounding away' with my interpretations while she plays her own game – cures herself with her own phantasies – this threat is relieved, because in that case she can feel that she has incorporated (pirated) my interpretations as a part of her self, as a kind of background that she already 'knows'. She then needn't feel any love for the analysis.

I believe that if this patient can equate herself with me, she feels comfortable in a way. But on a deeper level she is then in despair, since then the analysis can't offer her anything she doesn't already 'know'. On the other hand, if she feels I do have something new to offer (as she had felt in the previous session), she feels more hope, but at the same time feels captured by the analysis (or rather her love for it). The part of her that feels captured must then escape, but this means attacking both the analyst (the two aliens) and the part of herself that needs help (the groundlings destroyed in the explosion).

She responded to this interpretation after another silence by saying that I was 'probably exactly right'. What impressed me more than her words was the fact that her voice sounded sober and reflective, and had lost the edge of sullen hostility and despair that it had at the beginning of the session.

My interpretation helped her to experience her phantasy that she and the object are part of each other as just that – a phantasy – whereas before, her concept of her mind was dominated by that phantasy. She could then have a relationship with me as an object under the aegis of the oedipal father – i.e., as a true object.

On many occasions when the patient is able to hold on to the feeling of being helped, she is attacked by severe headaches. This dream gave some insight into the etiology of her headaches: an internal situation dominated by concrete, omnipotent phantasies of attacking herself. When she is able to allow herself to feel helped, she feels like a groundling, and she fire-bombs herself internally. The concreteness of the phantasies is also indicated by the fact that they give rise to a somatic symptom.

Splitting and concrete identification with an object may be necessary tactics for preserving *some* sort of good relationship with the good object in the face of the type of attack on the true object (and true self) seen in this dream. But it is a type of identification that ultimately cannot form the basis of mental stability. True mental stability occurs only through mourning the loss of one's identity with the good object, so that one can have a non-concrete relationship with it – a relationship in which the object can be experienced as something that one has a link to, without concretely identifying it with a part of one's mind. What is lost and must be mourned in the depressive position is the illusion that one is somehow the same as the needed object. This loss corresponds to Winnicott's notion of disillusionment (1953, p. 240).

9.5 Recapitulation

To summarize my argument to this point: identification in the paranoid-schizoid position is a product of omnipotent unconscious phantasies of concretely incorporating the object into one's body in a physical sense, which gives rise to a confusion between self and object. Having installed the object inside ourselves, we feel that we possess it, but also that it possesses us in return: we feel that the object is capable of controlling us by purposefully creating emotions and sensations inside us. Furthermore, we don't feel that we can resist these states of mind, since we experience such objects as being able to induce them regardless of what we wish. These last two characteristics of internal objects imply that the unconscious phantasy of incorporating these objects is connected to an unconscious wish to enter and control the object (and in particular its mind) in the manner that is familiar to us in the concrete type of projective identification that Melanie Klein described in 1946.

In the depressive position, however, the situation is quite different. In the place of narcissistic and grandiose phantasies producing a delusion that one possesses the object, we find *links* to (not narcissistic identifications with) the object. In this state of mind, one can have a relationship with a true object, i.e., an object not experienced as part of, or belonging to the self. The focus of anxiety shifts from whether or not one owns and controls the needed object (or is owned and controlled by it) to a conflict between the aspects of the self that love it and those that hate it – ultimately, between one's capacity for object relatedness and one's narcissism.

9.6 The internal world and the Oedipus complex

One of the ways in which the contrast between the type of internal object found in the paranoid-schizoid and the type found in the depressive position

106

shows up clinically is in the difference between the early and later stages of the resolution of the Oedipus complex.

Freud believed that the formation of the superego permitted the child to resolve his oedipal dilemma. He felt that the superego was formed through an identification with the parents, and that this identification represented a regression of the child's libido from genital to pre-genital (oral) forms, an event that ushers in the latency period. If we trace out the implication of this, we find that it encompasses two very different scenarios, depending on the type of identification involved. If the identification is narcissistic, its product is a superego that falls into the category of paranoid-schizoid internal objects (the archaic superego). In this case, the child gives up his desire for a genital sexual relationship with the parent by retreating to omnipotent phantasies of projection and introjection, which together create a state of mind in which he feels he has a version of his parents actually residing inside him as a concrete a part of his self.

In this case, the resolution of the Oedipus complex and the establishment of the superego would not be due simply to a regression from a genital to an oral sexual relationship with the parents (as Freud believed), but a regression to a relationship with the parents that is narcissistic and omnipotent, as well. This is not the same as an oral relationship to the object. Recall that an infant may have a pre-genital, oral relationship with the breast as an external object that it recognizes as such, as in the example I gave above where the infant feeds from the breast to take in only milk and understanding, while the breast remains separate, intact and uninvaded following the experience, as does the self. In the same way, an adult may take in new knowledge from an external object, also recognized as such. These are both manifestations of oral libido in a non-narcissistic relationship with the object.

The solution of the Oedipus complex by a retreat to omnipotent phantasy is not therefore a regression to an earlier, pre-genital type of libidinal relationship to an object, but an *abandonment of a link* to one's objects as objects separate from the self (a true object relationship), in favor of a relationship to an object that is experienced as part of oneself – that is, a narcissistic equation of self and object (a pseudo-object relationship).

The *equation* of the self with the parents avoids the painful loss of omnipotence inherent in a *link* with them by a maneuver that might be summarized as 'I am the object.' This represents a pseudo-resolution of the problem of the oedipal father's relationship to the mother. It is attained through narcissistic identification with the parents, who are then reduced to internal pseudo-objects (the archaic superego).

This early type of resolution of the Oedipus complex, based on a narcissistic identification, ushers in latency. The constriction of the child's spontaneity and creativity that typify the latency period are a result of the child's mind being controlled by the superego, the controlling nature of which arises largely from the manner in which the identification was achieved. (It is the establishment of this type of superego that accounts for the observation that latency-age children are teachers' dreams and analysts' nightmares.)

The latency child projects into and introjects the parents, as part of a phantasy of owning and controlling them, so that he may maintain *some* sort of good relationship with them in the face of his still overwhelming narcissism and his jealousy and envy of them. This tendency toward identification with objects as a substitute for libidinal relationships with them as separate individuals extends beyond the parents, and contributes to the extreme vulnerability to group pressure that one observes in latency and early adolescence.

The triumph of identification over object relationships is not complete, of course, and this narcissistic resolution of the Oedipus complex is normally just provisional. True object relationships do survive throughout latency, to flower once again in late adolescence, when a reworking of the first oedipal resolution becomes possible. This permits the possibility of a later, less omnipotent, resolution, with the eventual achievement of genitality in the full sense, which is equivalent to psychological maturity and true object relationships.

By late adolescence, the child's envy, jealousy and feelings of smallness have subsided to the point where it begins to be possible to have a relationship with the parents as true objects in place of the narcissistic identification that was formerly required. Now he is better able to experience the boundaries and differences between himself and his objects, which means he has a clearer picture of them, and of himself. At the same time, he is able to have a relationship with his objects that is not claustrophobic, to mourn their loss as internal possessions, and to experience reparative urges, now that he recognizes the destructive components of his ideas and feelings as his own. (Ronald Britton [1992, p. 35] has expressed the relationship between the resolution of the Oedipus complex and the depressive position in the following way: 'As I see it these two situations are inextricably intertwined in such a way that one cannot be resolved without the other: we resolve the Oedipus complex by working through the depressive position and the depressive position by working through the Oedipus complex.')

This development permits a second type of resolution of the Oedipus complex, based on an identification with the parents in which the child *aspires or wishes* to be somehow like his parents, while still remaining aware that he and his parents are separate – in other words, a relationship in which he still retains them as true internal objects. This kind of identification involves mourning the loss of one's omnipotent identification with the parents and an acceptance of the reality of the oedipal father and his psychological heirs. This is not a regression to a pre-genital libidinal relationship with the parents, or an abandonment of a relationship to them as objects, but a kind of identification that preserves their status as objects: they are not confused with the self, and not felt to have been concretely ingested or controlled by the self. At the same time, and in the same way, it preserves the self from the kind of domination by the object described by Tausk and Heimann.

The concrete superego of the early oedipal resolution has become mentalized as a consequence of the later oedipal resolution. It can now be thought about, doubted and evaluated because it is experienced as mental – part of one's mind – instead of as a concrete thing-in-itself. This type of superego does not possess the mind, but influences the mind because it embodies qualities that the child values and wishes to emulate. It leads naturally to the development of values based on one's own sense of what is realistically good and bad. The depressive superego tends in time to merge into the ego, to become the part of the ego that is encompassed by the term 'values', and to guide one's thinking. (The paranoid-schizoid superego, in contrast, tends to take over and dominate the ego, to *replace* one's thinking with moralism, a process that Bion [1965, p. 64n] called 'usurpation of ego function by superego'). When we speak of a 'good internal object' in the depressive position, referring to something in the mind that is essential to the survival of the ego as well as for the growth of its object relationships, we are speaking of an object formed by depressive identification, of which the mature superego is an example.

A depressive identification with an object, while incompatible with an equation between self and object, leads paradoxically to the object's becoming available to the ego. The good internal object in the depressive position acts as an inspiration or ideal. It becomes more like the 'parents' voices in the mind' that give one strength and encouragement but do not take over or dominate the ego.

Love for the good internal object in the depressive position must be maintained in the face of one's narcissistic hatred of the object for being good, needed, and at the same time not a part of the self. In my view, this hatred is identical to Klein's 'internal persecutors', the destructive forces within the personality that are felt to threaten the good object and the healthy parts of the self that love the good object in the depressive position. When one's love for the good object predominates over one's hatred for it in the depressive position, the result is what we commonly call healthy self-esteem. What is esteemed then in self-esteem is one's capacity to defend the loved object and the part of the self that loves it from internal destructive narcissistic attacks.

I have described these developments and regressions in terms of omnipotent and non-omnipotent identification, latency and adolescence, only for the sake of clarity. In fact, my description is much too schematic; these phenomena occur throughout life. The depressive type of object relationship that I attribute to late adolescence really only begins to predominate then. Its earliest manifestations occur long before latency, and may be seen, albeit fleetingly, even in the oral stage, as I suggested above. And narcissistic pseudo-object relations persist in the most mature person, erupting in moments of severe anxiety throughout life.

Our attempts to have both subjectivity and objectivity – both a mind of our own and a passionate relationship with our objects, succeeds and miscarries on a small scale many times throughout life. Very often patients come to analysis because their object relationships have not progressed beyond the type seen in

109

the latency-type resolution of the oedipal situation. They are too equated with their objects, and consequently too influenced by them and too little able to have a mind of their own and a full relationship with their objects.

I believe that one may give up the omnipotent phantasy that one has incorporated one's objects – that one's object is concretely inside one – even though this brings in its train feelings of smallness and inadequacy, and of a painful awareness of one's hostility toward the now separate good object, because it permits one to have something that no omnipotent phantasy can: a mind of one's own, a passionate relationship with one's objects, and a sense of sanity.

A mind of one's own

10.1 Introduction

In this chapter, I will try to explore the relationship between depressive awareness, or the awareness that an object is separate from oneself, and the oedipal
situation, or the awareness that the object has relationships with other objects
in which one does not partake. I will begin by reviewing certain ideas about
paranoid-schizoid and depressive object relationships with an eye toward clarifying what I mean by depressive awareness.

As we know, in paranoid-schizoid object relations, splitting, projection and
introjection are all active. Both the object and the self are split into good and bad
parts, and these parts are then merged into new combinations: the bad parts of the
self are merged with the bad parts of the object, while the good parts of the self
are merged with the good parts of the object. Despite its complex origin, we tend
to speak of the bad self merged with the bad object as the 'bad object', and of the
good self merged with the good object as the 'good object'. In doing so, we are
describing things from the point of view of the part of the personality that is using
paranoid-schizoid mechanisms. From an objective point of view, the good and
bad objects are not distinct objects, but confused mixtures of self and object.

The splitting of the self and object into good and bad parts destroys the
integration or wholeness of self and object. Following this, parts of the self are
recombined with parts of the object. This produces a confusion between self
and object. The aspect of paranoid-schizoid object relationships that I would
like to focus on in this chapter is the confusion that arises from the combination
of parts of the self with parts of the object. (In separating the splitting of self and
object from the subsequent confusion of parts of the self with parts of the
object, I am drawing a schematic picture that makes discussion of this complex

---

* This is a slightly revised version of a paper that appeared in the *International Journal of
Psycho-Analysis* 78(2), 265–78 (1997).

phenomenon easier, but which may have no counterpart in reality. Splitting of self and object seems always to entail confusion between self and object, so the two processes are really only parts of a single, indivisible process.)

The movement from the paranoid-schizoid to the depressive position involves an undoing of these confusions and splits within and between the self and the object. This produces a greater ability to see the object as a whole. A whole object is whole in two senses: it is not only more integrated, meaning that its formerly split-up parts are now experienced as more together, but it also has greater integrity, meaning that it is less confused with other things, such as parts of the self. The same considerations apply to the whole self: it is experienced as having all its parts, but also as not being confused with the object, as not having parts of the object mixed up with it. The ability to see the self and object as a whole – as integral – is therefore inseparable from the ability to accept the distinction between self and object – their integrity.

What I propose is that one experiences the separateness of the self from the object and the object from the self – what I am calling the integrity of self and object – by acknowledging that one's object has relationships with other objects from which one is excluded. Put another way, one attains a depressive relationship with an object (or a depressive awareness of an object) by experiencing it as separate from the self, and one experiences it as separate from the self by experiencing it as having relationships to objects of its own (internal or external) in which one does not participate. This latter experience is, of course, the oedipal situation in its broadest form.

The depressive position has an interesting and complex relationship to the oedipal situation. Melanie Klein has discussed some aspects of this relationship in her papers 'On observing the behaviour of young infants' (1952a) and 'Some theoretical conclusions regarding the emotional life of the infant' (1952c). Most analysts agree that one's ability to experience the oedipal situation depends on one's emergence into the depressive position (since, after all, one cannot experience oneself in a dyadic situation, let alone a triadic one, unless one can recognize objects distinct from the self). I propose to put the case the other way around by saying that emergence into the depressive position depends on one's being able to have a realistic experience of the oedipal situation, at least in its most rudimentary form. This idea is also consistent with Britton's (1992) observation that emergence into the depressive position enables one to work through oedipal anxieties and vice versa, and implies that not only do these two processes support each other, as Britton pointed out, but that they are in fact the same thing.

10.1.1 Narcissistic aspects of the transference

Some observations about the transference may help to tie these ideas to clinical realities. In the transference, the patient projects into the analyst (in phantasy) one or another of his internal objects, which are, as we know, parts of himself. He then comes to experience the analyst – an external object – unconsciously as the part of himself that he has projected. There is an aspect of the patient's personality for which these projections turn the analyst quite concretely into what Strachey (1934 [1969]) called an external phantasy object, an object that is experienced as an external version of an internal object. This aspect of the patient's personality needs the analyst to be what it has projected into him, and it has a great capacity to make the most of whatever evidence the analyst gives that this is so, and an equally great capacity to ignore evidence to the contrary. But the means by which it turns the analyst into an external phantasy object go beyond selective attention. In the process of forming the transference, the patient induces in the analyst (in reality) certain states of mind that correspond to the transference role into which the patient is casting him (in phantasy). This interpersonal aspect of the transference owes its effectiveness to the patient's use of his intuition and perceptiveness to assess trends and forces in the analyst's personality, including some of which the analyst may be unconscious. He then behaves in various ways, often quite subtle, to massage or manipulate these forces so they produce in the analyst a state of mind that corresponds in reality to what he is projecting into him in phantasy. This is part of what has been called 'role actualization' in Britain (Sandler 1976), or 'role responsiveness' in the US.

The analyst's receptivity to the patient's unconscious states of mind – which falls somewhere in the area of what we call intuition, listening to the patient or being in contact with the patient – depends in part on his capacity to be affected by these projections. But this receptivity is complicated by the tendency of these projected states of mind to produce in the receptive analyst what Bion (1961, p. 149) called a 'numbing feeling of reality' about themselves. That is, the analyst may end up feeling not simply *as if* he were the patient's external phantasy object, he may end up feeling that he *is* that object, and begin to act accordingly. This suggests that the projection has not only produced a certain state of mind in the analyst, but that it has also met with something in the analyst that combines with it to nullify his reality-testing as far as the projection is concerned. This fairly well-recognized occupational hazard of doing analysis manifests itself as an acute loss of intelligence on the part of the analyst (see also Chapter 4). This effect is seen most strikingly in group supervision, where almost everyone in the group has a clearer idea about what is being projected into the analyst than the analyst does.

This means that, while no one is in a better position to understand a patient than the analyst who is in the room with him (which is obvious), it is no less true (though perhaps less obvious and quite paradoxical) that no one is in a worse position either. The tendency of the analyst to identify with the patient's projections is due partly to the specific nature of what the patient is projecting – the extent to which the projection touches on the analyst's own unconscious complexes, to use a slightly archaic term. But even after this specific factor is accounted for, something more general still seems to be left over. It is something that is connected to the high degree of intimacy and rapport that typifies the analytic milieu, and that seems to sway the analyst into identifying with the patient's projections. This tendency toward identification is automatic and spontaneous, requiring no conscious thought or effort on the part of either participant. When the analyst joins the patient in experiencing himself unconsciously as what the patient has projected into him, we have in the clinical situation something that seems to correspond to our theoretical notion of a confusion between self and object in the paranoid-schizoid position: the patient identifies the analyst with what he has projected into him, and the analyst identifies himself with the same projections.

Under favorable conditions, however, the analyst is able to carry the analysis further by bringing into play a second capacity alongside his receptivity to the patient's projections that keeps it from simply sliding over into an identification with them. (A large part of the effort required to do analysis might be said to consist of trying *not* to identify with the patient and trying to get the patient not to identify with us. This is one of the main distinctions between psychoanalysis and non-analytic psychotherapies.) This second capacity is his ability to establish enough distance from the patient's projections to permit him to recognize that they *are* projections, and that the state of mind he is experiencing has arisen from outside himself. To summarize this process, the analyst tends to fall spontaneously into a countertransference illness as part of his receptivity to the patient's projections, and he must cure himself of it if the analysis is to progress. The 'cure' consists of a reversal of the spontaneous process that produced the illness, and requires a certain amount of psychological work on the part of the analyst. (It has been suggested by some authors – for example, Ogden [1996] – that the analyst must become *quite* identified with the patient's projections and work through this illness laboriously if his understanding of the patient's projections is to be therapeutically effective. I disagree with this position. What is important is only the fact that the analyst has been able to think about the patient's projections, not how much (or little) trouble he has had to go to in doing so.)

While the analyst's receptivity to the patient's projections allows him to establish contact with the patient's mind, his capacity to *not* identify with them forms a barrier between his mind and the patient's. The patient experiences this barrier or boundary as something in the analyst that he cannot penetrate with his projections. The analyst demonstrates both his receptivity to the patient's projections and his capacity to not identify with them by interpreting the patient's unconscious phantasies. This means treating the patient's unconscious communications as objects of knowledge, rather than as indications of a need the analyst should fill (aside, of course, from the need for self-knowledge). In other words, the analyst must be sensitive to the role he is meant to play as the patient's external phantasy object, and must at the same time be role-*un*responsive. The effect of such an interpretation (if it hits home) is to make the patient aware that the analyst is not the external phantasy object that he unconsciously took him to be, that he is not identified with the patient's projections, and that there is therefore at least some part of the analyst's mind that is outside the projective system with which the patient has identified him. A successful interpretation makes the patient aware that he and the analyst are separate. This brings about the complex set of emotions that fall under the heading of depressive anxiety: fear, persecution, loss, loneliness, guilt, remorse and mourning.

But often the transference interpretation does not hit home and does not have this effect. This may occur for a number of reasons, but the one of particular interest for our discussion is based on the fact that often the patient will attempt to retreat to a paranoid-schizoid relationship with the analyst by immediately identifying with the analyst who has just made the interpretation. This identification makes the patient into the analyst who 'knows' the interpretation that the analyst just made, who 'sees what the analyst means'. It is a kind of false insight into himself that fails to lead to psychological development because, while he understands the interpretation, he does not really experience it as being about himself in a live or real way. An extreme example of this kind of identification is the patient who, instead of using the interpretation to gain insight into himself, becomes a version of the analyst and develops a false insight into his friends and relations (really projects into them what he should be having insight into within himself), often becoming a plague to them all.

Whether the patient makes the analyst into an external phantasy object or himself becomes the analyst through identification, his relationship with the analyst is the same: a type of identification that we might call simple like-mindedness. It is a phantasy that the patient's mind and the analyst's are somehow the same, and it takes advantage of the analyst's receptivity to the patient's projections to reinforce itself. When this phantasy is in full force, it has a characteristic emotional tone that I will now try to describe: there is a feeling of mutual identification, of a relationship between two people who know, understand and love one another (the patient will, in fact, often describe the emotional state that accompanies this like-mindedness as 'being understood', or more emphatically, 'finally being understood'); there is a feeling of relief and of rapport with the analyst; the patient may feel that the analyst has been able to articulate what he has always known and wanted to articulate for himself, but has not theretofore been able to find the words for. What is missing from this emotional state is just as noteworthy as what is present: there is no anxiety, guilt, depression or resistance to interpretation. There is often a subtle us-against-them quality to this type of rapport, the 'us' being the patient and the analyst who understand each other, and the 'them' being those who don't. The sense of understanding and of being understood is associated with a positive moralistic

115

tone, in the spirit of 'tout savoir, c'est tout pardonner.' To be completely under-stood is to be forgiven everything. The analyst and the patient form a 'good' couple, the 'us', whose mutual understanding of the patient allows them to forgive him.

But, while it is obviously the business of psychoanalysis to understand, it is just as obviously not the business of psychoanalysis to use understanding to forgive, any more than it is its business to use it to condemn. This 'understand-ing' couple is therefore not an analytic couple, but something else: the merger of the patient who loves the analyst with the analyst who loves the patient, the 'good' patient merged with the 'good' analyst to form the good object (or rather good self/object) of the paranoid-schizoid position. Since this merger between good self and good object is a narcissistic object relationship, we may call the aspect of the patient that wants to reduce the analysis to this kind of relationship the narcissistic aspect of the personality.

These considerations apply to transference situations in which the analyst is the patient's narcissistic good object (or self/object). There are, of course, other trans-ference situations in which the analyst is the patient's bad object. In these cases, the patient has something other than the analyst as a good self/object. This role may be filled by a spouse, a child, a career, a drug, the self, or practically anything else which the patient can idealize, and with which he can form an addictive relation-ship. He then feels that the analyst is full of envy of his possession of the good object, and the transference acquires a distinctly paranoid tinge in which the analyst often feels that the patient is engaging in a pseudo-analysis, keeping the analyst at bay in order to protect his 'good' internal objects from him.

Whether the narcissistic aspect of the transference is idealizing or paranoid, it is marked by a delusional state in which the analyst is concretely felt to be an external phantasy object, and evidence that the analyst is able to detach himself from this role — to have a mind of his own — causes great upset and is usually avoided. The narcissistic aspect of the patient needs to have a delusional object (preferably one that is deluded as well) to maintain its delusions, and it achieves this through a combination of selective attention and active intervention in the object's internal object world. This seems to be true whether the delusional object is a good one or a bad one, or whether it is the analyst or someone else in the patient's life.

10.1.2 Non-narcissistic aspects of the transference

Alongside the narcissistic aspect of the patient's personality, there is a non-narcissistic aspect that is capable of forming a relationship with the analyst other than identification or union. It is not like-minded, that is, it does not identify the analyst with its projections, and does not identify itself with the analyst's insights. This aspect of the patient enables him to experience the interpretation as having originated from someone else, and as being about himself. For the non-narcissistic aspect of the patient, the analyst is an object that is distinct from itself, what we might call a proper external object. (I am using the term 'proper' in its dictionary sense of 'belonging to the person or thing in question distinctively [more than to any other], or exclusively [not to any other]; special, particular, distinctive, characteristic, peculiar, restricted, private, individual, of its own. Opposite to common' [*Oxford English Dictionary*, second edition].) The emotional tone of this type of relationship, unlike that associated with narcissistic identification, is complex and contains painful elements (see 5.2), but the non-narcissistic aspect of the patient welcomes it because, among other things, if the patient is not confused with the analyst in a system of identification, he can have an identity and a mind of his own. When this state is newly arrived at, when some narcissistic identification has given way to a depressive awareness, the patient experiences it as a feeling of sanity. It is very difficult to overestimate the importance of this state of mind to the non-narcissistic part of the patient's personality, or the degree to which it motivates the patient to do the hard work of analysis. This aspect of the patient feels that its good object is not the merger of two people, the narcissistic union or confusion of the loving patient with the loving analyst, but the union or coming together of two distinct capacities *within* the analyst – the union of the analyst's receptivity to the patient's projections with the analyst's capacity to distance himself from them.

There is a powerful conflict between the narcissistic and non-narcissistic aspects of the patient's personality that may perhaps be most clearly seen in the fact that the good object for the non-narcissistic aspect of the personality – the analyst whose receptivity combines with his ability to distance himself enough from the projection to interpret it – destroys the narcissistic union between patient and analyst and is therefore a bad object from the point of view of the narcissistic aspect of the patient. Similarly, the good object from the point of view of the narcissistic aspect of the personality – the narcissistic union of the patient and analyst – is a bad object from the point of view of the non-narcissistic aspect of the personality, since this union prevents the analytic work that brings sanity. This conflict seems to me to be both unavoidable and incessant. Whichever aspect of the patient's personality is dominant at the moment, the other experiences very real anxiety for the survival of what it feels to be its good object and therefore of itself.

10.1.3 Oedipal aspects of the transference

I would like now to explore briefly the state of mind that allows the analyst to be receptive to the patient's projections and at the same time to distance himself from them. As Hanna Segal pointed out at the International Psychoanalytic Congress in Amsterdam (1993), the analyst is linked to the patient via his sensitivity to the patient's projections, but at the same time he has a link with his own internal objects, from which the patient is excluded. What we call the emotional distance or barrier between analyst and patient is a way of speaking of these links to his internal objects. The patient experiences the analyst's receptivity to his projections as a relationship that the analyst has with him, and he experiences the analyst's distance from his projections as a relationship that the analyst has with something or someone else. This is a realistic perception: the analyst does indeed have these two kinds of relationship – one with his patient and one with his internal objects – and he must be able to maintain them both simultaneously if he is to be able to analyze (as distinct from merely being receptive to or identified with) the patient's unconscious transference.

I suggest that the internal object that helps the analyst sustain his internal barrier against the patient's projections is psychoanalysis itself as a specific type of empirical investigation. It functions this way only if it is an internal object for the analyst, and it becomes an internal object for the analyst only if he loves it. This love of psychoanalysis is acquired and strengthened through the analyst's own analysis, and its presence seems to be a good criterion of that elusive state called 'being analyzed', or 'having an identity as a psychoanalyst'. (I am using the term 'love' here to mean a relationship with psychoanalysis that, while it is positive, does not idealize it and does not lead to an identification with it. That would be a narcissistic relationship with psychoanalysis, which would, of course, prevent contact with the real patient.) I want to emphasize that psychoanalysis as an internal object is not something that one acquires merely by having been analyzed, it it something that one has only if one has an active passion for the type of knowledge it brings.

I use the word 'passion' here because I am trying to describe something that is capable of counteracting the powerful and mind-numbing pull that operates on the analyst in the analytic setting to identify with the patient's projections – to enjoy the intimacy and sense of power of a narcissistic merger instead of treating the patient's state of mind as an object of knowledge.

In turning the analyst into an external phantasy object, the patient is entering a delusional relationship with him. To the extent that he is able to recruit the analyst as a narcissistic object (whether in phantasy or reality), he must nullify the analyst's reality-testing about what the patient has projected into him (in phantasy or reality). This means undermining the link that the analyst has to psychoanalysis as an internal object that represents his passion for knowledge or reality-testing. The analyst will be able to interpret the transference, that is, restore the analytic relationship in the patient's mind to a depressive one, to the extent that he is able to maintain his link with analysis as this type of internal object in the face of the patient's projections.

This situation has an obvious oedipal character. Bion (1967b, pp. 35–6) used an explicit oedipal metaphor of mother, infant and father in representing his experiences as an analyst with his patient when he wrote: 'when the mother

118

loves the infant, what does she do it with? Leaving aside the physical channels of communication, my impression is that her love is expressed by reverie.' By 'reverie', Bion seems to mean a state of mind that is receptive to the infant's state of mind. He went on, 'if the feeding mother cannot allow reverie or if the reverie is allowed but is not associated with love for the child or its father this fact will be communicated to the infant even though incomprehensible to the infant.' At first Bion's inclusion of the mother's love for the father as a requirement for adequate maternal reverie is puzzling. Does the infant really need the mother to love its father, in addition to loving it? It is striking that, in many discussions of Bion's ideas about maternal reverie, this idea is simply overlooked. But I believe it is an essential component of the whole process. Translating Bion's metaphor into the realities of the analytic situation, the analyst must be in a state of mind in which he is receptive to the patient's projections and in which he has an internal object that he loves and that this love must come between him and the projections.

This suggests that the analyst must have a passionate relationship with his internal objects – a mind of his own – that excludes the patient if he is to help the patient move from the paranoid–schizoid, narcissistic fusion with him into a realistic depressive contact with him as a proper object. This depressive contact with the analyst helps the patient to establish proper contact with *himself* (i.e., with his own internal objects) separate from his external objects – to have a mind of *his* own. Put another way, one of the tasks of the analyst is to not identify with the patient (or rather to identify with him in a limited and circumscribed way). He is able to do this by having a mind of his own – relationships with his internal objects that exclude the patient. If he can do this, he is in a position to help the patient not identify with him, and this allows the patient to identify with himself, and to have a relationship with his own internal objects instead of an identification with the analyst. The following clinical illustration will help to clarify some of the details of this process.

10.2 Clinical illustration

The patient from whose analysis this illustration is taken is a young woman who, at the time of her analysis, was working toward a degree in ancient history. One of her major symptoms was an inhibition of self-expression. This symptom was connected to a fear that her ideas would not harmonize with the listener's, and that the listener would then attack her because of the difference. At times, this inhibition led her to become confused about what her ideas really were.

She began a Monday session by saying that she had spent the weekend attending a seminar in her field. It was 'OK', she said, but she found that during the seminar she had gotten into an unpleasant, 'spaced-out' state of mind that she could not bring herself out of. All she could say about it was that she felt that one of her professors had been too solicitous of everyone, that this 'drove her crazy', and that the spaced-out state of mind seemed to take her over shortly afterwards. This spaced-out state of mind was familiar from previous work in the analysis. It usually meant that she had lost contact with her inner world – her thoughts and emotions. But beyond this general assessment, nothing emerged.

In the following session, however, she reported a dream in which *she was about to have sexual intercourse with a man she loves, when she noticed that there was a child in the room. It seemed to be about one and a half or two years old – she wasn't sure. Just as her lover was about to penetrate her, she found she could not let him with the child in the room.* She awoke at this point, fell asleep again and had the same dream. This time *she was turned away from the child, attempting to ignore it, but the same thing happened again: the child's presence played on her mind and stopped her love-making.*

In the third session of the week, she said that she found herself spacing out again the previous night, as she had during the weekend seminar. This occurred while she had been talking to a friend about a historian whose views on Athenian democracy she consciously believed she shared. She began to feel bored, and this led to the spaced-out feeling of detachment from herself. She said this was odd, because she had always been interested in the ideas that this author discusses. She had felt detached from herself since then. Her interest in the author's work was based on a feeling that his ideas led naturally to certain ideas of her own about the paradoxical co-existence of democracy and slavery in ancient Athens. The problem of an aristocratic slave-based system existing within a democracy was important to her because she felt it had practical implications for the race problem in the United States. In fact, she had recently thought of someday writing something that would bring the author's ideas together with hers – to show the harmony between them. But what emerged after some discussion (and considerable resistance) was that she was denying that the author was working very hard *not* to talk about the ideas that are so important to her, even when they appear to follow from what he is saying – that he is actually hostile to them. This surprised her greatly, but she realized it must be true, and after some reflection she said that she thought she was trying to eliminate some important differences between herself and the author to avoid the possibility of conflict between herself and him because she admired much of what he had to say. She then realized that this is what annoyed her about her professor over the weekend – he wanted everyone at the seminar to be one big happy family, but in a crazy way. He seemed to feel responsible for bringing everyone into harmony and making them all comfortable with each other's views. The link between the weekend situation and the dream was now evident: in the dream her intercourse was stopped by her fear that it would cause a disharmonious relationship with the child. She was unable to let herself feel real passion for someone she loved because that would interfere with the requirement that she create one big family that brought the sexual couple together with the left-out child in a completely harmonious way, free of jealousy and envy. In the same way, she had muted her passion for her internal objects – the ideas and values she loved – in order to create a spurious harmony with the historian she admired.

In retrospect, we may see that she was doing in her dream what her professor had done at the seminar, and that she was driven by a need to maintain harmony, as she felt her professor was. This need for harmony revealed itself in a more subtle ways elsewhere in the analysis. This patient often identifies with my interpretations in a way that is often quite difficult to detect. While appearing to agree with them, she will bend their meaning slightly so that it becomes hard to distinguish them from what she was already conscious of. At the same time, she appears to make an effort to accommodate herself to some part of the interpretation – to make herself fit it. The result is something that sounds reasonable, but only in a superficial way. On other occasions, she will focus on some peripheral part of the interpretation, often quibbling about it so that the main point – the point that had really differed from what she consciously thought – gets lost. These maneuvers create a spurious like-mindedness between us. There is a feeling that she knows what I am talking about and agrees with it. I am left with a feeling that this may be true in a way, but that there is a way in which it is not true, that there is something in what I was saying that she didn't know, but it had gotten lost, and I was unable to pinpoint it. The result is that I am left feeling that I had been unable to establish proper contact with her, and was no longer in contact with myself. This is, of course, the symptom that plagues the patient, and that she describes as a spaced-out feeling. At this point, I had not only not cured the patient of her symptom, I had begun to acquire it myself. I had succumbed to the transference role of a like-minded, narcissistic good object.

I had been drawn into this state of mind by an aspect of her personality that wished to make us like-minded, so that differences and distinctions that might give rise to disharmonies in the analytic 'family' could be denied. This was, of course, my problem and not hers. That is, it was my problem that I had gotten drawn into. But her problem was related to mine: it was her tendency to draw me in, which was a problem for her because it had a profound effect on her mind. Her attempt to make me think like her was an acting-in that corresponded to what she had done in her mind to the author. With him, she had denied the aspect of his work or attitude that would have produced an unavoidable conflict with hers. In other words, she (mentally) disrupted his contact with some of his internal objects, the ideas or attitudes that were important to him because they conflicted with the ideas and attitudes that were important to her. But one could just as well say that her attempts at homogenization were a denial of the aspect of *her* work or attitude that would have made evident its conflict with his. Viewed from this perspective, she would be disrupting her contact with *her* internal objects. It was not that she knew what she thought, and that she felt the author's ideas agreed with hers because she had a delusion that the

121

author agreed with her. She was simply unable to think clearly in this area at all – she was unable to have a clear idea of what *either* of them thought.

Her attempt to be like-minded with the author – to be identified with him – requires a breaking of the passionate links that *both* of them have with their internal objects. She does this in her mind, of course, but while doing it to the author in her mind has no effect on his actual state of mind, doing it to herself in her mind has a profound effect. It prevents her from making proper contact with her internal objects. What I mean by proper contact with her internal objects is contact that is clear and passionate. This is what was represented by sexual penetration in the dream. But this kind of contact with one's internal objects – including ideas and values that one is passionate about – is also exclusive. It sets up a barrier between herself and her external objects, insofar as *their* internal objects – their cherished ideas and values – differ from hers.

Despite her desire to homogenize her ideas with mine so she may feel that they are really just extensions of each other, this patient is also very grateful when she feels that I have been able to make an interpretation with enough clarity and conviction to make it obvious that it is not something she already knows. My conviction arises, I believe, from my being able to establish a clear enough contact with my unconscious as it is affected by her unconscious projections and communications. This is *not* precisely the same as like-minded contact with her, and this is a critical point. It is contact with an aspect of myself – my unconscious commitment to psychoanalysis – that enables me to make proper analytic contact with her. The confusion that she draws me into as part of her resistance interrupts the solid contact with my internal objects that I require to make proper analytic contact with her. She is aware (thought not always consciously) that my ability to analyze her depends on my being in contact with something in myself, and that this contact excludes her.

The situation I am trying to describe in the analysis would be well represented by picturing the analyst as a parental *couple*, a mother who receives the infant's (patient's) projections, but who is also in relation to a father, who prevents the projections from taking the receptive mother over. That is, the baby is able to *communicate* to the mother, but is not able to get inside her and fill her completely with its projections. To say the same thing in different terms, it is the mother's love for the father that establishes him as an internal object for her. Her love for the baby allows her to be receptive to it, and her love for the father as an internal object protects her from being dominated by the baby. (This is consistent with Britton's [1989] and Feldman's [1993] observations that the patient experiences the analyst being able to think on his own as an oedipal situation.)

The patient's dream was therefore also a portrayal of the situation in her analysis, where I am trying to establish contact with psychoanalysis as a loved internal object, while she attempts to interrupt this contact so she may homogenize us into a narcissistic 'good' object. The problem I face in the analysis, being in contact with her without losing my own mind, is parallel to her problem of being in contact with herself – having a mind of her own – while in contact with an external object. But I suspect that this is not just a problem of hers, or of mine when I am trying to analyze her, but a problem in all object relationships.

The next day, she began her session by saying that she felt much better. She now found herself feeling quite angry with the author. This anger seemed to be due to an appreciation of the differences between her and the author, and specifically to a new awareness of his hostility to ideas and values that are very important to her. She then related a dream in which *she was given a box by an old friend whose face had always 'looked much younger than his age'. He warned her that the box contained scorpions, but when she accidentally dropped it, she found that it was actually full of harmless spiders instead. The sight of them crawling all over the carpet 'made her itch'. She tried to blow them into a corner, in an attempt to gather them back into the box, but without success. Then someone said they were dangerous and must be burned. There was a fiery explosion and she ran away, fearing that her nightgown, flowing behind her, had caught fire and that she would burn.* She associated the spiders to a recent family gathering, where two or three babies were crawling on the carpet. She said she was distressed when she realized that the babies' mothers were ignoring them, so they could talk to each other.

In this dream, the baby-faced friend represents the aspect of herself that drives her crazy – the child of the first dream that interrupts her contact with her internal and external objects. It presents itself in this dream as a powerful and dangerous scorpion (i.e., as a scorpion that she *feels* is powerful and danger-ous). When she realizes that it is really a harmless crawler, associated to a neglected baby, she tries to put it back in its place. But there is an explosion apparently connected to a resurgence of the feeling that the baby is dangerous. The result-ing fire threatens to burn her nightgown, and her along with it.

The scorpion's sting was connected to the pang of (perverse) guilt that my patient felt in the first dream over exposing the child to adult sexuality – that is, over presenting the narcissistic aspect of herself with a creative analytic couple that it could not homogenize itself with. When she recognized in the previous session how destructive this homogenization can be to her contact with herself, she was able to overcome the perverse guilt (perhaps more accurately a sense of persecution about being sane), and the scorpion once more became just a left-out, harmless spider-baby. But the baby, as if enraged by her progress in detaching herself from it, then counterattacks with a fire-storm, a form of attack that is again directed against her sexuality (the nightgown). Her sexuality, as we have seen from the first dream, is connected to her ability to make contact with herself, to think and have insight. It is important to see that from the point of view of the patient's unconscious, this attack is real and very dangerous, and that she lives in very real terror of what the baby will do to her if she has passionate links with her internal or external objects. Behind the superficially warm ambience of the narcissistic union lies the threat of great violence against those who refuse to participate in it.

I felt that the scorpion/arsonist also represented an aspect of herself that she felt was able to put a stop to her actual parents' sexuality. When I interpreted this aspect of her dream, she was interested, but unmoved, which was not surprising because she was not conscious of ever having felt jealous of her parents' sexual relationship, never having consciously believed there was much to be jealous about. A few weeks later, however, she had another dream in which *she saw her mother emerge from a room, shirtless, with a man who placed his hand on her bare breast. The patient 'got hysterical and threw a fit', yelling and screaming at her mother for 'betraying her father'. Later in the dream, she tells her father of the betrayal, but he seems oddly philosophical about it.* In her associations, his sang-froid raised her suspicion that the man with whom her mother committed her act of betrayal was the father himself (disguised as someone else in line with her denial that her parents were ever passionate with each other) and the betrayal over which she became so upset was a betrayal of the patient herself: her mother's feeding breast (which she could feel was all hers) becoming a sexual breast (which she could not feel was all hers). The violence of her reaction, which was what impressed the patient most of all about the dream, corresponds to the fire-bombing in the last dream.

The patient was very struck by her reaction in this dream. She had not recalled ever having such strong feelings about her mother's sexuality, but now she felt they were unmistakable. But in all likelihood her oedipal feelings were now *less* violent than they were in the past, when they had actually succeeded in eliminating her awareness of her parents' sexuality altogether. We might say that she had emerged from her narcissistic identification with her parents, and was able to experience her oedipal jealousy. But we could also say that, by virtue of her now being able to experience her mother as having a sexual relationship with a father that excluded her, she had been able to emerge from a narcissistic identification with a desexualized mother (i.e., one that could be all hers) so that her mother could now become a proper object – an object distinct from herself – that she could be jealous *of*. Her emergence *into* an oedipal (three-person) situation seems to coincide precisely with her emergence *out of* a narcissistic (pseudo-one-person) relationship.

10.3 Discussion

To summarize my main points so far: in the transference, the patient unconsciously identifies the analyst with what he has projected into him, creating what Strachey called an external phantasy object. This is a narcissistic object relationship, in which the object is confused with a part of the self, as distinct from what might be called a proper object relationship, in which the object is experienced as distinct from the self. In the intimate rapport of the analytic session, the analyst tends to identify with these projections as well, which brings him into a relationship with the patient that compliments the patient's narcissistic object relationship with him. The analyst's identification with the patient's projections is a type of pathology of his receptivity to the patient. It is based on the analyst's tendency to confuse the patient with *his* internal objects – to make the patient into an external phantasy object of *his* (I will elaborate on this point shortly). It is exacerbated by the patient's skill at producing states of mind in the analyst that the analyst is supposed to identify with. He exercises this skill by manipulating the analyst's relationships with his internal objects.

Insofar as the analyst is able to distance himself from the patient's projections, he is in a position to interpret them. The analyst's ability to do this depends on his having links to his internal objects that survive the patient's projections and his unconscious manipulations. Especially important is his link to psychoanalysis as a good internal object, since it is this link that allows him to treat the patient's projections as objects of knowledge, and hence to interpret them. These interpretations make the patient aware that he and the analyst are separate. They also make the patient aware that the analyst has a link to internal objects that have not been controlled by the patient's attempts to make the analyst into an external phantasy object. I argue that these two 'awarenesses' are really the same – that to say that the patient is aware the analyst is separate from him and to say that the patient is aware that the analyst has relationships with his own internal objects that are immune from the patient's projections is really just saying the same thing in two different ways.

If merger or identification with an object means denying that it has a mind of its own, that it has as part of its very nature *proper* links with other objects that exclude us, then emergence into the depressive position must involve acknowledgment of the object's sovereign internal object relationships. And if awareness of these relationships places the patient in a triangular situation in the transference, then emergence into the depressive position is the same as accepting one's position in the oedipal situation. This conclusion is in agreement with Britton (1989), who described a patient for whom 'any move of mine towards that which by another person would have been called objectivity could not be tolerated. We were to move along a single line and meet at a single point.' It was consequently intolerable to feel that her analyst was communing with himself about her. When he demonstrated that he had been by describing her in analytic terms, she became violent, and later, when she was able to express her feeling in words, did so by demanding that he 'stop that fucking thinking!'

I would like to conclude with an observation about what I have called the pathology of the analyst's receptiveness to the patient's projections. I said above that the analyst's identification with the patient's projections is determined by two factors. One is the patient's skill at manipulating the analyst's state of mind, or more precisely, the analyst's internal object relationships. The other is the degree to which the analyst's mind provides fertile ground for this type of manipulation. This second factor seems to depend on the degree to which the analyst is engaged in trying to manipulate the *patient's* internal object relationships.

The most common way in which the analyst does this is by attempting to 'cure' the patient (Chapter 3). Here I am distinguishing curing the patient from analyzing him: a cure is based on manipulation of the patient's internal object relationships – or, if you prefer, his mental structure – into a configuration that the analyst deems healthy or desirable. The analyst who is trying to 'cure' the patient is acting the part of the patient's archaic superego, making the patient feel that certain of his internal object relationships are 'good', and that others are 'bad' and therefore in need of alteration. Analysis is based strictly on describing the patient's internal object relationships to him, without trying to alter them.

The crucial difference is that by doing analysis and refraining from attempts to 'cure' the patient, the analyst is recognizing that the patient has a mind of *his* own. This means that he has succeeded in removing himself from a paranoid-schizoid object relationship with the patient, in which no one really has a mind of their own, and one feels that one can invade and control the mind of one's objects, and also feels that they can do the same in return. If the analyst can adopt this attitude (and regain it over and over when he loses it, as he inevitably does under the pressure of his countertransference), his work will manifest a deep respect for the patient's internal object world – a deep awareness of who the patient is and isn't and who the analyst is and isn't. This type of respect tends to foster in the patient both a sense of freedom or separateness from his objects, and its corollary, a sense of responsibility for himself. Together these two senses help him to have a mind of his own.

— 11 —

On alpha function*

11.1 Introduction

It is possible to regard Bion's theory of the container as a kind of inter-personal dreaming: the patient unconsciously projects what Bion called beta elements (which are themselves by definition incapable of being meaningful or even being thought about) into the unconscious mind of the analyst (using what Bion called realistic projective identification), following which the analyst, through the use of what Bion called alpha function, converts the projected beta elements into what he called alpha elements. These alpha elements, according to Bion, are something like latent dream-thoughts – they are such stuff as dreams are made of.

The alpha elements that have newly formed in the analyst's mind as a result of his processing the patient's projections through his alpha function act as something like the latent content of a dream. The analyst may then 'have' the dream that the patient can't have. By having this dream, the analyst is in a position to become vicariously conscious of the contents of the patient's unconscious – contents that the patient is unable to be conscious of, or even unconscious of, since, while in the patient, these contents were still in the form of beta elements, which Bion felt could not hold any conscious or unconscious meaning. They are quite literally unthinkable. (It is important to keep in mind that Bion was trying to understand phenomena that are essentially psychotic. The clinical experiences that stimulated his theorizing were with psychotic patients, and beta elements are thrown up by the psychotic aspect of the personality.) So in this sense the analyst derives his interpretation from a 'dream' that he has under the impact of the patient's projections – a joint dream.

---

* This is a revised version of a paper presented at a panel on 'Interpretação: Revelação ou Criação?', as part of the symposium 'Bion em São Paulo: Ressonâncias', sponsored by the Sociedade Brasileira de Psicanálise de São Paulo, November 14, 1996.

The patient's role in this process is to contribute beta elements – mental contents that he is himself incapable of dreaming or thinking about. The analyst's role is to convert these beta elements into alpha elements which, according to Bion, are not themselves thoughts or dreams, but something with the potential to become thoughts or dreams with all their emotional ramifications. Once this conversion is complete, the analyst returns to the patient the alpha element. The net result of this process is that the patient is rendered capable of having an emotional experience – a dream or a thought – of which he was previously incapable. Note that the analyst's interpretation does not give the patient an emotional experience *per se*, but only renders him capable of experiencing something he was literally incapable of experiencing before.

The analyst's function then is to receive the patient's beta elements – mental contents that for the patient are unthinkable and un-experienceable – and convert them to a form in which they are thinkable and experienceable. (Whether the patient does think, experience or dream them is beyond the analyst's scope. He relies on something in the patient that is inclined to do so.) What is the nature of the transformation that the analyst performs?

There are two important differences between alpha elements and beta elements. The first is that alpha elements are capable of carrying and transmitting meaning, while beta elements are incapable of doing so. The second is that, while beta elements cannot link up with one another or with anything else, alpha elements can cohere or link with each other.

Bion leaves the specific nature of beta elements, alpha elements and alpha function deliberately unclear: he was not trying to arrive at a specific theory of the psychoanalysis of psychotic phenomena. He was trying to outline a theory that would serve as a sort of prolegomenon to a specific theory or theories. One of the things I will try to do in this chapter is fill in some of the area circumscribed by Bion's theory of alpha function.

In Bion's outline, alpha function is simply something that is supposed to convert beta elements – unthinkable mental contents that cannot be connected with each other – into alpha elements – thinkable mental contents that *can* be connected with each other. But we might be able to learn something about the precise nature of alpha function if we consider what we might mean by thinkable (a property of alpha elements) and unthinkable (a property of beta elements), what the difference between them is, and how something unthinkable might be converted into something thinkable.

11.2 Alpha elements

To begin with, what do we mean when we say that something is 'unthinkable'? I don't believe that we mean anything like 'too terrible to contemplate', as it would if we were to say that modern weapons have made all-out warfare be-

tween nuclear powers unthinkable, or that a traumatic experience is too terrifying or painful to be thought about. It seems to me that this way of looking at
it misjudges the problem that Bion was trying to understand with his theory of
alpha function. He was trying to understand situations in which certain things
could not be thought about, not because of the painful affects accompanying
them, but because thinking itself had become impossible: *the very apparatus for
thinking was not working. This is simply a way of saying that the theory of alpha
function is concerned with psychotic, rather than neurotic, phenomena.*

What Bion himself tells us is that alpha elements, whatever they are, are
meaningful, while beta elements, whatever they are, are not, and that alpha
elements can connect with each other (perhaps like atoms linking together in
specific ways to form molecules), while beta elements cannot (perhaps like the
atoms of inert gases, destined forever to remain solitary). This sounds as though
meaningfulness and thinkability in the senses in which Bion was using them are
connected to connections, that an idea is meaningful if it can be connected to
other ideas. This corresponds, of course, to a common-sense idea of meaningfulness, in which we learn the meaning of something by noting how it is used,
and what it is used in connection with. If we didn't know what cathode-ray
tubes were, we could learn by observing that they are placed in television sets
and computer monitors and that, when the devices are turned on, we see an
image forming on the faces of the cathode-ray tubes, which is why they are
commonly called picture tubes. But if we *really* want to understand what a
cathode-ray tube is, we would have to make other connections, which would
perhaps lead us into the theories of electrical fields, of the electron, fluorescence,
excited states of atoms, quantum mechanics, and so on. In other words, an
infinite network of connections. We learn the meaning of words in a similar way.
When we look up the definition of a word in the dictionary, we are seeing the
other words that the lexicographer has connected it to. But if we really want to
know what a word means in all its nuances, we must learn a whole language,
read its literature, listen to everyday speech, and so on *ad infinitum*.

The idea that an idea is meaningful if it is connected to other ideas has been
elaborated in a more rigorous way by Quine (1961), who has argued that, at
least in the empirical arena, an idea is meaningful *only* by virtue of its being
connected to other ideas. Quine holds that one cannot appreciate the meaning
of any idea in a complete sense unless one takes into account its connections
with all other ideas. He therefore held (p. 41) that the smallest unit of empirical
significance is not a concept, but rather an entire body of knowledge. No idea
is an island, entire of itself. (John Donne [1571–1631]: 'No man is an Island,
entire of itself; every man is a piece of the Continent, a part of the main.')

It seems to me that it makes sense to assume that an idea is meaningful – that
is, potentially thinkable – if it is a member of an interconnected community of
ideas. Such ideas can be defined in terms of how they fit in with other ideas (an
example of a system for doing this is Bion's grid [Bion 1963]), and their truth

or falsity can also be evaluated by examining their connections to other ideas. (This is the sense of the physicist Arthur Eddington's puckish warning that 'we must never accept a new observation until it has been carefully checked against existing theory'.) A meaningful or intelligible idea would then be one that is susceptible to critical thought, or, in other words, susceptible to being placed into some context in which it may be evaluated. This is consistent with Bion's idea that alpha elements are both meaningful and connected to other alpha elements, whereas beta elements are both meaningless and unconnectable.

In fact, he used the idea that alpha elements can connect with one another when he devised the idea of an alpha screen, which is simply a network composed of interconnected alpha elements. He felt that something like this alpha screen forms the boundary between the conscious and the unconscious parts of the mind. I think that what he had in mind here was not just something that separates the conscious from the unconscious in the topographical or descriptive sense, but something that separates what Freud called the system Ucs. from the system Cs., which are two very different *forms* of mental life that operate according to very different rules. According to Freud (1915, p. 186), 'there is in [the system Ucs.] no negation, no doubt, no degrees of certainty … there are only contents … '

Bion described the alpha screen as a sort of contact-barrier (a term he borrowed from Freud's *Project for a Scientific Psychology*). The alpha elements cohere to form a barrier that separates conscious from unconscious, while at the same time permitting some kind of contact between the two. It permits this contact by creating consciously representable derivatives of unconscious contents, which, while they may themselves still be unconscious, can at least be *represented* consciously, for example, in the way in which the (unconscious) latent content of a dream may be represented in the dream's manifest content.

We might note in passing that this contact-barrier is like Segal's (1957) notion of the capacity to form symbols. If symbolic function is intact, one may make conscious symbolic contact with one's unconscious, while the unconscious itself remains unconscious. We recall that Bion called the activity or capacity in the mind that converted meaningless beta elements into meaningful alpha elements the alpha function. But alpha function is precisely what the alpha screen does. This suggests that alpha function is something that a network of ideas – that is, a group of ideas that are actually or potentially connected to each other – is able to do.

We have now arrived at the notion of a network of meaningful ideas whose meaning depends on their being linked with each other. This network is connected to alpha function. Bion, as we know, used the ideas of alpha elements, beta elements and alpha function not just as part of his theory of the analytic process – the container and the contained – but also as part of his theory of thinking. The analyst's alpha function is an interpersonal version of the process that Bion believed was required if normal dreaming were to be possible. In the intrapersonal version, an unthinkable mental content (a beta element) must be converted within the mind of the dreamer (or thinker) by his alpha function into an alpha element which is then dreamable or thinkable. Bion believed that when the analyst performs alpha function on the beta elements that the patient has projected into him, he is doing something like what he does in his own mind as a prerequisite for dreaming or thinking.

11.3 Beta elements

The effect of the analyst's alpha function is to convert the patient's beta elements which are not suitable for dreaming or thinking, into alpha elements, the material that is suitable for dreaming and thinking. While we can say what a thought or a dream is clinically, what is the clinical significance of something that is not capable of being thought about? I suggest that what corresponds to this clinically are delusions. Someone in the grip of a delusion cannot think about it, which is why they are in its grip. A delusion is not an ordinary wish, phantasy or thought, but something experienced as quite concretely real. What makes a delusion a delusion is that its reality may not be questioned or subjected to critical thought. (Again, compare Freud [1915, p. 186]: 'The nucleus of the Ucs. consists of instinctual representatives which seek to discharge their cathexis; that is to say, it consists of wishful impulses ... there is in this system no negation, no doubt, no degrees of certainty ... there are only contents.' These contents, in other words, are all absolutely 'true' in and of themselves, they have no connections with one another or with anything else, and cannot even contradict one another.)

Roger Money-Kyrle (1968) has argued that the task of analysis is precisely to help the patient to recover from his unconscious delusions. A delusion by definition exists on its own. It is immune from the kind of connection with other ideas that permits it to be thought about in a critical manner. A delusion *is* an island, entire unto itself. In this sense, it has a narcissistic or autistic character.

The task of correcting it obviously requires means other than ordinary critical thought. A delusion is not simply a false belief, it is a false belief that is clung to in the face of contradictory evidence as a result of emotional forces. Correcting it requires an analysis of its roots. But this analysis of the unconscious roots of a delusion implies that it *has* roots, which must be connections to other ideas. Since a delusion by definition has no connections to other ideas, the idea of analyzing a delusion would seem to be a contradiction. This apparent contradiction is resolved by noting that the delusion is absolute and rootless only from the point of view of the person who is held in its grip. From the analyst's point of view, it is a belief that arises from certain motivations in the patient, which is what we mean by its roots. The difference, of course, is that in the analyst's mind, the patient's delusional idea is an alpha element: he has in mind a *representation*

131

of the patient's delusion, which permits him to know it is a delusion, while in the patient's mind the delusion is a beta element – simply a delusion.

I can illustrate this point with some vignettes taken from the analysis of a fourteen-year-old girl (this example is taken from Caper 1981) who was hospitalized for treatment of drug abuse and life-threatening depression. Following her eventual discharge from the hospital, she continued her analysis as an office patient for a total of three years.

During the first six months of treatment, she arrived at sessions late, left early, shouted me down and attempted escapes from the hospital, which forced the hospital staff into restraining her instead of using their considerable ability and willingness to understand her. Alternatively, she would become docile and well mannered, a 'model child' (as she had been when she was little), while secretly violating some major hospital rule, usually after recruiting other patients in the effort, and feeling great triumph when she got away with it. When these activities were discovered, however, her triumph quickly turned to terror.

The power this secretly triumphant aspect of her personality had over her was seen in the transference in a session during the sixth month of her analysis, when I made an interpretation connecting her secret triumph over the hospital staff and myself, representing her parents, with her subsequent fear of them. She became quite confused, in contrast to the usual clarity of her thinking, despite the fact that the interpretation itself was quite simple and straightforward. Since there was plenty of evidence for the interpretation, I suggested that she felt the interpretation was correct, which made her aware of her dependence on me as a source of correct information about herself. This led the part of her personality that was addicted to being triumphant to mangle her ability to think and be aware of what was correct.

She reacted to this further interpretation with anger and contempt. The following day, however, after I announced that I would be taking a week's vacation later in the month, she became acutely depressed and lamented that all she ever loved was always getting lost.

This understanding of how strongly this triumphant part of her personality affected her, even to the point of depriving her of her ability to think, led her to a series of insights about how humiliated she felt (i.e., precisely the opposite of triumphant) if she was forced to wait for what she wanted.

At this point she began to express 'heartache' at the slowness of her progress. She associated this to a memory of suffering frustration at the hands of her mother, then kicking a soccer ball so hard she hurt her ankle, which slowed her progress when she tried to walk. I interpreted this as a communication about the part of her that kicks the mother and the analyst in her mind in response to frustration, leading to a bad internal relationship with them that slows her attempts to grow and causes heartache for having hurt someone she cares about. Her immediate response was to become offended, as though I had just assaulted her.

132

Her experience of the interpretation turned out to be that of a quite concretely dangerous assault. This was revealed a few months later, when she described a 'crazy guy' whose car she had bumped in a parking lot, causing no visible damage. He accused her of 'gashing' his car, chased her and actually dented hers. I connected this to her reaction to the interpretation concerning her heartache, saying that it must have made her feel guilty, that she experienced the interpretation as a very damaging assault, and that the only thing she could do with it was assault me back with it by making me feel that I had done the injury. She responded by saying, in such a sad and thoughtful way that it was painful to hear, that she didn't see how doctors could stand to treat people who were dying. I told her that this was an expression of appreciation for the difficulties that her parents and I had to tolerate in order to help her, including having to face the realization that she may never recover. This was the first definite sign of her coming into contact with the pain she caused others.

I believe that what had happened when she began to be able to experience concern for her objects and the 'heartache' and guilt that ensued, as part and parcel of this process, was that her omnipotent belief – her delusion – that the interpretations were attacks on her was replaced by an awareness that this was only an *idea* of hers, and furthermore an idea that she could consider critically, and think of as something that might be incorrect and even damaging.

A representation of an omnipotent wish or delusion, unlike the delusion itself, can be placed in the context of, or linked with, other ideas, or, in other words, be thought about in a critical manner. This suggests that we may regard beta elements as unconscious delusions. Alpha function would then act through rooting delusions, which are absolute, narcissistic and *sui generis*, in a network of ideas. Alpha function converts an isolated belief, unconnected to other beliefs and immune to their effects, into an idea that can be linked to other ideas. Alpha function does something to beta elements that renders them linkable into the network or community of ideas that Bion called the alpha screen, where, by virtue of their being part of this network, their meaning can be defined and examined (and their validity determined).

11.4 Beta elements and countertransference

A projected beta element, until it is subjected to alpha function, acts in the recipient's mind like an unconscious delusion, with all the emotional compulsion and intellectual restriction that this implies. When we speak of the patient projecting beta elements into the analyst, we are speaking of the patient using projective identification to create a sort of induced unconscious delusion in the analyst. This induced delusion is the unconscious component of the analyst's countertransference. That is, when the patient projects beta elements into the analyst's mind (prior to their being worked on by the analyst's alpha function), he produces in the analyst a countertransference, the mark of which is a loss of his ability to think critically. This is a kind of intellectual deterioration in the analyst that we are all familiar with, and that we become aware of through the experience of having made an interpretation after considerable work, and then, having made it, seeing that it's so obvious that we can't understand why it wasn't obvious to us to begin with. It is as though we had just recovered from an acute deterioration of our intelligence, that had prevented us from seeing what is now clearly the case (for an example of this, see the clinical illustration given in Chapter 4, and more extensively in Chapter 7). This deterioration is a sign that the analyst had been in the grip of what we would call in Bionian terms an unprocessed beta element.

In the case mentioned above, I would, at certain times, begin to feel guilty over the 'needless' restrictions that the treatment was placing on a young patient's life, and the suffering that resulted from them. I felt an urge to shorten or even abandon the treatment on the grounds that it was too much of an imposition on an adolescent. I might have rationalized this at certain points on the ground that she had made considerable improvement already, which may have been quite true, however irrelevant to the issue of a stable recovery.

An analyst in the grip of an unprocessed beta element feels a compulsion to *act* on the patient. This action is something intended to generate a certain state of mind in the patient, an activity similar to what the patient did in projecting the beta element in the first place. It represents a re-evacuation of the beta element (which, unless it is subjected to alpha function, is the only thing he can do with it).

In this instance, it turned out that she was inducing guilt in me in the countertransference instead of experiencing her own guilt over the damage that her behavior was doing to her objects and her mind. The temptation here was to evade the guilt by doing something to the patient: to create an image of myself in her mind as a 'good' (meaning compliant) object with whom she could have a 'positive' relationship, instead of tolerating it long enough to realize that it was delusional and to understand what made it so. This is similar to the clinical problem I described in Chapter 4.

The way in which the analyst generates a state of mind in the patient is through the use of a pseudo-interpretation. Bion made a most interesting and important observation about psychoanalytic interpretation when he said that an interpretation is the precise opposite of propaganda. Pseudo-interpretations are marked by their tendency to make the patient feel a certain way about himself, in much the same manner as effective propaganda can make one feel what the propagandist wants one to feel. (This may be seen most readily in non-analytic forms of psychotherapy (even those cloaked in analytic terminology), which depend on this kind of action for their therapeutic effect.) We may note that here the analyst would be inducing a state of mind in the patient about which the patient is not supposed to be able to think critically, that is, a state of mind similar to the countertransference that the patient has induced in the analyst. The force behind this induced state of mind, whether it is the patient inducing it in the analyst, or vice versa, is the same as the force behind propaganda: a kind or moral bullying and/or seduction.

The analyst's only other option is to convert the beta element he has received into an alpha element by exercising his alpha function. The analyst's alpha function converts this unconscious delusion into a representable form, that is, a form that can be represented in the process of thinking or dream work. A representation of something – even of a delusion – is merely an idea that one can think about critically. If the analyst has been able to exercise his alpha function successfully, he will be able to think about or know something about the induced delusion he was in the grip of. This loosens the grip of the patient's projections on his mind, and allows his mind to get a grip on them instead.

He is now in a position in which he can begin to formulate a proper interpretation. How does he know when he has arrived at an interpretation, that is, how does he know when the countertransference has been adequately transformed? One of the ways in which he might know is connected to the fact that, while a pseudo-interpretation has the propagandistic effect of making the patient feel that he should think or be a certain way, a real interpretation does not. It is nothing more than a bare, evenhanded description of the patient's unconscious psychic reality. An interpretation should convey no more exhortation or suggestion about what the patient should feel or do than a line call in tennis. The linesman should simply report on whether the ball looked in or out from his point of view, with no claim to omniscience, and with no implication of what it *should* have been. The impact that a good interpretation has on a patient is partly due to the fact that it *is* so free of exhortation, a fact that contributes to its being such a unique way of talking about intimate matters.

Another way in which the analyst can know that he has arrived at a real interpretation is connected to Bion's observation that an interpretation should describe something 'obvious [to the analyst] but unobserved [by the patient]'. The reason that something about the patient is obvious enough to be detected by the analyst, but unobserved by the patient is not that the analyst is especially perceptive or intellectually acute, but because the patient is especially *un*perceptive in the area needing to be interpreted. The patient's lack of perceptiveness is connected to his being in the grip of his own unconscious delusions, which makes critical, perceptive thought about them impossible. The analyst's perceptiveness (when it arrives) is a product of his having freed himself of the delusions that the patient's beta elements tend to produce in him, through the use of his alpha function to convert them from delusions into mere representations of delusions, which are something that he can think perceptively about.

The analyst's transformation of the delusion that the patient has induced in him into something he can think about and interpret is what Bion meant by containment. Containment is the opposite of the state of mind the analyst is in

135

when in the grip of a countertransference (or projected beta elements): when the analyst has successfully contained the patient's projections, he is able to think clearly about his own state of mind and does not feel the urge to alter the patient's. ('One should let the patient work on one's mind until one is *about* to do something to the patient, then not do it, but analyze the impulse to do it instead, and use this analysis as the basis of an interpretation' [A. A. Mason, personal communication]. See also Chapter 3.)

The analyst *hopes* that the interpretation will eventually diminish the patient's anxiety (or produce it when it is inappropriately absent), but he cannot allow his interpretation to be distorted in an attempt to *make* the patient less (or more) anxious. Anything in the interpretation that causes it to deviate from a mere description of the patient's unconscious psychic reality makes it less of an interpretation, and more of something else, such as an attempt to manipulate the patient's mind.

To summarize: beta elements are ideas that are simultaneously meaningless (in the sense of being incapable of being thought about) and extremely potent. This makes their meaninglessness rather peculiar: it is not the same as the meaninglessness of a series of random sounds or gestures, since literal non-sense has no impact on the mind of the recipient, while beta elements have a very powerful impact on the recipient. They act as a kind of hypnotic suggestion, as foreign bodies in the mind that are *sui generis* and therefore not susceptible to criticism by other members of a community of ideas, since they are part of no community. This gives them the absolute quality, the immunity from skeptical criticism, that characterizes delusions. Both their power and their meaninglessness are consequences of what we might call their narcissistic character, the fact that they exist as absolute ideas, unconnected to and unaffected by other ideas. The source of their 'meaninglessness' (that is, their insusceptibility to critical thought) is also the source of their power.

Alpha elements *are* meaningful, and are linkable with one another. Their meaningfulness is a consequence of their links with one another. But because they are not absolute, but only members of a community of ideas, their impact on the mind is less absolute in itself, and more connected to their connections with other alpha elements. An idea that can combine with other ideas can also be evaluated in terms of other ideas. Its validity is *relative* to that of other ideas. Alpha function converts unconscious delusions that grip the mind into unconscious ideas that the mind can get a grip on. It reduces omnipotent wishes, which are indistinguishable from indisputable facts, to mere wishes. The exercise of alpha function requires one to work to recover one's wits from the effect that beta elements have on them. This is not done easily, and it exposes one to a certain psychological danger. The emotional forces behind the delusion are obviously quite powerful – one must have a real emotional investment in one's delusions, or they wouldn't have such power – and withstanding them is always associated with anxiety and dis-equilibration.

A delusion is a kind of sacred cow, and it is clung to with religious conviction. The forces militating against the conversion of a delusion into an ordinary criticizable thought therefore take the form of moral pressure; one feels as though one were committing a sacrilege. The psychoanalyst who is analyzing a delusion is exposed to the opposition not only of the patient's archaic superego (the source of the moralistic pressure), but to his own as well.

To be able to think in such circumstances, one must emerge from being dominated by moralistic considerations into a state of mind where ideas can be considered in a realistic manner without fear of moral censure for doing so. I believe that this emergence is the *clinical* meaning of Bion's idea of alpha function. Bion was a tank commander in France during the First World War. Because the visibility from within a tank was severely restricted in those days, it was necessary for the commander to walk in front of the tank, guiding the driver with gestures. He was therefore exposed directly to enemy fire, and if he was hit and fell, ran a substantial risk of being run over by his own tank (Bion 1982). The psychoanalyst, like the First World War tank commander, exposes himself openly to the fire of the patient's archaic superego, and if he is hit, runs the risk of also being crushed by his own. He must try to do this without panicking.

12

A theory of the container*

12.1 Introduction

12.1.1 *Freudian repression and Kleinian splitting and projection*

Bion's theory of the container is based on the observation that certain states of mind are inherently unbearable. This does not mean that they are merely painful, frightening or difficult, but literally incapable of being borne in the mind. This observation is hardly new. Freud made it more than 100 years ago, and formulated his theory of repression to explain what happens to states of mind that cannot be borne.

In Freud's theory, intolerable states of mind are disposed of by being divorced from consciousness and repressed into the unconscious, where they take on a life of their own. Once repressed, a thought is no longer subject to the rules that govern conscious, rational thought: it is immune from contradiction by other thoughts and from the corrective effects of subsequent experience. A repressed thought nonetheless continues to exert an impact on the mind, the power of which stems precisely from the fact that it has been repressed and thereby removed from the moderating influences of conscious ideas and perceptions (Freud 1915; Gardner 1993).

Repression damages the ego by removing what would otherwise have been an idea from its domain, leaving only what Freud called a thing-representation (*Dingvorstellung*) that affects the ego, but cannot be evaluated (thought about) by it in the light of other ideas and experiences because it lacks the capacity to be linked with other ideas and experiences. (Freud thought that this was because the thing-representation could not be linked with words.) Today, we would be

---

* This is a revised version of a paper presented at *Sympósio Commemorativo: W.R. Bion 100 Anos* sponsored by the Sociedade Brasileira de Psicanálise de Rio de Janeiro, November 21, 1997.

more inclined to speak not of thing-representations, but of omnipotent unconscious phantasies, i.e., phantasies that are experienced not as phantasies, but as concretely real entities, and are isolated from contact with experience that might contradict them. This state of affairs distinguishes pathological repression (in Freud's terminology) from normal repression; normally repressed experiences are not experienced as concretely real, and are not isolated from contact with other emotional experiences and beliefs, but are connected to them through the process of symbol formation.

Bion's theory of the container shares certain elements with Freud's theory of repression, but its most direct roots are found in Melanie Klein's theory of splitting and projection. Where Freud believed that intolerable thoughts are pushed into the unconscious, Klein emphasized the projection of intolerable parts of the self into an object. This process also involves a splitting of the ego, followed by projection of the part of the ego that is attached to (i.e., values) the idea as well. As a result of splitting and projection, both the idea and the part of the personality that has an emotional link to it are attributed to the object. No matter how phantastic the attribution of an aspect of one's personality to the object might be, the projector nonetheless believes in his projections, unconsciously if not consciously.

Klein's emphasis on projection into an object does not imply a contradiction with Freud's emphasis on repression into the unconscious. One of the ways of rendering an attribute of oneself unconscious of oneself is precisely by attributing it to an object in place of oneself. In this case, the object functions as a receptacle in the same way as Freud's repressed unconscious. Klein's notion of splitting and projection fleshes out one aspect of Freud's notion of pathogenic repression by taking into account the role of the object, or at least of one's phantasies about the object, in the process of rendering something unconscious.

Splitting off and projecting an unbearable part of the personality into an object damages or impoverishes both one's personality (due to the fact that a part of the personality that we cannot bear may nonetheless contain valuable attributes), and one's object relationships (by creating an unbearable object). The type of splitting and projection that leads to confusion between what belongs to the self and what to the object is characteristic of a paranoid-schizoid object relationship. Many authors, especially in Latin America, refer to this as the schizo-paranoid position, a terminology which gives precedence to splitting, and characterizes the paranoia as a secondary phenomenon. This usage better describes the actual chain of events, since the unbearable, persecuting object is *created* by the splitting off and projection of unbearable aspects of the self into an object.

Another consequence of the view that what is projected is an unbearable aspect of the personality, and that what it is projected *into* is an object, is that the formation of unconscious omnipotent phantasies is no longer an individual matter, as is the case in Freudian pathological repression. Since these unconscious phantasies are about the patient's present-day objects, they therefore have

139

a real impact on one's relationship to the object, which means that the object is inevitably involved in splitting and projection.

This involvement of the object is a complex matter. Strictly speaking, splitting and projection are only unconscious phantasies that an aspect of one's personality can be extruded from the personality and relocated in an object. But the phantasy is very often accompanied by behavior calculated to evoke the projected state of mind in reality in the object. There is now a sizable and growing literature on the specific and accurate evocation of a state of mind in another, beginning with the work of Paula Heimann (1950) and Heinrich Racker (1968). Rather than attempt to review it, I will only say that there need be nothing mysterious or telepathic about the patient's capacity to actually evoke a given state of mind in the analyst, even though it may require a great deal of careful investigation to elucidate the precise way in which it is done.

Bion called this phenomenon realistic projective identification. The fact that projective identification has a realistic component means that the capacity to split off and project an aspect of one's personality into an object requires a certain degree of (usually unconscious) compliance on the part of the object. Realistic projective identification is a circumscribed *folie à deux*. This means that the 'success' of realistic projective identification depends not only on the state of mind of the projector (as it would if the projection were completely phantastic), but also on the object's state of mind. One of the consequences of this is that the object's state of mind can affect the subject's use of projective identification, and hence his state of mind. This was the launching point for Bion's work on the container.

According to Bion, the 'realistic' projection of states of mind that are unbearable for the projector creates the possibility that they might still be borne by the mind of another, who receives them, converts them into a form that is more bearable ('detoxifies' them) and returns the more bearable form to the personality from which they originated. This interaction constitutes a means whereby the process of splitting of the personality and projection into an object may be reversed: splitting and projection becomes introjection and integration. This conclusion has obvious implications for the possibility of therapeutic influence. This is the theory of the container.

Bion called the ability of the object to convert unbearable states of mind into bearable ones by the non-committal terms 'alpha function' or 'containment'. He went on to suggest that the personality to which the formerly unbearable state of mind is returned after modification by an external object not only introjects the modified state of mind, but also introjects the *function* of the external container at the same time. It is not clear from his account whether the function of the container is simply introjected, or whether it already exists, in however rudimentary a form, in the mind of the patient. Certainly, in the case of anyone who has developed any capacity at all to bear emotional states, an internal container function must be present. In this case, what we call containment would amount only to the analyst supporting or defending a process already inherent in the mind of the patient.

In any event, the experience of being contained by an external object either causes or reinforces the capacity for *self*-containment. If we assume that the therapeutic action of psychoanalysis depends at least in part on containment of the patient by the analyst, a working analysis should not only make formerly unbearable states of mind more bearable, but should also increase the patient's capacity for rendering his own unbearable states of mind more bearable. That is, proper containment should not only help a patient bear a current state of mind, but also help him to better bear future ones without help from an external object.

The picture that Bion gave us of containment really consists of no more than this: the analyst does something to the state of mind that the patient has split off from himself and projected into the analyst. The result of whatever the analyst has done is returned to this patient, who can now bear whatever it was that he previously could not bear. He can also better bear future instances of the same thing. Considering the impact that this theory has had on psychoanalytic thinking, it is surprisingly sketchy, and it is remarkable how little it tells us about how containment is actually supposed to work. This sketchiness was probably deliberate: Bion phrased his concept of the container to be like what he called an 'empty thought'. It is an outline of an idea that must be filled in by psychoanalytic experience.

12.1.2 The theory of the container

I propose in this chapter to develop Bion's ideas of containment and alpha function in the light of psychoanalytic experience. My development of these ideas is obviously not the only one possible, but I hope that, whatever its shortcomings, it will at least be clear enough to stimulate a meaningful discussion and further development.

The idea I propose is that the object contains or detoxifies what has been projected into it simply by being realistic about it. Recalling the Kleinian view of the role of splitting and projection in making one unaware or unconscious of certain parts of one's mind, and that this is not an individual matter, but one that inevitably involves one's objects, i.e., that splitting and projection, insofar as it goes beyond pure phantasy, is a system that requires the participation of at least two people, we can say that, while the object obviously cannot bring about changes in the subject's mind by *fiat*, it *can* control to a certain extent the role it plays in the system of splitting and projection. If an object such as the analyst is able to play a role in the analytic relationship that is governed by a realistic attitude about who is really who in the analytic relationship, then he will be able to transform his part of the *folie à deux*, the role into which he is unconsciously molded by the patient's realistic projective identification, into an interpretation. This offers the possibility of preventing or reversing the dis-integration of the patient's personality.

When I say that the object contains the projection simply by being realistic about it, what I have in mind is that, if the analyst can keep clear in his own mind who he really is, despite the pressure exerted on him by the patient's realistic projective identification to feel like the patient's projected internal object – to feel in the countertransference that he is what Strachey called an 'external phantasy object' of the patient's – then he will be able to have some conviction about the difference between what he is and what is the patient's phantasy about what he is. What is of central importance here is not the projector's state of mind, but the object's state of mind. It is the analyst's state of mind that allows him to have a conviction about who he is and isn't, and therefore to have a conviction about the patient's unconscious projected phantasy.

In this way, he deprives the patient's projection of the support that he might otherwise give it by being part of the *folie à deux*. This disparity between the role the analyst is supposed to be playing in the patient's projective system and the realistic role he is actually playing allows the patient (if he is able to appreciate it) to begin to imagine that his projections, which up to that point he has been unable to doubt or even think about (since he experiences his omnipotent phantasies as givens, indubitable psychological facts of life), might not represent a concrete reality. From the patient's point of view, this alters the character of what has been projected by allowing him to feel less that it is concretely real.

12.1.3 Urgent and aggressive projective identification

Broadly speaking, states of mind may be split off and projected for two reasons. One may evoke an unbearable state of mind in the object in the (unconscious) hope it will be transformed into something more bearable and then returned. This type of projection is based on urgency, and corresponds to Klein's 'inter-action of introjection and projection' (Klein 1932) and to Bion's 'normal projective identification'. Alternatively, one may evoke an unbearable state of mind in the object in the (unconscious) hope that the object will be unable to effect this transformation, and will simply be controlled by the projection. This type of projection is based on aggression, and corresponds to what Klein (1946) called 'the prototype of an aggressive object relationship', and what Bion called 'excessive projective identification'.

The capacity of the external container to transform the state of mind that has been evoked in it is, in principle, independent of whether the state of mind has been projected for reasons of urgency or for reasons of aggression: an urgent projection (i.e., something intended for communication and transformation) may fail to be properly understood and transformed, so that the recipient is more or less controlled by it, and an aggressive projection (i.e., something intended to dominate the container as an unbearable state of mind and not to be transformed) may yet be borne and transformed by the container.

Although the function of the external container is relatively independent of the reason that a state of mind has been projected into it, the projector's *response* to containment of his unbearable states of mind by an object is highly dependent on the motive for the original projection. Insofar as a state of mind is projected aggressively, containment of it (should it occur) will not be welcomed by the sender. This unwelcoming attitude will interfere with the ability of the sender to receive back the state of mind after it has been contained, as well as with his ability to introject the containing function of the container. In other words, the beneficial effects of otherwise adequate containment are limited by the potential beneficiary's interest in aggressive (as opposed to urgent) projection of mental contents.

In practice, urgent projection of an unbearable state of mind almost always co-exists alongside aggressive projection of it, and there is almost always a conflict between the part of the patient that wants the object taken over by the projection, so it may have more verisimilitude, and the part of the patient that wants the projection contained or transformed into something truly real. The degree to which each motive is present in a given patient at a given moment may be estimated clinically by observing the patient's response (welcoming or otherwise) to adequate containment.

This implies that the analyst must have some means of deciding whether he has contained the patient's state of mind that is independent of a positive response from the patient. In other words, he must be able to assess for himself the adequacy of his contact with the patient's state of mind. How one might do this is a topic that would require another paper to explore fully. I will say here only that the analyst's independent judgment of the adequacy of his contact with the patient's unconscious is indispensable to analytic containment. This judgment is a function of the analyst's own capacity for reality-testing, a subject I explore in the following pages.

While containment by an object may succeed temporarily regardless of the balance of forces in the mind of the projector, for containment by another to lead to an increase in the capacity for self-containment (i.e., for it to result in analytic growth), the sender must be able to recognize that an object has performed a function that is necessary for its well-being or survival, and yet beyond his own capabilities (namely containment of states of mind it cannot contain). If this recognition is not present, in other words, if the container's capacity for containment is denied, what will be introjected will be a debased version of the container whose capacities are not felt to exceed those of the personality needing containment. In this case, growth in the capacity for self-containment will

143

not occur. In other words, the wish to be contained, and gratitude and admiration for the capacity of the object to contain one's unbearable states of mind (which lie behind the desire to *urgently* project an unbearable state of mind) must be stronger than one's envious hatred for the container, the wish to feel superior to it, or the narcissistic wish that the object's grasp of painful states of mind not exceed one's own (which lie behind the desire to *aggressively* project an unbearable state of mind). Aggressive projection of a state of mind and the associated response to adequate containment was illustrated by Bion's patient who insisted that the analyst actually go through experiences that he himself was unable to bear, and, when he felt that Bion had done so without breaking down, was filled with hate (1959, p. 105).

Certain aspects of Bion's idea of normal projective identification and containment by the mind of another were anticipated in Melanie Klein's discussion of introjection and projection in *The Psychoanalysis of Children*:

> In consequence of the interaction of introjection and projection – a process which corresponds to the interaction of super-ego formation and object-relationship – the child finds a refutation of what it fears in the outer world, and at the same time allays its anxiety by introjecting its real, 'good' objects. ...
>
> According to my observation of children, the mother has to prove again and again by her presence that she is not the 'bad', attacking mother. The child requires a real object to combat its fear of its terrifying introjected objects and of its super-ego. Furthermore, the presence of the mother is used as evidence that she is not dead ... What happens is that in its efforts to master anxiety, the child's ego summons to its assistance its relations to its objects and to reality. Those efforts are therefore of fundamental importance for the child's adaptation to reality and for the development of its ego.
>
> (Klein 1932, pp. 178–180)

The capacity to bear (or have borne for one) states of mind that were formerly unbearable allows one to have a more realistic view of both internal and external reality, the former because states of mind may now be held within the personality instead of being projected, and the latter because external reality is more accurately apprehended when it has not had pieces of internal reality ejected into it. These more realistic views are more bearable because they are less concrete (a point I elaborate below).

12.1.4 Alpha function and beta elements

Before going on, I would like to clarify some of the terms of the discussion. Bion used the term 'alpha function' to denote the complex processing that renders unbearable states of mind bearable (for example, when he says that 'reverie is a factor of the mother's alpha-function' [Bion 1962, p. 36]). But he also used the same term in quite a different way, to designate a process whereby raw physiologic sensation is converted into something that is psychologically meaningful. The conversion of an unbearable state of mind into a bearable one is clearly different from the conversion of a raw sensation or perception, something that is *not* a state of mind (and therefore neither bearable nor unbearable) *into* a state of mind.

It seems to me that the use of the same term to denote these two quite different types of mental activity has given rise to a certain amount of confusion. To add to the confusion, Bion also used a single term – 'beta element' – to designate the raw material on which alpha function operates. But if what Bion called alpha function is really two functions, and the two types of alpha function operate on two different types of raw material, unbearable states of mind in one case, and non-states of mind (meaningless sensation), in the other, the use of the same term for both types of raw material also contributes to the confusion. To avoid propagating this confusion, I will denote the type of alpha function that makes raw sensations or perceptions psychologically meaningful 'synthetic alpha function' and the type that makes unbearable states of mind bearable 'analytic alpha function' (with apologies to Kant).

In the following sections, I will describe in more detail my view on the two types of alpha function and how they are related to each other, beginning with synthetic alpha function.

12.1.5 Synthetic alpha function

I propose that synthetic alpha function operates by mating a sensory perception with an instinctual drive, both of which are in themselves without psychological meaning, to form an unconscious phantasy, which does have psychological meaning. The model for this process is Freud's theory of dreaming, in which some perhaps otherwise insignificant percept (a part of the day residue) is linked to an unconscious instinctual impulse to form a latent dream-thought. Without the unconscious impulse to adopt it, the day residue would remain without psychological significance and undreamable, and without the day residue to act as a vehicle (or language or model) for its expression, the unconscious impulse would remain inarticulate and undreamable. This aspect of dream formation – the mating of an unconscious impulse with an external perception – is unconscious, and its product has been variously called a latent dream-thought, an unconscious phantasy or an alpha element. Once unconscious phantasies (alpha elements) are formed, they may in turn be mated with new sensations or perceptions to produce new unconscious phantasies or alpha elements. On the level of the development of unconscious phantasy and thought from material that is not phantasy and not thought, this mating has an oedipal character: perception and instinct are allowed to mate to produce a live birth—a live mental entity called an alpha element. Synthetic alpha function requires little or no psychological work; it is as easy as dreaming. It also does not itself require the function of a container, although, as I suggest below, a container may be required to protect synthetic alpha function from other forces in the mind.

12.1.6 *The role of unconscious phantasy in the sense of reality*

The mind is not a Baconian observer, learning by passively gathering and cataloging observations, but an active investigator, making and testing hypotheses about itself and the outside world. Unconscious phantasies (the products of synthetic alpha function) act as hypotheses that are indispensable for learning from experience (reality-testing). They are tested by being projected into objects, following which the object is observed for 'goodness of fit' to the projection. In this way, we learn something about the correspondence (or lack of it) between our inner world of unconscious phantasy (alpha elements) and the outer world of external objects. This use of unconscious phantasy as hypothesis to be tested against perception is scientific in its essence. It is one of the main the architects of one's sense of reality and of one's creativity, a point I elaborate in Chapter 8, 'Play, creativity and experimentation'.

More specifically, the acquisition of a sense of reality (what Freud called the development of the reality principle) depends on having the experience of one's unconscious hypotheses about the object being *dis*proven. If our hypotheses about the object are never disproven, the distinction between external and internal reality will not develop, perception will be indistinguishable from hallucination and the sense of reality will suffer. To be able to know what is real, one must be able to phantasize, then to compare the phantasy with perception, and then to see the difference. The establishment of a sense of reality is synonymous with 'seeing the difference' – with the establishment of the distinction between external and internal reality. This is what Bion meant when he suggesetd that frustration is necessary for the development of thoughts and the capacity to think.

12.2 Anti–alpha function

The drawing of a line between internal and external reality conflicts with the operation of what Bion called omnipotent projective identification and Klein the prototype of an aggressive object relationship, or, in other words, with the operation of omnipotent splitting and projection, the *modus operandi* of which is the permanent blurring of the border between external and internal reality. I will call this blurring anti–alpha function.

Anti–alpha function attacks the scientific interplay of unconscious phantasy and perception by agglomerating the two together. The effect of this is not only to destroy the interplay between the two, but also to destroy unconscious

146

phantasy and perception themselves. To use an anthropomorphic analogy, it is as if, angered by the failure of phantasy and perception to correspond exactly (in accordance with its demands), omnipotent splitting and projection makes them correspond with a vengeance by violently agglomerating the two to form a psychological monster or chimera. These monstrosities are neither phantasies nor perceptions, but the products of a violent fusion of what used to be phantasies and perceptions. Since they are neither phantasy nor perception, they are completely useless for either hypothesis or observation.

Anti-alpha function eliminates the possibility of having dreams, imagination, perception, frustration or satisfaction. It prevents one from investigating the meaning of one's phantasies and perceptions scientifically (the only way their meaning can be investigated) by destroying both the capacity to form hypotheses (in the form of unconscious phantasies) and the capacity to make measurements (in the form of the apprehension of external reality). Without unconscious phantasy, we cannot even imagine what our experiences might mean, and without the ability to apprehend external reality, we cannot know what is imagination and what is perception.

Under the impact of the blurring of who is who and what is what that anti-alpha function produces, perception is agglomerated with phantasy so that the ego, which is able to learn in an experimental way about what is real, is replaced by a narcissistic 'super'-ego, the function of which is to make learning from experience impossible. In the domain of the 'super'-ego, the mental means by which experimentation can be conducted, phantasy and perception, are replaced by concrete mental entities, that is, entities whose reality or lack of reality cannot be explored because the means by which they might be explored (imagination and observation combining to produce learning from experience) have been destroyed. In line with Bion's terminological conventions, I shall call the products of anti-alpha function anti-alpha elements. They consist of delusions, hallucinations and bizarre objects. (This concept of anti-alpha function agrees on some points with the one recently introduced by Sandler [1997].)

The production of anti-alpha elements corresponds to what Bion called a reversal of alpha function. But the term 'reversal' cannot be taken in a strict sense, since the reversal of alpha function, as Bion himself points out, does

> not produce a simple return to beta-elements [raw sensory impressions], but objects which differ in important respects from the original beta-elements which had no tincture of the personality adhering to them. The beta-element differs from the bizarre object in that the bizarre object is beta-element plus ego and superego traces. The reversal of alpha function does violence to the structure associated with alpha function [i.e. the scientific ego].
>
> (Bion 1962, p. 25)

147

Anti–alpha function, in other words, does not simply undo the work of synthetic alpha function: it does not convert an unconscious phantasy back into a sensory perception plus an instinctual drive or unconscious phantasy. It produces delusions, hallucinations and bizarre objects, the effect of which is to obstruct the evolution of unconscious phantasy and its scientific use in conjunction with sensation.

We are now in a position to approach the question of what makes unbearable states of mind literally unbearable. I suggest that, while dreams, perceptions, knowledge and moral values may cause psychological pain, they are not in themselves literally unbearable. Truly unbearable states of mind fall into the category of anti–alpha elements. A state of mind becomes unbearable when it consists of unconscious delusions, hallucinations, bizarre objects and moralistic hatred. Properly speaking, these are not states of mind at all, but concrete experiences that cannot be encompassed (borne) by the mind, i.e., thought about, doubted or tested, because they encompass, invade and deaden the mind instead.

12.3 Analytic alpha function

The production of anti–alpha elements by anti–alpha function calls into operation the second type of alpha function, which operates upon anti–alpha elements to restore the alpha elements (unconscious phantasies) from which they were derived, and therefore the possibility of thought. This type of alpha function, acting upon anti–alpha elements (bizarre objects, hallucinations, delusions and the 'super'-ego) rather than upon raw perception and instinct or unconscious phantasy, is what I call analytic alpha function. Analytic alpha function must work against the force of anti–alpha function. I propose that *the function of the container is precisely analytic alpha function and the material it works on – the type of beta elements it contains – are precisely anti–alpha elements*.

The effect of anti–alpha function is to confuse phantasy with external reality – to produce chimerical agglomerations of the two that obstruct learning from experience. What the container contains is the tendency of anti–alpha function to confuse internal and external reality and thereby to interfere with the capacity to dream and perceive. This containment amounts to the de-confusion of internal from external reality. This is the type of alpha function needed for the detoxification of unbearable mental contents.

By de-confusing internal from external reality, analytic alpha function improves contact with internal reality, including the aspect of the personality engaging in anti–alpha function. This contact with a part of the personality that destroys one's own capacity for thought and true contact with objects (i.e., true object relationships) produces guilt and insecurity. But, at the same time, the awareness of the destructive nature of this part of the personality and the guilt that it entails also brings relief because it diminishes the effectiveness of anti-alpha function, including its attacks on the ego for exercising alpha function.

The operation of analytic alpha function *within* the mind is the aspect of ego functioning that constitutes self-containment. Increased contact with internal and external reality brought about by analytic alpha function makes frustration more bearable in two ways. On one hand, increased contact with internal reality permits one to think, and also to think objectively about one's thinking, as Britton (1989) has pointed out, both incalculable advantages when trying to cope with frustration. And on the other, increased contact with external reality allows one to have real experiences of satisfaction, i.e., experiences of satisfaction with real external objects.

12.4 Clinical illustrations

A clinical illustration taken from the analysis of a three-year-old boy might help to clarify some of these points. The boy was brought for analysis because of night terrors, defiance of parental authority, especially that of his mother, unmanageability and chronic restlessness and misery. During his first year of life his mother was quite ill and had to be hospitalized a number of times for repeated surgical procedures. In addition, his father's work required him to be away from the home for long periods of time so that the parents were more often apart than together. The session I will describe occurred early in his second year of analysis, on a Monday.

He entered the playroom ahead of me and ordered me to remain standing outside saying, 'It all adds up – everything ends up the same.' After a while, he allowed me in, but insisted I sit precisely where he directed, and not move without his express permission. He told me he was a camp counselor and began to draw, telling me I must copy his drawing precisely on my own paper. I started to make an interpretation, but he stopped up his ears and drowned my voice out with his, scolding me for 'messing up everyone's good time.' He then drew a large eye on a piece of paper and on the reverse side, a mushroom with the sun shining on it, called a 'rainbow mushroom'. He then drew the outline of a house, filling it in with two upstairs windows and curtains, and drawing a mushroom-shaped front door. He said his mother was inside the house, then quickly said she was outside with the flowers. He quickly drew a balcony, saying mother was on the balcony, overlooking the mushrooms and flowers, then said the house had many balconies. During this time, he was getting more and more anxious and confused. I began to say something about the inside of the house, but he abruptly stopped me, saying the house had no inside at all. I could then interpret the house as representing both his mother's body and my mind, standing for his mother's body. When he had to wait to see me over the weekend, it reminded him of how he felt when he had to wait for mother and felt that daddy was

149

getting between him and her, blocking her doorway-vagina with his mush-room-penis. He became much calmer and looked at me with evident interest. I said that 'adding it all up' meant making me have the left-out feelings he had had over the weekend, and also the feeling that we were leaving him out on purpose, to spoil his good time. This made him want to 'add it all up' by spoiling our good time, by making us into things he could run and boss around. This way, he wouldn't have to feel jealous.

He picked up a drawing of a large eye and taped it to the wall, using double and triple layers of tape, obviously meaning it to be a permanent installation. I said that his left-out feelings were not so terrible now, and he could now feel them himself, and could also let me have a good time. But now he needed to keep an eye on me so he could see what was going on when he was gone and wouldn't then have to feel so left out.

He then told me of a story he had heard in which a robot had had its head cut off, yet was still alive. He said it was 'scary like "Twilight Zone".'

The headless robot was a good description of how I had felt during most of the session, and encompassed both his controlling of my movements and his attempts to prevent me from thinking about the session in my own way. (It was, incidentally, quite characteristic of this patient to react to an interpretation by denying that he had said what he had, saying I had misheard him and offering the 'correct' version in its place, a situation well-designed to keep me from being able to think about him in any way, since I was always 'wrong.') One effect of this kind of relationship to me was to make him afraid that I wanted to take away his ability to think – I was often accused of talking all the time and never letting the 'other children' have a turn, even when I was barely able on those occasions to get a word in edgewise. It is, however, the robot aspect of the transference that I wish to emphasize. It suggests a relationship based on the phantasy that an object may be rigidly controlled, denied a life of its own and (what is almost the same thing), turned into a machine.

He had, in phantasy, projected into me the helpless, jealous feelings which the weekend had stimulated. The weekend represented in the transference the parental intercourse which he experienced as virtually continuous and respon-sible for much of his frustration and troubles. My being able to think for myself (to put my ideas together without him) also had the significance of parental intercourse for him, leading to an attack on my thinking. In consequence of the projection and attacks, I became incorporated as a terrifying, controlling and omnipotent internal object. Such an internal object was similar to that which his parents had become in his infancy. It changed his personality from its normal developmental lines into one characterized by nightmares, restlessness and fear-ful defiance of imagined parent-monsters.

The motive for forming this kind of relationship may, as in this case, be a defense against jealousy (of the daddy who is felt to be able to have a relation-ship with Mommy's inside) and envy (the desire to spoil my good time over the weekend, and also the good time I have thinking in the session). The headless robot being 'scary like "Twilight Zone",' was an indication that this type of phantasy was related to his night terrors.

At the beginning of the session, he experienced me concretely as an omnipotent, left-out baby who wanted to spoil his fun and turn him into a robot (and, he felt, could do so at will). This was the result of his having projected into me an aspect of himself that he believed could quite concretely do this to me and his parents during our weekend/intercourse. One consequence of this was a terrifying set of twilight parents. He needed urgently to project this aspect of himself, not because it was simply painful to feel left out and jealous, but much more so because it produced unbearable terror. But the result of the projection was that he felt quite concretely that now *I* was doing something like this to *him*.

In both its projected and unprojected forms, the phantasy was quite omnipotent and concrete. When I was able to identify and describe it, he was able to feel that I could 'get my mind around it', as the saying goes, instead of it encompassing and deadening my mind. This converted it for him as well from an omnipotent phantasy into an ordinary one, one that might be encompassed in the mind instead of having to be a concrete, unthinkable thing. This produced real relief, and a feeling that perhaps *neither* of us were condemned to be under the control of our objects, i.e., that he could perhaps live in a world free of terrifying, headless robots. I would emphasize here that what needed containment was not his jealousy, but his terror that resulted from the concreteness of his phantasies of his controlling his objects (and its sequel, his objects controlling him).

A second clinical example from a more disturbed patient will illustrate a few more points about containment. A patient who had been denied permission by the staff for a weekend pass from the hospital became extremely upset, and began to complain to his analyst of the unfairness of the refusal. The more he spoke, the more upset he became: he began talking of the conflicts between himself and the hospital staff, then went on to other conflicts, each more dangerous than the last, and finally predicted that the United States and the Soviet Union would eventually destroy each other in a nuclear war.

The analyst said that he understood that the patient was upset and angry over his request having been turned down, that this had brought him into conflict with the hospital staff, and that this seemed to the patient to be a conflict that would lead to a wider and wider breach between himself and the staff, and that this situation seemed both very dangerous and quite hopeless to him. The patient appeared to be reassured by this. But even so, the analyst added, it wasn't the Third World War, not the end of the world, and that no one was going to die as a result of it. At this, the patient relaxed visibly, but shortly afterward, began to look troubled.

It is possible to see a complex set of forces at work in this simple vignette. The patient told the analyst about his conflict with the hospital staff. The analyst expressed his understanding of the patient's state of mind, which helped the

151

patient to feel that the analyst was not rejecting it. This corresponds to my tolerating the role I was cast into in the three-year-old's play.

It is obviously not necessary for the analyst to endorse the patient's state of mind. It is only necessary for him to convey that he doesn't reject it. The reason that this is both necessary and effective as a prologue to further interpretation is that, at first, the patient fears and expects that the analyst will reject his point of view as violently as he had rejected the hospital staff's. In a state of mind dominated by omnipotence and anti-alpha function, disagreements or differences cannot be resolved, because they cannot be brought into relation with each other; they can only annihilate each other. As far as the patient is concerned, this makes the analyst something like another mad nuclear power.

In other words, the patient has a paranoid relationship to the analyst – he expects an annihilating attack from him – and it is necessary for the analyst to convey his understanding of the patient's point of view (meaning simply not to blame the patient) in order to reassure the patient that what he fears and expects the analyst to be is not the case. Without this step, the patient will remain too paranoid – too much in a universe in which any disagreement between wish and perception is equivalent to a nuclear attack – to take anything further in from the analyst. (This corresponds to what Strachey called the first phase of a mutative interpretation.)

Up to this point, the analyst had succeeded in 'holding' the patient (in Winnicott's term), but had not yet contained him. It is the patient's paranoid relationship to the analyst (and his other objects), due to his omnipotent state of mind, that requires the analyst to 'hold' the patient by expressing an understanding of the patient's point of view.

But this holding and reassurance only conveys to the patient that the analyst is not hostile toward him. At this point, the patient still had the feeling that the analyst was a nuclear power, and all he had gained was the the reassurance of being able to feel that he was at least a non-hostile nuclear power. The next step occurs when the analyst went on to show the patient that he was *not* in agreement with his unconscious belief about the nuclear character of his anger. He was able to do this by first recognizing in himself the anxiety that the patient's threatening posture had caused, identifying the phantasy in himself that had caused this anxiety, and then comparing this phantasy with his perception of the actual patient. He recognized that this phantasy about the patient was part of a projective system in which the analyst played the role of terrified victim, and then realized that the patient must be under the sway of the same phantasy. He could then make an interpretation based on his awareness that the patient's estimate of the power of his destructiveness was phantastic. This realistic non-rapport with the patient's point of view broke the 'holding' relationship with the patient (because it violated Winnicott's condition that the analyst adhere to what he supposed to be the infant's 'lack of knowledge of anything other than the self' (Winnicott 1965, p. 49).

But it was precisely this non-rapport that provided the patient with something other than reassurance that the analyst was not attacking him for his feelings; it provided him with real relief from the anxiety connected to his believing in the omnipotence of his phantasies. Now the patient could feel that no one concerned was a nuclear power – that anger was not a nuclear weapon – and that hostility (his or any one else's) was, for better or worse, not a life and death matter *per se*. (This corresponds to the first patient's being able to feel that no one was a terrifying, headless robot.) I suggest that this identification of a phantasy for what it was is the essence of containment: the analyst had said to the patient (in effect), 'I know you feel you're engaged in a potential nuclear holocaust, but it's just a phantasy that you have about the nature of anger, yours and others'.' While this obviously reassures the patient (which accounts for his visible relaxation), once the full implications of the interpretation sink in, it also makes him aware of the limitations of his powers (which accounts for the troubled look that followed shortly after).

I believe that the patient's troubled look resulted from the fact that the patient recognizes his relief as a sign that the interpretation was something he needed, and also as something beyond his own capabilities. This had the further consequence of making him aware that the analyst was not part of the system in which his omnipotent phantasies were believed to be real, and was therefore beyond whatever control the patient felt he exerted on his objects through projective identification. In one stroke, the analyst gave the patient something that relieved him of his anxiety, showed him what he could not provide for himself (and for which he must therefore depend on the analyst) and demonstrated that he was not under the patient's control.

12.5 Containment, security and insecurity

This combination of factors introduces an element of insecurity alongside the relief that the patient experiences. This insecurity is not present in simple holding, because holding is characterized by a maximal adaptation of the analyst to the patient – a reassurance that the analyst is capable of seeing things from the patients' point of view and is therefore not hostile to the patient – without adding any new perspectives. One of the essential tactics of holding is to selectively and deliberately minimize awareness of those aspects of the relationship in which the analyst disagrees with the patient's point of view.

Certain patients need the analyst to hold their anxiety for a considerable period of time before it can be contained. In such patients, the effect of the analysts' holding their anxiety – that is, the the enhancement by holding of patients' ability to view the analyst in a non-paranoid way – tends to evaporate quickly. Such patients must be reassured frequently by analytic holding that the analyst is not a paranoid bad object. They are difficult to contain, since the

153

container–analyst is felt to be both needed, and beyond the patient's control – what I have elsewhere called a true object (Chapter 10). Proper good objects rapidly become paranoid objects for the narcissistic aspects of the patient's personality, which tends always to experience proper good objects as bad objects, since an object that is both needed and non-self *is* bad from the point of view of narcissism. The duration of this holding period (or the ratio of holding to containment that is required by the patient) is a measure of the degree of entrenchment of the patient in paranoid-schizoid or narcissistic mechanisms.

We may be able to get a fuller idea of why insecurity is associated with analytic containment, but not analytic holding, if we review certain aspects of the processes of holding and containment in greater detail. Holding does not, by definition, present the patient with a proper object. Its purpose is to accommodate to the patient in order to reassure him that the analyst is not hostile, and for this reason the analyst identifies with the patient's state of mind, and conveys to the patient that he has done so. So far the analyst has not moved the patient into territory that is unfamiliar to him, but has on the contrary moved himself into what is already familiar to the patient. This does not produce any real change in the patient's relationship with the analyst, which remains at the paranoid-schizoid level. It merely brings about a shift *within* the patient's paranoid-schizoid world-view by fostering the impression in the patient's mind that the analyst is a good paranoid-schizoid (or narcissistic) object (i.e., one that is identified with the patient's point of view). In other words, it tends to move the analyst toward the good side of the patient's splitting (while leaving his other objects to absorb the bad side of the splitting).

Containment, on the other hand, does move the patient into unfamiliar territory. It presents the patient with an object that has gone beyond identifying with him to gain some insight into what the patient himself is unable to know, namely his own unconscious. This puts the analyst in the position of being a proper object, an object that the patient experiences as distinct from himself – in other words, not a narcissistic or paranoid-schizoid object. At the same time, containment provides the patient with an experience of a proper self: he now knows who's who both in terms of the object and of himself. This makes him aware, in Bion's words, that 'the circumstances that have led to analysis and the consequences that may in future arise from it are a responsibility that can be shared with nobody'. This awareness produces the 'sense of isolation within the intimate relationship of analysis' that Bion felt distinguished true analysis from an imitation of it' (Bion 1963, p. 15).

Being a proper object makes the analyst a bad object for the narcissistic aspect of the patient (the aspect of the patient that uses projection aggressively), for which only someone *not* distinct from the self can be a good object. At the same time, the non-narcissistic or depressive aspect of the patient (the aspect of the patient that is motivated by urgency to use realistic projective identification, and wishes for containment) experiences the analyst who has actually been

154

helpful as a container as a good object. Now the patient has a conflict about the analyst: he simultaneously feels persecuted by the bad–object analyst, helped by the good–object analyst, attacks the bad–object analyst, feels helplessness at the danger in which this places the good object, and feels guilt and remorse over his role in creating this danger. Collectively, these feelings constitute what Klein called the depressive state: 'the result of a mixture of paranoid anxiety and of those anxiety-contents, distressed feelings and defences which are connected with the impending loss of the whole loved object' (Klein 1935, p. 275).

This combination of feelings contributes to the peculiar insecurity that char-acterizes analytic alpha function or containment. I suggest that this sense of insecurity (which exists alongside the sense of security that is connected to the feeling that, for example, differences and disagreements are not catastrophic) is a hallmark of containment or analytic alpha function. The absence of this sense of insecurity indicates that analytic containment has not succeeded, and that only something like holding is occurring. Analytic containment converts a state of mind that is unbearable (because it destroys one's capacity to think, perceive and phantasize) into a state of mind that is merely insecure. This corresponds (on perhaps a deeper level) to Freud's observation that much is gained if analysis succeeds in converting hysterical misery into ordinary unhappiness.

Bibliography

Bick, Esther (1964) 'Notes on infant observation in psychoanalytic training', the *International Journal of Psycho-Analysis* 45, 558–66.

Bion, Wilfred (1961) *Experiences in Groups*, Basic Books, New York.

—— (1962) *Learning from Experience*, Heinemann, London (also in *Seven Servants*, Jason Aronson, New York, 1977).

—— (1963) *Elements of Psychoanalysis*, Heinemann, London (also in *Seven Servants*, Jason Aronson, New York, 1977).

—— (1965) *Transformations*, Heinemann, London (also in *Seven Servants*, Jason Aronson, New York, 1977).

—— (1967a) 'Attacks on linking,' in *Second Thoughts*, Jason Aronson, New York, pp. 93–109. Originally published in the *International Journal of Psycho-Analysis* 40, 1959.

—— (1967b) 'A theory of thinking,' in *Second Thoughts*, Jason Aronson, pp. 110–19. Originally published in the *International Journal of Psycho-Analysis* 43, 1962.

—— (1982) *The Long Week-End 1897–1919*, Fleetwood Press, Abingdon.

Bower, T.G.R. (1977) *A Primer of Infant Development*, W.H. Freeman, San Francisco.

Britton, Ronald (1989) 'The missing link: parental sexuality in the Oedipus complex,' in J. Steiner, ed., *The Oedipus Complex Today*, Karnac, London, pp. 83–101.

—— (1992) 'The Œdipus situation and the depressive position,' in R. Anderson, ed., *Clinical Lectures on Klein and Bion*, Tavistock/Routledge, London and New York, pp. 34–45.

—— (1994) 'Psychic reality and unconscious beliefs', the *International Journal of Psycho-Analysis* 76, 19–24.

Caper, Robert (1981) 'The interaction of drug abuse and depression in an adolescent girl,' in *Adolescent Psychiatry* vol IX, University of Chicago Press.

Chasseguet-Smirgel, Janine (1984) *Creativity and Perversion*, W.W. Norton, New York.

Emde, Robert (1988a) 'Development terminable and interminable: I. innate and motivational factors in infancy', the *International Journal of Psycho-Analysis* 69, 23–42.

—— (1988b) 'Development terminable and interminable: II. recent psychoanalytic theory and therapeutic considerations', the *International Journal of Psycho-Analysis* 69, 283–96.

Faimberg, Haydée (1996) 'Listening to Listening', the *International Journal of Psycho-Analysis* 77(4), 667–77.

Feldman, Michael (1993) 'The dynamics of reassurance', the *International Journal of Psycho-Analysis* 74, 275–85.

Ferenczi, Sándor (1909) 'Introjection and transference', *Jahrbuch der Psychanalyse*. Translated in: S. Ferenczi, *First Contributions to Psycho-Analysis*, London, Hogarth Press, 1952, pp. 35–93.

Freud, Sigmund (1905) *Three Essays on the Theory of Sexuality*, The Standard Edition of the Complete Psychological Works of Sigmund Freud, ed. James Strachey, 24 volumes, Hogarth Press, London, 1953–73, vol. 7

—— (1908) 'Creative writers and day-dreaming', *The Standard Edition of the Complete Psychological Works of Sigmund Freud*, vol. 9.

—— (1909) 'Analysis of a phobia in a five-year-old boy', *The Standard Edition of the Complete Psychological Works of Sigmund Freud*, vol. 10.

—— (1911) 'Formulations on the two principles of mental functioning', *The Standard Edition of the Complete Psychological Works of Sigmund Freud*, vol. 12.

—— (1912) 'Recommendations to physicians practising psychoanalysis', *The Standard Edition of the Complete Psychological Works of Sigmund Freud*, vol. 12.

—— (1915) 'The unconscious', *The Standard Edition of the Complete Psychological Works of Sigmund Freud*, vol. 14.

—— (1915–17) *Introductory Lectures on Psycho-Analysis*, The Standard Edition of the Complete Psychological Works of Sigmund Freud, vols 15–16.

—— (1917) 'Mourning and melancholia', *The Standard Edition of the Complete Psychological Works of Sigmund Freud*, vol. 14.

—— (1918) 'From the history of an infantile neurosis', *The Standard Edition of the Complete Psychological Works of Sigmund Freud*, vol. 17.

—— (1921*a*) 'Group psychology and the analysis of the ego', *The Standard Edition of the Complete Psychological Works of Sigmund Freud*, vol. 18.

—— (1921*b*), 'Massenpsychologie und Ich-Analyse,' in *Gesammelte Werke*, S. Fischer Verlag, Frankfurt am Main, 1945, pp. 71–121.

—— (1925) 'An autobiographical study', *The Standard Edition of the Complete Psychological Works of Sigmund Freud*, vol. 20.

—— (1926) *Inhibitions, Symptoms and Anxiety*, The Standard Edition of the Complete Psychological Works of Sigmund Freud, vol. 20.

—— (1927) Postscript to 'The question of lay analysis", *The Standard Edition of the Complete Psychological Works of Sigmund Freud,* vol. 20.

—— (1930) *Civilization and its Discontents*, The Standard Edition of the Complete Psychological Works of Sigmund Freud, vol. 21.

—— (1933) *New Introductory Lectures on Psycho-Analysis*, The Standard Edition of the Complete Psychological Works of Sigmund Freud, vol. 22.

—— (1939) 'Findings, ideas, problems', *The Standard Edition of the Complete Psychological Works of Sigmund Freud*, vol. 23.

—— (1985) *The Complete Letters of Sigmund Freud To Wilhelm Fliess 1887–1904*, translated and edited J.M. Masson, Harvard University Press, Cambridge, MA.

Gardner, Sebastian (1993) *Irrationality and the Philosophy of Psychoanalysis*, Cambridge University Press, Cambridge.

Gill, Merton (1990), 'The analysis of transference,' in A. H. Esman, ed., *Essential Papers on Transference*, Essential Papers in Psychoanalysis, New York University Press, New York, pp. 362–91.

Gleick, James (1992) *Genius: The Life and Science of Richard Feynman*, Pantheon Books, New York.

Glover, Edward (1931) 'The therapeutic effect of inexact interpretation: a contribution to the theory of suggestion', the *International Journal of Psycho-Analysis* 12, 397.

Grinberg, Leon (1962) 'On a specific aspect of countertransference due to the patient's projective identification', the *International Journal of Psycho-Analysis* 43, 436–40.

Heimann, Paula (1942) 'A contribution to the problem of sublimation and its relation to processes of internalization', the *International Journal of Psycho-Analysis* 23, 8–17.

—— (1950) 'On countertransference', the *International Journal of Psycho-Analysis* 31, 81–4.

—— (1956) 'Dynamics of transference interpretation', the *International Journal of Psycho-Analysis* 37, 303–10.

Hinshelwood, R.D. (1997) 'The elusive concept of "internal objects" (1934–1943): its role in the formation of the Klein group', the *International Journal of Psycho-Analysis* 78(5), 877–97.

Isaacs, Susan (1952) 'The nature and function of phantasy,' in *Developments in Psychoanalysis*, Hogarth Press, London.

Joseph, Betty (1985) 'Transference: the total situation', the *International Journal of Psycho-Analysis* 66, 447–54.

—— (1989) *Psychic Equilibrium and Psychic Change*, Tavistock/Routledge, London and New York.

Kanner, Leo (1944) 'Early infantile autism', *Journal of Pediatrics* 25, 211–17.

Klein, Melanie (1921), 'The development of a child,' in *The Writings of Melanie Klein, Volume 1: Love, Guilt and Reparation and Other Works, 1921–1945*, Hogarth Press, London, 1975, pp. 1–53.

—— (1926), 'The psychological principles of early analysis,' in *The Writings of Melanie Klein, Volume 1: Love, Guilt and Reparation and Other Works, 1921–1945*, Hogarth Press, London, 1975, pp. 128–38.

—— (1930), 'The importance of symbol formation in the development of the ego,' in *The Writings of Melanie Klein, Volume 1: Love, Guilt and Reparation and Other Works, 1921–1945*, Hogarth Press, London, 1975, pp. 219–32.

—— (1931), 'A contribution to the theory of intellectual inhibition,' in *The Writings of Melanie Klein, Volume 1: Love, Guilt and Reparation and Other Works, 1921–1945*, Hogarth Press, London, 1975, pp. 236–47.

—— (1932) *The Psycho-Analysis of Children*, Hogarth Press, London, 1975.

—— (1935), 'A contribution to the psychogenesis of manic-depressive states,' in *The Writings of Melanie Klein, Volume 1: Love, Guilt and Reparation and Other Works, 1921–1945*, Hogarth Press, London, 1975, pp. 262–89.

—— (1936a), 'The early development of conscience in the child,' in *The Writings of Melanie Klein, Volume 1: Love, Guilt and Reparation and Other Works, 1921–1945*, Hogarth Press, London, 1936, pp. 290–305.

—— (1936b), 'Weaning,' in *The Writings of Melanie Klein, Volume 1: Love, Guilt and Reparation and Other Works, 1921–1945*, Hogarth Press, London, 1975, pp. 290–305.

—— (1937), 'Love, guilt and reparation,' in *The Writings of Melanie Klein, Volume 1: Love, Guilt and Reparation and Other Works, 1921–1945*, Hogarth Press, London, 1975, pp. 306–43.

—— (1940), 'Mourning and its relation to manic-depressive states,' in *The Writings of Melanie Klein, Volume 1: Love, Guilt and Reparation and Other Works, 1921–1945*, Hogarth Press, London, 1975, pp. 344–69.

—— (1946), 'Notes on some schizoid mechanisms,' in *The Writings of Melanie Klein, Volume 3: Envy and Gratitude and Other Works, 1946–1963*, Hogarth Press, London, 1975, pp. 1–24.

—— (1952a), 'On observing the behaviour of young infants,' in *The Writings of Melanie Klein, Volume 3: Envy and Gratitude and Other Works, 1946–1963*, Hogarth Press, London, 1975, pp. 94–121.

—— (1952b), 'The origins of transference,' in *The Writings of Melanie Klein, Volume 3: Envy and Gratitude and Other Works, 1946–1963*, Hogarth Press, London, 1975, pp. 48–56.

—— (1952c), 'Some theoretical conclusions regarding the emotional life of the infant,' in *The Writings of Melanie Klein, Volume 3: Envy and Gratitude and Other Works, 1946–1963*, Hogarth Press, London, 1975, pp. 61–93.

—— (1957), 'Envy and Gratitude,' in *The Writings of Melanie Klein, Volume 3: Envy and Gratitude and Other Works, 1946–1963*, Hogarth Press, London, 1975, pp. 176–235.

Kohut, Heinz (1959) 'Introspection, empathy and psychoanalysis', *Journal of the American Psychoanalytic Association* 7, 459–83.

—— (1979) 'The two analyses of Mr Z', the *International Journal of Psycho-Analysis* 60, 3–27.

Mason, A. A. (1994) 'A psychoanalyst looks at a hypnotist: a study of *folie à deux*', *Psychoanalytic Quarterly* 53, 641–79.

McDougall, Joyce (1995) *The Many Faces of Eros: A Psychoanalytic Exploration of Human Sexuality*, W. W. Norton, New York.

Meltzer, Donald (1966) 'The relation of anal masturbation to projective identification', the *International Journal of Psycho-Analysis* 47, 335–42.

—— (1967) *The Psycho-Analytical Process*, Heinemann, London.

—— (1972) *Sexual States of Mind*, Clunie Press, Strath Tay, Perthshire, Scotland.

Meltzer, Donald and Meg Harris Williams (1988) *The Apprehension of Beauty: The Role of Aesthetic Conflict in Development, Art and Violence*, Clunie Press, Strath Tay.

Money-Kyrle, R. E. (1956) 'Normal counter-transference and some of its deviations', the *International Journal of Psycho-Analysis* 37, 360–6.

—— (1968) 'Cognitive development', the *International Journal of Psycho-Analysis* 49, 691–8.

Ogden, Thomas H. (1994) 'The analytical third: working with intersubjective clinical facts', the *International Journal of Psycho-Analysis* 75, 3–19.

—— (1996) 'The perverse subject of analysis', *Journal of the American Psychoanalytic Association* 44(4), 1121–46.

Pick, I. (1985) 'Working through in the counter-transference', the *International Journal of Psycho-Analysis* 66, 157–66.

Quine, Willard van Orman (1961), 'Two dogmas of empiricism,' in *From a Logical Point of View*, Harper & Row, New York, pp. 20–46.

Racker, Heinrich (1968) *Transference and Counter-transference*, Hogarth Press, London.

Rosenfeld, Herbert (1971) 'Contributions to the psychopathology of psychotic states: the importance of projective identification in the ego structure and object relations of the psychotic patient', in P. Doucet and C. Laurin, eds, *Problems of Psychosis*, Excerpta Medica, Amsterdam, pp. 115–28 (also in E. Bott Spillius, ed., *Melanie Klein Today, Volume 1*, Routledge, London, 1988).

Sandler, Joseph (1976) 'Countertransference and role-responsiveness', *International Review of Psycho-Analysis* 3(1), 43–7.

Sandler, Paulo Cesar (1997) 'The apprehension of psychic reality: extension of Bion's theory of alpha-function', the *International Journal of Psycho-Analysis* 78(1), 43–52.

Segal, Hanna (1952) 'A psychoanalytical approach to aesthetics,' in *The Work of Hanna Segal*, Jason Aronson, New York, 1981, pp. 185–206.

—— (1957) 'Notes on symbol formation', the *International Journal of Psycho-Analysis* 38, 391–7 (also in *The Work of Hanna Segal*, Jason Aronson, New York, 1981).

—— (1974) 'Delusion and artistic creativity', in *The Work of Hanna Segal*, Jason Aronson, New York, 1981, pp. 207–16.

—— (1977) 'Countertransference,' in *The Work of Hanna Segal*, Jason Aronson, New York, 1981, pp. 81–7. (Originally published in the *International Journal of Psychoanalytic Psychotherapy*, 1977).

—— (1993), 'A dialogue on countertransference', unpublished panel discussion at the 1993 International Psychoanalytic Congress, Amsterdam.

Spillius, Elizabeth Bott (1988) *Melanie Klein Today, Volume 1: Mainly Theory*, Routledge, London.

Stern, Daniel N. (1985) *The Interpersonal World of the Infant*, Basic Books, New York.

Stoller, Robert (1994 [1986]) *Perversion: The Erotic Form of Hatred*, Brunner-Mazel, New York.

Stolorow, Robert D., Bernard Brandchaft and George E. Atwood (1987) *Psychoanalytic Treatment: an Intersubjective Approach*, Analytic Press, Hillsdale, NJ.

Strachey, James (1934 [1969]) 'The nature of the therapeutic action of psychoanalysis', the *International Journal of Psycho-Analysis* 50, 275.

Tausk, Victor (1919 [1933]) 'On the origin of the influencing machine in schizophrenia', *Psychoanalytic Quarterly* 2, 519–56.

Trevarthen, Colwyn (1993) 'The self born in intersubjectivity: the psychology of an infant communicating', in U. Neisser, ed., *The Perceived Self: Ecological and Interpersonal Sources of Self-knowledge*, Emory Symposia in Cognition, no. 5, Cambridge University Press, New York, pp. 121–73.

Trevarthen, Colwyn and Katerina Logotheti (1989) 'Child and culture: genesis of co-operative knowing,' in A. Gellatly, ed., *Cognition and Social Worlds*, *Keele cognition seminars*, vol. 5, Clarendon Press, Oxford, pp. 37–56.

Winnicott, D.W. (1953) 'Transitional objects and transitional phenomena', the *International Journal of Psycho-Analysis* 34. Reprinted in *Collected Papers: Through Paediatrics to Psycho-Analysis*, London, Tavistock, 1958, pp. 229–42.

—— (1965), 'The theory of the parent–infant relationship,' in *The Maturational Process and the Facilitating Environment*, Hogarth Press and the Institute of Psycho-Analysis, London. Originally published in the *International Journal of Psycho-Analysis* 41, 585–95.

Index

abnormal mental states 72–3
aesthetic conflict 3; case study 51–4
aesthetics 92
affective attunement 71
aggressive object relationship 142–4,
  146–8; *see also* anti-alpha function
aggressive projective identification 142–4
alpha elements 6–7, 40, 43, 127–31, 136,
  145, 148; *see also* unconscious
  phantasies
alpha function 6–7, 42, 127–37, 140–1,
  144–5; analytic 7–8, 145, 148–9;
  reversal of 147; synthetic 7, 145–6;
  see also containment; interpretations;
  mutative interpretation; reality-testing
alpha screen 130
analysis *see* psychoanalysis
analyst *see* psychoanalyst
analytic alpha function 7–8, 145, 148–9;
  case studies 149–53; *see also* alpha
  function
analytic receptivity 15; *see also*
  containment
analytic third 67
anti-alpha function 7–8, 146–8, 152; *see*
  also aggressive object relationship
archaic superego 2, 99, 137; analysis
  of 67–9; basic-assumption
  mentality 39; and beta elements 41;
  mutative interpretation 32–3, 37–8,
  41–2; *see also* auxiliary superego; beta
  elements; mature superego
attributive projective identification 60
auxiliary superego 14; in mutative

interpretation 36–9, 44; *see also* archaic
  superego; ego; mature superego

bad objects 154–5
basic-assumption groups 2, 9–10, 16, 17,
  39, 44, 100
beta elements 6, 40–4, 127–8, 129, 131–3,
  144–5; countertransference 133–7; *see*
  also archaic superego
Bion, Wilfred R.: alpha function 127–37,
  144–5; basic-assumption groups 2, 9,
  39; containment 40, 138–55;
  interpretation 52, 135; learning from
  experience 72; 'numbing feeling of
  reality' 34, 113; psychoanalysis 50–1;
  realistic projective identification 2, 86,
  140; reality-testing 40–3; reverie
  118–9; reversal of alpha function 147;
  transformations 62, 74
bizarre objects 8, 147–8
blame 68
Britton, Ronald: analyst's internal
  objects 125; objective thought 149;
  Oedipus complex 108, 112;
  unconscious phantasies 89

case studies; aesthetic conflict 51–4;
  containment 149–53; creativity 92;
  delusions 89, 132–3; internal
  objects 98–9, 104–6; mutative
  interpretation 35–6, 74–7; oedipal
  situation and depressive awareness
  119–24; psychosis 84–5, 89, 93;
  splitting 25; superego 99–100;

161